Martha Stewart's
CUPCAKES

Martha Stewart's
CUPCAKES

175 Inspired Ideas for Everyone's Favorite Treat

From the Editors of
Martha Stewart Living

Photographs by Con Poulos and others

BANTAM PRESS

LONDON · TORONTO · SYDNEY · AUCKLAND · JOHANNESBURG

TRANSWORLD PUBLISHERS
61–63 Uxbridge Road, London W5 5SA
A Random House Group Company
www.rbooks.co.uk

First published in the United States 2009 by
Clarkson Potter/Publishers, an imprint of the
Crown Publishing Group, a division of Random
House, Inc., New York

First published in Great Britain
in 2010 by Bantam Press
an imprint of Transworld Publishers

Some photographs and recipes originally
appeared in *Martha Stewart Living*
publications.

Design by Amber Blakesley, Yasemin Emory and
Matthew Papa

A CIP catalogue record for this book
is available from the British Library.

ISBN 9780593065655

Addresses for Random House Group Ltd
companies outside the UK can be found at:
www.randomhouse.co.uk
The Random House Group Ltd Reg. No.
954009

The Random House Group Limited supports
the Forest Stewardship Council (FSC), the
leading international forest-certification
organization. All our titles that are printed
on Greenpeace-approved FSC-certified paper
carry the FSC logo. Our paper procurement
policy can be found at www.rbooks.co.uk/
environment

Printed and bound in Great Britain by
Butler, Tanner and Dennis Ltd, Frome

2 4 6 8 10 9 7 5 3 1

ACKNOWLEDGMENTS

Many people contributed to the creation of this wonderful book,
particularly food and entertaining editorial director Jennifer
Aaronson; special projects group editors Evelyn Battaglia, Ellen
Morrissey, Sarah Rutledge Gorman, Christine Cyr, and Stephanie
Fletcher; art directors William van Roden, Matt Papa, Yasemin
Emory, and Amber Blakesley; editorial and creative director Eric
A. Pike; and photographers Con Poulos and Raymond Hom,
along with photo assistants Marc McAndrews and Christina
Holmes. Others who provided ideas, guidance, and support
include:

The talented team at Martha Stewart Living Omnimedia:
Mary Cahill, Denise Clappi, Marissa Corwin, Alison Vanek Devine,
Lawrence Diamond, Catherine Gilbert, Katie Goldberg, Heloise
Goodman, Elizabeth Gottfried, Julie Ho, Marcie McGoldrick,
Heather Meldrom, Sara Parks, Ayesha Patel, Dawn Perry,
Lucinda Scala Quinn, Megan Rice, Gael Towey

Our partners at Clarkson Potter:
Rica Allannic, Amy Boorstein, Angelin Borsics, Doris Cooper,
Jenny Frost, Derek Gullino, Mark McCauslin, Marysarah Quinn,
Lauren Shakely, Patricia Shaw, Jane Treuhaft, Kate Tyler

CONVERSION CHART

Oven temperatures	Spoon measures
130°C = 250°F = Gas mark ½	1 level tablespoon flour = 15g
150°C = 300°F = Gas mark 2	1 heaped tablespoon flour = 28g
180°C = 350°F = Gas mark 4	1 level tablespoon sugar = 28g
190°C = 375°F = Gas mark 5	1 level tablespoon butter = 15g
200°C = 400°F = Gas mark 6	
220°C = 425°F = Gas mark 7	
230°C = 450°F = Gas mark 8	

American solid measures	Liquid measures
1 cup rice US = 225g	1 cup US = 275ml
1 cup flour US = 115g	1 pint US = 550ml
1 cup butter US = 225g	1 quart US = 900ml
1 stick butter US = 115g	
1 cup dried fruit US = 225g	
1 cup brown sugar US = 180g	
1 cup granulated sugar US = 225g	

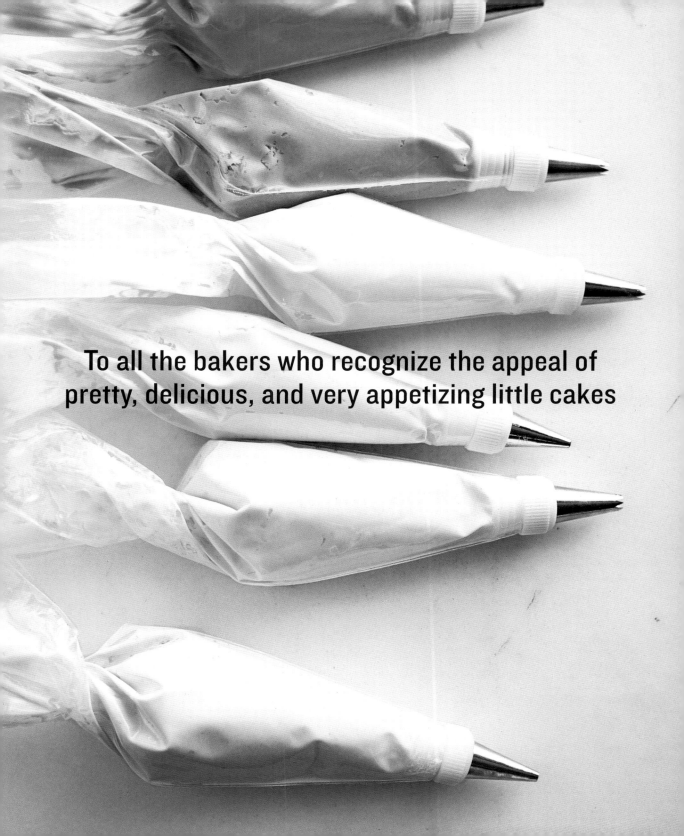

To all the bakers who recognize the appeal of pretty, delicious, and very appetizing little cakes

contents

dipped AND glazed

PAGE 58

simple AND sweet PAGE 88

filled AND layered

piped AND topped

birthdays PAGE 160

holidays

celebrations

introduction

At the end of a dinner at my home, while we were all devouring a very rich and lovely chocolate cupcake topped with chocolate glaze poured over a thick coating of ganache and served with a dollop of whipped cream and a quenelle-shaped scoop of caramel ice cream, I asked my guests to describe what cupcakes meant to them. Their remarks were charming, and given the wild popularity of cupcakes as a dessert or a snack, not surprising. Adjectives like *mouthwatering*, *rich*, *moist*, *dense*, and *flavorful* were tossed about. *Decadent*, *with lots of frosting*, *filled*, *cute*, *covered with sprinkles*, *pretty*, and *evocative of childhood* were also offered up as descriptive and appealing words and phrases relating to the subject under discussion, the now ubiquitous cupcake.

What is it, really, about these small cakes that is so appealing that people stand in line at certain bakeries, waiting for their favorite cupcake to come out of the oven and cool before it's ready to go through the decorating process? The patience displayed by these aficionados, while the next batch of freshly baked cakes—in pretty and practical fluted or pleated paper wrappers, some specially designed for that bakery—emerges from tiny or vast ovens, is not typical, especially in New York, where everyone is usually in a hurry. But for a cupcake, a special reserve of patience is somehow dredged up, and smiles and idle conversation with other customers ensue, while the reality of biting into the cupcake of choice, the favorite, nears.

A cupcake is, indeed, a small and perfect indulgence for those of us who love something sweet and pretty and unique. Magnolia Bakery, Billy's Bakery, Cupcake Café, BabyCakes Bakery, Kara's Cupcakes, SusieCakes, Happy Cakes, Violet's Cakes, ChikaLicious, Crumbs Bake Shop, and Sprinkles Cupcakes are just a few of the bakeries that have brought their little cakes to my television show and demonstrated how to create their distinctive and special decorations. And now, we at *Martha Stewart Living* have collected all of our favorite techniques and recipes—175 of them—in one volume to inspire you to bake and decorate your very own cupcakes at home.

Martha Stewart

CUPCAKES FOR
any day

You don't have to wait for a special occasion to enjoy a cupcake—although you might find that sharing a batch makes even an ordinary day seem that much more sweet. The cupcakes in the first half of this book are suitable for just about any gathering, but they are also fuss-free enough to bake and enjoy as a mid-morning snack, an afternoon companion to a cup of coffee or tea, or a tasty finish to dinner any night of the week. And their potential as heartwarming gifts cannot be overlooked. Whether you are looking for a friendly way to welcome a new neighbor or a surprise treat to tuck into a lunch box, you're sure to find just the thing in the five chapters that follow: Swirled and Sprinkled, Dipped and Glazed, Simple and Sweet, Filled and Layered, and Piped and Topped. Turn to these "any day" options whenever you want something comforting and sure to please.

swirled AND sprinkled

There are few things more delightfully nostalgic than an old-fashioned cupcake. The diminutive dome-shaped dessert generously spread with creamy frosting serves as an instant reminder of a grandmother's kitchen or a childhood bake sale. But don't be fooled by its humble appearance: A cupcake can still be fresh and modern, whether it pairs the tried-and-true (Yellow Buttermilk Cupcakes with Fluffy Vanilla Frosting) or more inspired components (Date-Nut Mini Cupcakes with tangy crème fraîche). Decorating the cupcakes in this section requires no special training—for the most part, the frostings come together quickly, and can cover a cake in one fell swoop. Many are sprinkled with a little something on top, such as nonpareil candies or toasted coconut flakes. Although optional, these finishing touches contribute additional texture and flavor—and a memorable bit of charm.

Chocolate Chip Cupcakes

Kids of all ages are bound to adore white cupcakes studded with chocolate morsels. Whipped egg whites folded into the batter produce a light and airy crumb. Tossing the chocolate chips with a bit of flour helps ensure they will be distributed throughout, rather than sink to the bottoms as they bake. The chocolate frosting is so rich and satiny, you'll want to pair it with other cupcakes in this book, especially yellow buttermilk (page 26) and devil's food (page 34). MAKES 30

3¼ cups plus 1 tablespoon sifted cake flour (not self-rising)

4½ teaspoons baking powder

¼ teaspoon salt

1 tablespoon pure vanilla extract

1 cup plus 2 tablespoons milk

½ cup plus 6 tablespoons (1¾ sticks) unsalted butter, room temperature

1¾ cups sugar

5 large egg whites, room temperature

2 cups (12 ounces) semisweet chocolate chips

Dark Chocolate Frosting (page 302)

Round candy sprinkles (nonpareils), for decorating (optional)

1. Preheat oven to 350°F. Line standard muffin tins with paper liners. Whisk together 3¼ cups cake flour, the baking powder, and salt. Stir the vanilla into the milk to combine.

2. With an electric mixer on medium-high speed, cream butter until smooth. Adding the sugar in a steady stream, beat until pale and fluffy. Reduce speed to low. Add flour mixture in three batches, alternating with two additions of milk mixture, and beating until just combined after each.

3. In another bowl, with an electric mixer on medium speed, whisk the egg whites until stiff peaks form (do not overmix). Fold one-third of the egg whites into the batter to lighten. Gently fold in the remaining whites until just combined. Toss chocolate chips with remaining tablespoon cake flour, and gently fold into batter.

4. Divide batter evenly among lined cups, filling each three-quarters full. Bake, rotating tins halfway through, until a cake tester inserted in centers comes out clean and the tops are springy to the touch, about 22 minutes. Transfer tins to wire racks to cool completely before removing cupcakes. Cupcakes can be stored overnight at room temperature, or frozen up to 2 months, in airtight containers.

5. To finish, use a small offset spatula to spread cupcakes with frosting. Refrigerate up to 3 days in airtight containers; bring to room temperature and, if desired, decorate with sprinkles before serving.

Carrot Cupcakes

A well-loved American layer cake is scaled down to cupcake form. Golden raisins give these cakes added texture, but you can omit them. You can also add one cup walnuts or pecans; toast them as directed on page 323, let cool, then finely chop before stirring into the batter at the end, after the flour mixture. Unfrosted carrot cupcakes make delicious snacks. **MAKES 24**

1 pound carrots, peeled and finely grated

3 large eggs, room temperature

1/3 cup buttermilk

2 cups sugar

1 1/2 cups vegetable oil

1 vanilla bean, halved length-wise, seeds scraped and reserved (or 1 1/2 teaspoons pure vanilla extract)

1/2 cup golden raisins

3 cups all-purpose flour

1 teaspoon baking soda

2 teaspoons baking powder

1 teaspoon salt

1 teaspoon ground cinnamon

1 teaspoon ground ginger

1/8 teaspoon ground cloves

Cream-Cheese Frosting (page 303)

Sweetened shredded coconut, toasted (see page 323), for garnish (optional)

1. Preheat oven to 325°F. Line standard muffin tins with paper liners. Whisk together carrots, eggs, buttermilk, sugar, oil, vanilla-bean seeds, and raisins. In another bowl, whisk together flour, baking soda, baking powder, salt, cinnamon, ginger, and cloves. Stir flour mixture into carrot mixture until well combined.

2. Divide batter evenly among lined cups, filling each three-quarters full. Bake, rotating tins halfway through, until a cake tester inserted in centers comes out clean, 23 to 28 minutes. Transfer tins to wire racks to cool 10 minutes; turn out cupcakes onto racks and let cool completely. Cupcakes can be stored overnight at room temperature, or frozen up to 2 months, in airtight containers.

3. To finish, use a small offset spatula to spread cupcakes with a mound of frosting. Refrigerate up to 3 days in airtight containers; bring to room temperature and, if desired, garnish with toasted coconut (press gently to adhere) before serving.

Yellow Buttermilk Cupcakes

You will likely make these cupcakes again and again, varying the frosting (say, dark chocolate, page 302) and sprinkles (sparkly, multicolored, or otherwise) to suit your whim or fancy. Two types of flour contribute to the cupcakes' singular texture: Cake flour makes for a delicate crumb, while all-purpose flour keeps them from being too tender. MAKES 36

3 cups cake flour (not self-rising)

1½ cups all-purpose flour

¾ teaspoon baking soda

2¼ teaspoons baking powder

1½ teaspoons coarse salt

1 cup plus 2 tablespoons (2¼ sticks) unsalted butter, room temperature

2¼ cups sugar

5 large whole eggs plus 3 egg yolks, room temperature

2 cups buttermilk, room temperature

2 teaspoons pure vanilla extract

Fluffy Vanilla Frosting (page 302)

Round candy sprinkles (nonpareils), for decorating (optional)

1. Preheat oven to 350°F. Line standard muffin tins with paper liners. Sift together both flours, baking soda, baking powder, and salt.

2. With an electric mixer on medium-high speed, cream butter and sugar until pale and fluffy. Reduce speed to medium. Add whole eggs, one at a time, beating until each is incorporated, scraping down sides of bowl as needed. Add yolks, and beat until thoroughly combined. Reduce speed to low. Add flour mixture in three batches, alternating with two additions of buttermilk, and beating until combined after each. Beat in vanilla.

3. Divide batter evenly among lined cups, filling each three-quarters full. Bake, rotating tins halfway through, until cupcakes spring back when lightly touched and a cake tester inserted in centers comes out clean, about 20 minutes. Transfer tins to wire racks to cool 10 minutes; turn out cupcakes onto racks and let cool completely. Cupcakes can be stored overnight at room temperature, or frozen up to 2 months, in airtight containers.

4. To finish, use a small offset spatula to spread cupcakes with frosting. Refrigerate up to 3 days in airtight containers; bring to room temperature and, if desired, decorate with sprinkles before serving.

Coconut Cupcakes

Calling all coconut lovers: These cupcakes get intense flavor from ground sweetened coconut and coconut milk in the batter, billowy seven-minute frosting spiked with coconut extract, and a garnish of unsweetened coconut flakes (available at natural-food stores). Be sure to buy only unsweetened coconut milk, not the sweeter varieties (such as Coco Lopez) used to make mixed drinks. MAKES ABOUT 20

1¾ cups all-purpose flour

2 teaspoons baking powder

½ teaspoon salt

½ cup packed sweetened shredded coconut

¾ cup (1½ sticks) unsalted butter, room temperature

1⅓ cups sugar

2 large whole eggs plus 2 egg whites, room temperature

1½ teaspoons pure vanilla extract

¾ cup unsweetened coconut milk

Seven-Minute Frosting (coconut variation, page 303)

1⅓ cups unsweetened flaked coconut, for garnish (optional)

1. Preheat oven to 350°F. Line standard muffin tins with paper liners. Whisk together flour, baking powder, and salt. Pulse shredded coconut in a food processor until finely ground, and whisk into flour mixture.

2. With an electric mixer on medium-high speed, cream butter and sugar until pale and fluffy. Gradually beat in whole eggs, whites, and vanilla, scraping down sides of bowl as needed. Reduce speed to low. Add flour mixture in three batches, alternating with two additions of coconut milk, and beating until combined after each.

3. Divide batter evenly among lined cups, filling each three-quarters full. Bake, rotating tins halfway through, until a cake tester inserted in centers comes out clean, about 20 minutes. Remove from oven; turn out cupcakes onto wire racks and let cool completely. Cupcakes can be stored overnight at room temperature, or frozen up to 2 months, in airtight containers.

4. To finish, use a small offset spatula to spread a generous dome of frosting onto each cupcake, and, if desired, garnish with flaked coconut (press gently to adhere). Cupcakes are best eaten the day they're frosted; store at room temperature until ready to serve.

Red Velvet Cupcakes

Food historians may differ about the origin of red velvet cake, but one thing is certain: The cupcakes have gained widespread popularity in recent years. Many believe the name comes from the naturally reddish hue of cocoa powder, which is enhanced by a chemical reaction between vinegar and baking soda. Today, most versions rely on food color (although some bakers use beet juice) to achieve a vivid shade. Gel-paste food color is much more concentrated than the supermarket liquid variety; if you substitute the liquid, you may need to add an entire bottle (1.5 ounces) to achieve the desired shade. Cream-cheese frosting is the classic choice.

MAKES 24

2½ cups cake flour (not self-rising), sifted

2 tablespoons unsweetened Dutch-process cocoa powder

1 teaspoon salt

1½ cups sugar

1½ cups vegetable oil

2 large eggs, room temperature

½ teaspoon red gel-paste food color

1 teaspoon pure vanilla extract

1 cup buttermilk

1½ teaspoons baking soda

2 teaspoons distilled white vinegar

Cream-Cheese Frosting (page 303)

1. Preheat oven to 350°F. Line standard muffin tins with paper liners. Whisk together cake flour, cocoa, and salt.

2. With an electric mixer on medium-high speed, whisk together sugar and oil until combined. Add eggs, one at a time, beating until each is incorporated, scraping down sides of bowl as needed. Mix in food color and vanilla.

3. Reduce speed to low. Add flour mixture in three batches, alternating with two additions of buttermilk, and whisking well after each. Stir together the baking soda and vinegar in a small bowl (it will foam); add mixture to the batter, and mix on medium speed 10 seconds.

4. Divide batter evenly among lined cups, filling each three-quarters full. Bake, rotating tins halfway through, until a cake tester inserted in centers comes out clean, about 20 minutes. Transfer tins to wire racks to cool completely before removing cupcakes. Cupcakes can be stored overnight at room temperature, or frozen up to 2 months, in airtight containers.

5. To finish, use a small offset spatula to spread cupcakes with frosting. Refrigerate up to 3 days in airtight containers; bring to room temperature before serving.

Rhubarb Cupcakes with Whipped Cream

A harbinger of spring, rhubarb flavors these deliciously sweet-tart cupcakes. Ruby-red stalks are diced, then mixed into the cupcake batter as well as a vanilla-flecked syrup that tops a puff of whipped cream. Save any extra rhubarb topping to serve with ice cream. **MAKES 16**

1½ cups all-purpose flour

¼ teaspoon baking soda

¼ teaspoon baking powder

½ teaspoon coarse salt

½ cup (1 stick) unsalted butter, room temperature

2 cups sugar

2 large eggs, room temperature

1 teaspoon pure vanilla extract

½ cup sour cream, room temperature

¾ pound rhubarb, stalks trimmed and cut into ¼-inch dice (3 cups)

1 vanilla bean, halved lengthwise

1 cup water

Whipped Cream (unsweetened; page 316)

1. Preheat oven to 350°F. Line standard muffin tins with paper liners. Whisk together flour, baking soda, baking powder, and salt.

2. With an electric mixer on medium-high speed, cream butter and 1 cup sugar until pale and fluffy. Add eggs, one at a time, beating until each is incorporated, scraping down sides of bowl as needed. Beat in vanilla extract. Reduce speed to low. Add flour mixture in two batches, alternating with the sour cream, and beating until combined after each. Stir in 2 cups diced rhubarb.

3. Divide batter evenly among lined cups, filling each three-quarters full. Bake, rotating tins halfway through, until a cake tester inserted in centers comes out clean, about 25 minutes. Transfer tins to wire racks to cool completely before removing cupcakes. Cupcakes can be stored up to 3 days at room temperature in airtight containers; remove liners before topping.

4. To make rhubarb topping, use the tip of a paring knife to scrape vanilla-bean seeds into a saucepan, reserving pod for another use (such as vanilla sugar; see page 292). Add the water and remaining 1 cup sugar, and bring to a simmer, stirring to dissolve sugar. Remove from heat, and stir in remaining 1 cup rhubarb. Let cool completely. Remove rhubarb with a slotted spoon, and reserve. Return liquid to a simmer, and cook until reduced by half, 5 to 8 minutes. Let cool slightly, then return rhubarb to syrup. Once cool, rhubarb can be refrigerated in syrup up to 1 week in an airtight container; bring to room temperature before using.

5. To finish, dollop a generous amount of whipped cream onto each cupcake, and top with rhubarb and some syrup. Serve immediately.

Devil's Food Cupcakes

Some believe devil's food cake got its name because it was so tempting; others think that the deep, dark color is "devilish." Whatever its history, the cake is typically made with melted butter (instead of oil) and a hefty amount of cocoa powder. This version mixes sour cream into the batter to add moistness and a subtle tang. Silky smooth ganache makes a rich topping; other options include seven-minute frosting (page 303) and cream-cheese frosting (page 303). The chocolate curls are easily made with a few strokes of a vegetable peeler, but you can omit them. MAKES 32

3/4 cup unsweetened Dutch-process cocoa powder

3/4 cup hot water

3 cups all-purpose flour

1 teaspoon baking soda

1 teaspoon baking powder

1 1/4 teaspoons coarse salt

1 1/2 cups (3 sticks) unsalted butter

2 1/4 cups sugar

4 large eggs, room temperature

1 tablespoon plus 1 teaspoon pure vanilla extract

1 cup sour cream, room temperature

Chocolate Ganache Frosting (page 313)

Chocolate Curls, for decorating (optional; page 323)

1. Preheat oven to 350°F. Line standard muffin tins with paper liners. Whisk together cocoa and hot water until smooth. In another bowl, whisk together flour, baking soda, baking powder, and salt.

2. Melt butter with sugar in a saucepan over medium-low heat, stirring to combine. Remove from heat, and pour into a mixing bowl. With an electric mixer on medium-low speed, beat until mixture is cooled, 4 to 5 minutes. Add eggs, one at a time, beating until each is incorporated, scraping down sides of bowl as needed. Add vanilla, then cocoa mixture, and beat until combined. Reduce speed to low. Add flour mixture in two batches, alternating with the sour cream, and beating until just combined after each.

3. Divide batter evenly among lined cups, filling each three-quarters full. Bake, rotating tins halfway through, until a cake tester inserted in centers comes out clean, about 20 minutes. Transfer tins to wire racks to cool 15 minutes; turn out cupcakes onto racks and let cool completely. Cupcakes can be stored overnight at room temperature, or frozen up to 2 months, in airtight containers.

4. To finish, use a small offset spatula to spread cupcakes with frosting. Refrigerate up to 3 days in airtight containers; bring to room temperature and garnish with chocolate curls just before serving.

Chocolate Malted Cupcakes

Malted milk powder gives these chocolate cupcakes a nostalgic flavor reminiscent of a soda-fountain favorite. So as not to overpower the taste of malt, use a mild-tasting Dutch-process cocoa powder, such as Droste. MAKES ABOUT 28

2 1/4 cups all-purpose flour

3/4 cup unsweetened Dutch-process cocoa powder

1/2 cup granulated sugar

3/4 cup packed light-brown sugar

1 1/2 teaspoons baking soda

1/2 teaspoon salt

1 cup milk

1 1/4 cups malted milk powder

1 cup vegetable oil

3 large eggs, room temperature

1 cup sour cream, room temperature

1 teaspoon pure vanilla extract

Fluffy Vanilla Frosting (page 302)

Candy sprinkles, for decorating (optional)

1. Preheat oven to 350°F. Line standard muffin tins with paper liners. Whisk together flour, cocoa, both sugars, baking soda, and salt. In another bowl, whisk together milk and malted milk powder until powder is dissolved.

2. With an electric mixer on medium-high speed, beat flour mixture, milk mixture, and oil until combined. Add eggs, one at a time, beating until each is incorporated, scraping down sides of bowl as needed. Add sour cream and vanilla, and beat until just combined.

3. Divide batter evenly among lined cups, filling each halfway. Bake, rotating tins halfway through, until a cake tester inserted in centers comes out clean, about 20 minutes. Cupcakes can be stored up to 3 days at room temperature, or frozen up to 2 months, in airtight containers.

4. To finish, use a small offset spatula to spread frosting over each cupcake. Refrigerate up to 3 days in airtight containers; bring to room temperature and, if desired, decorate with sprinkles before serving.

Tiramisu Cupcakes

Ethereal mascarpone frosting blankets sponge cake in this adaptation of a famous Italian dessert. Extra yolks in the batter make the cake sturdy enough to hold a generous dose of coffee-liqueur syrup without becoming too soggy. Freshly brewed coffee or espresso would be a natural accompaniment, as would little glasses of marsala, a fortified Italian wine used in the soaking syrup. MAKES 18

1¼ cups cake flour (not self-rising), sifted

¾ teaspoon baking powder

½ teaspoon coarse salt

¼ cup milk

1 vanilla bean, halved lengthwise, seeds scraped and reserved

4 tablespoons (½ stick) unsalted butter, room temperature, cut into pieces

3 large whole eggs plus 3 egg yolks, room temperature

1 cup sugar

Coffee-Marsala Syrup (recipe follows)

Mascarpone Frosting (page 310)

Unsweetened cocoa powder, for dusting

1. Preheat oven to 325°F. Line standard muffin tins with paper liners. Sift together cake flour, baking powder, and salt. Heat milk and vanilla-bean pod and seeds in a small saucepan over medium just until bubbles appear around the edge. Remove from heat. Whisk in butter until melted, and let stand 15 minutes. Strain milk mixture through a fine sieve into a bowl, and discard vanilla-bean pod.

2. With an electric mixer on medium speed, whisk together whole eggs, yolks, and sugar. Set mixing bowl over a pan of simmering water, and whisk by hand until sugar is dissolved and mixture is warm, about 6 minutes. Remove bowl from heat. With an electric mixer on high speed, whisk until mixture is fluffy, pale yellow, and thick enough to hold a ribbon on the surface for several seconds when whisk is lifted.

3. Gently but thoroughly fold flour mixture into the egg mixture in three batches; stir ½ cup batter into the strained milk mixture to thicken, then fold milk mixture into the remaining batter until just combined.

4. Divide batter evenly among lined cups, filling each three-quarters full. Bake, rotating tins halfway through, until centers are completely set and edges are light golden brown, about 20 minutes. Transfer tins to wire racks to cool completely before removing cupcakes.

5. To finish, brush tops of cupcakes evenly with coffee-marsala syrup; repeat until all syrup has been used. Allow cupcakes to absorb liquid 30 minutes. Dollop frosting onto cupcakes; refrigerate up to overnight in airtight containers. Dust generously with cocoa powder just before serving.

. . . .

COFFEE-MARSALA SYRUP
MAKES ENOUGH FOR 18 CUPCAKES

⅓ cup plus 1 tablespoon freshly brewed very strong coffee (or espresso)

1 ounce marsala

¼ cup sugar

Stir together coffee, marsala, and sugar until sugar is dissolved. Let cool.

Banana-Pecan Cupcakes

Baking a batch of these ultra-moist cupcakes is a great way to use overripe bananas; keep a bunch in your freezer (unpeeled) and thaw when you're ready to use. You can substitute walnuts for pecans, or leave the nuts out entirely. Caramel buttercream makes a satisfyingly sweet topping; cream-cheese frosting (page 303) and chocolate–sour cream frosting (page 311) are also good choices. Left unfrosted, the cupcakes can be enjoyed any time of day. MAKES 28

3 cups sifted cake flour (not self-rising)

1½ teaspoons baking soda

¾ teaspoon baking powder

¾ teaspoon salt

1 teaspoon ground cinnamon

4 very ripe large bananas, mashed (about 2 cups)

¾ cup buttermilk

½ teaspoon pure vanilla extract

¾ cup (1½ sticks) unsalted butter, room temperature

1½ cups packed light-brown sugar

3 large eggs, room temperature

1 cup pecans (about 4 ounces), toasted (see page 323) and coarsely chopped

Caramel Buttercream (page 307)

1. Preheat oven to 350°F. Line standard muffin tins with paper liners. Whisk together cake flour, baking soda, baking powder, salt, and cinnamon. In another bowl, whisk together bananas, buttermilk, and vanilla.

2. With an electric mixer on medium-high speed, cream butter and brown sugar until pale and fluffy. Add eggs, one at a time, beating until each is incorporated, scraping down sides of bowl as needed. Reduce speed to low. Add flour mixture in two batches, alternating with banana mixture, and beating until just combined after each. Stir in pecans by hand.

3. Divide batter evenly among lined cups, filling each three-quarters full. Bake, rotating tins halfway through, until a cake tester inserted in centers comes out clean, about 20 minutes. Transfer tins to wire racks to cool completely before removing cupcakes. Cupcakes can be stored overnight at room temperature, or frozen up to 2 months, in airtight containers.

4. To finish, use a small offset spatula to spread cupcakes with buttercream. Refrigerate up to 3 days in airtight containers; bring to room temperature before serving.

Blueberries-and-Cream Cupcakes

The summery combination of blueberries and whipped cream tops berry-filled cupcakes. The muffin-like cakes, which can also be served for breakfast or brunch, are delightful as standard or mini cupcakes. MAKES 30 STANDARD OR 60 MINI

1½ cups all-purpose flour

1½ cups cake flour (not self-rising), sifted

1 tablespoon baking powder

½ teaspoon salt

1 cup (2 sticks) unsalted butter, room temperature

1¾ cups sugar

4 large eggs, room temperature

2 teaspoons pure vanilla extract

1¼ cups milk, room temperature

2 cups fresh blueberries, plus more for garnish

Whipped Cream (page 316)

1. Preheat oven to 350°F. Line standard or mini muffin tins with paper liners. Whisk together both flours, baking powder, and salt.

2. With an electric mixer on medium-high speed, cream butter and sugar until pale and fluffy. Add eggs, one at a time, beating until each is incorporated, scraping down sides of bowl as needed. Beat in vanilla.

3. Reduce speed to low. Add flour mixture in three batches, alternating with two additions of milk, and beating until combined after each. Fold in blueberries by hand.

4. Divide batter evenly among lined cups, filling each three-quarters full. Bake, rotating tins halfway through, until pale golden, about 25 minutes for standard and 15 for mini. Transfer tins to wire racks to cool completely before removing cupcakes. Cupcakes can be stored up to 3 days at room temperature in airtight containers.

5. To finish, dollop cupcakes with whipped cream, and garnish with berries. Serve immediately.

Courgette-Spice Cupcakes

Bake an unexpected alternative batch of treats using abundant seasonal courgettes from the farmstand or local market. Like their carrot counterparts, these are finished with cream-cheese frosting. For a more wholesome snack, forgo the frosting and lightly dust cupcakes with confectioners' sugar instead. MAKES 24

3 cups all-purpose flour

1 teaspoon baking soda

½ teaspoon baking powder

1 teaspoon salt

2 teaspoons ground cinnamon

½ teaspoon freshly grated nutmeg

¼ teaspoon ground cloves

1 cup vegetable oil

2 large eggs, room temperature

1 tablespoon pure vanilla extract

¾ teaspoon finely grated lemon zest

2 cups packed light-brown sugar

3 cups packed grated courgettes (about 1½ courgettes)

1 cup walnuts (about 3 ounces), toasted (see page 323) and coarsely chopped

Cream-Cheese Frosting (page 303)

1. Preheat oven to 350°F. Line standard muffin tins with paper liners. Whisk together flour, baking soda, baking powder, salt, cinnamon, nutmeg, and cloves. In another bowl, whisk together oil, eggs, vanilla, and zest until well blended; whisk in brown sugar until smooth. Stir in courgettes, then add flour mixture and stir until just combined. Stir in walnuts.

2. Divide batter evenly among lined cups, filling each three-quarters full. Bake, rotating tins halfway through, until a cake tester inserted in centers comes out clean, about 20 minutes. Transfer tins to wire racks to cool completely before removing cupcakes. Cupcakes can be stored overnight at room temperature, or frozen up to 2 months, in airtight containers.

3. To finish, use a small offset spatula to spread cupcakes with frosting. Refrigerate up to 3 days in airtight containers; bring to room temperature before serving.

Mocha Cupcakes

Dramatic peaks of coffee-flavored seven-minute frosting and a single coffee bean crown mocha cupcakes; the coffee variation of Swiss meringue buttercream (page 305) and chocolate-covered espresso beans would be delicious substitutions. MAKES 24

2$\frac{1}{4}$ cups cake flour (not self-rising), sifted

2 tablespoons unsweetened Dutch-process cocoa powder

$\frac{1}{2}$ cup (1 stick) unsalted butter, room temperature

1$\frac{1}{2}$ cups packed light-brown sugar

2 large eggs, room temperature

1 teaspoon pure vanilla extract

1$\frac{1}{2}$ teaspoons baking soda

$\frac{1}{4}$ teaspoon salt

$\frac{1}{2}$ cup sour cream, room temperature

$\frac{3}{4}$ cup freshly brewed espresso

1 tablespoon instant espresso powder (not instant coffee)

Seven-Minute Frosting (coffee variation, page 303)

Coffee beans, for garnish

1. Preheat oven to 325°F. Line standard muffin tins with paper liners. Whisk together cake flour and cocoa. With an electric mixer on medium-high speed, cream butter until smooth and light. Add the brown sugar and eggs; beat until fluffy, scraping down sides of bowl as needed. Add the vanilla, baking soda, and salt; beat to combine thoroughly.

FORMING FROSTING PEAKS

2. Reduce speed to low. Add flour mixture in three batches, alternating with two additions of sour cream, and beating until just combined after each. Mix together brewed espresso and espresso powder; add to batter, and beat until smooth.

3. Divide batter evenly among lined cups, filling each three-quarters full. Bake, rotating tins halfway through, until a cake tester inserted in centers comes out with only a few moist crumbs attached, about 22 minutes. Transfer tins to wire racks to cool completely before removing cupcakes. Cupcakes can be stored up to 3 days at room temperature, or frozen up to 2 months, in airtight containers.

4. To finish, use a small spoon to dollop cupcakes generously with frosting and make decorative peaks. Garnish each cupcake with a coffee bean before serving.

Tres Leches Cupcakes

Just like the Latin American cake on which they are based, these cupcakes are doused with a mixture of three milks ("tres leches"). Don't worry: The cupcakes will absorb the liquid without becoming soggy, but you will need to use paper-lined foil liners (plain ones will not hold up after soaking). Airy whipped cream dusted with ground cinnamon is a finishing touch.

MAKES ABOUT 20

6 large eggs, separated, room temperature

¼ teaspoon baking soda

¼ teaspoon coarse salt

1 cup sugar

½ cup (1 stick) unsalted butter, melted and cooled

1 cup all-purpose flour, sifted

1 can (12 ounces) evaporated milk

1 can (14 ounces) sweetened condensed milk (1¼ cups)

¾ cup heavy cream

Whipped Cream (page 316)

Ground cinnamon, for dusting

1. Preheat oven to 325°F. Line standard muffin tins with paper-lined foil liners. With an electric mixer on medium speed, whisk together egg whites, baking soda, and salt until soft peaks form. Reduce speed to low. Add yolks and sugar; whisk until completely combined. Fold in melted butter with a flexible spatula. Add flour in four batches, folding until just combined after each.

2. Divide batter evenly among lined cups, filling each halfway. Bake, rotating tins halfway through, until light golden brown, about 25 minutes. Remove from oven. Immediately poke holes in tops of cupcakes with a skewer.

3. Whisk together evaporated milk, condensed milk, and heavy cream. With cupcakes still in tins, brush milk mixture over cupcakes, repeating until all liquid has been used. Allow cupcakes to absorb mixture, at least 30 minutes (or up to 1 day in the refrigerator, wrapped tightly in plastic once completely cool; bring to room temperature before serving).

4. To finish, dollop whipped cream generously onto cupcakes, and dust with ground cinnamon. Serve immediately.

BRUSHING CUPCAKES WITH THREE-MILK MIXTURE

Date-Nut Mini Cupcakes

If you grew up eating tiny sandwiches made with date-nut bread and cream cheese—or even if you didn't—you'll appreciate the wonderful flavor combination of these tiny cupcakes. Crème fraîche is a rich and velvety update, and soft enough for dolloping on top of the spiced cakes. A little batter goes a long way when baked in mini muffin tins, but the cupcakes freeze well and thaw quickly, so you can serve some now and save the rest for later. Or, if you prefer, you can bake the batter in standard muffin tins for about thirty minutes; you'll end up with about three dozen. MAKES 75 MINI

1½ cups all-purpose flour

1 teaspoon baking soda

½ teaspoon baking powder

½ teaspoon salt

¼ teaspoon ground cardamom

10 ounces plump, moist dates, preferably Medjool, pitted and coarsely chopped

1½ cups boiling water

4 tablespoons (½ stick) unsalted butter, cut into small pieces

1 cup packed light-brown sugar

1 large egg, lightly beaten

1 teaspoon pure vanilla extract

1⅓ cups walnuts (about 4 ounces), toasted (see page 323) and coarsely chopped

1 cup crème fraîche

1. Preheat oven to 325°F. Line mini muffin tins with paper liners. Whisk together flour, baking soda, baking powder, salt, and cardamom.

2. In a large bowl, combine dates with the boiling water and butter. Stir until butter is melted and dates are soft, about 2 minutes. Stir in brown sugar, beaten egg, and vanilla. Add flour mixture, and stir just until combined. Stir in walnuts.

3. Divide batter evenly among lined cups, filling each three-quarters full. Bake, rotating tins halfway through, until a cake tester inserted in centers comes out clean, about 15 minutes. Transfer tins to wire racks to cool completely before removing cupcakes. Cupcakes can be stored overnight at room temperature, or frozen up to 1 month, in airtight containers.

4. To finish, dollop crème fraîche on top of each cupcake. Serve immediately.

Ginger and Molasses Cupcakes

Spicy cupcakes packed with a generous amount of fresh ginger are just right for cool-weather days. Choose fresh ginger that is plump with smooth skin. To peel, run the edge of a teaspoon along the length of a piece, working in and out of the crevices; use a firm but light touch to remove only the papery coating, not the flavorful flesh beneath. A mini chopper or food processor makes quick work of mincing the ginger. **MAKES 26**

3 cups all-purpose flour

2 teaspoons baking soda

1 teaspoon salt

1½ cups sugar

⅔ cup unsulfured molasses

2 large eggs

1 cup (2 sticks) unsalted butter, melted

⅓ cup hot water

9 ounces (about two 6-inch pieces) fresh ginger, peeled and minced (1 cup)

Whipped Cream (unsweetened; page 316)

Ground ginger, for dusting

1. Preheat oven to 350°F. Line standard muffin tins with paper liners. Whisk together flour, baking soda, and salt. In another bowl, whisk sugar, molasses, and eggs until smooth; whisk in melted butter and the hot water. Stir in flour mixture until just incorporated, then stir in ginger.

2. Divide batter evenly among lined cups, filling each three-quarters full. Bake, rotating tins halfway through, until a cake tester inserted in centers comes out clean, about 20 minutes (cupcakes will not be domed). Transfer tins to wire racks to cool completely before removing cupcakes. Cupcakes can be stored overnight at room temperature, or frozen up to 2 months, in airtight containers.

3. To finish, dollop whipped cream onto cupcakes, and dust lightly with ground ginger. Serve immediately.

Applesauce-Spice Cupcakes

Applesauce in the batter makes these cupcakes incomparably moist. Pecans add a bit of texture, but they can be omitted. The cream-cheese frosting gets a twist with the addition of brown sugar. MAKES 18

2 cups all-purpose flour

1 teaspoon baking soda

¾ teaspoon salt

2 teaspoons ground cinnamon

½ teaspoon freshly grated nutmeg

⅛ teaspoon ground cloves

½ cup (1 stick) unsalted butter, room temperature

1 cup granulated sugar

½ cup packed light-brown sugar

4 large eggs, room temperature

1½ cups unsweetened applesauce

1 cup pecans (about 4 ounces), toasted (see page 323) and chopped

Brown-Sugar Cream-Cheese Frosting (page 310)

1. Preheat oven to 350°F. Line standard muffin tins with paper liners. Whisk together flour, baking soda, salt, cinnamon, nutmeg, and cloves.

2. With an electric mixer on medium-high speed, cream butter and both sugars until pale and fluffy. Add eggs, one at a time, beating until each is incorporated, scraping down sides of bowl as needed. Reduce speed to low. Add applesauce and then flour mixture, beating until just combined after each. Stir in pecans by hand.

3. Divide batter evenly among lined cups, filling each three-quarters full. Bake, rotating tins halfway through, until a cake tester inserted in centers comes out clean, about 20 minutes. Transfer tins to wire racks to cool completely before removing cupcakes. Cupcakes can be stored overnight at room temperature, or frozen up to 2 months, in airtight containers.

4. To finish, use a small offset spatula to spread cupcakes with frosting. Frosted cupcakes can be refrigerated up to 3 days in airtight containers; bring to room temperature before serving.

Peanut Butter and Jam Cupcakes

Inspiration for new cupcakes can come from anywhere, even a popular childhood sandwich. The creamy peanut butter frosting may be crowned with any jam or jelly flavor; strawberry is pictured, but grape or raspberry would also be delicious. For the best flavor, use natural-style peanut butter in the cupcake batter. MAKES 22

1¾ cups all-purpose flour

¼ teaspoon baking soda

¾ teaspoon baking powder

½ teaspoon salt

¾ cup (1½ sticks) unsalted butter, room temperature

1⅓ cups sugar

⅔ cup creamy peanut butter, preferably natural-style

3 large eggs, room temperature

½ teaspoon pure vanilla extract

½ cup sour cream, room temperature

¾ cup coarsely chopped salted, roasted peanuts

Creamy Peanut Butter Frosting (page 310)

½ cup strawberry jam or jelly

1. Preheat oven to 375°F. Line standard muffin tins with paper liners. Whisk together flour, baking soda, baking powder, and salt.

2. With an electric mixer on medium-high speed, cream butter and sugar until pale and fluffy. Reduce speed to low. Mix in peanut butter. Add eggs, one at a time, beating until each is incorporated, scraping down sides of bowl as needed. Mix in vanilla. Gradually add flour mixture; beat until just combined. Mix in sour cream and peanuts.

3. Divide batter evenly among lined cups, filling each three-quarters full. Bake, rotating tins halfway through, until golden and a cake tester inserted in centers comes out clean, about 22 minutes. Transfer tins to wire racks to cool completely before removing cupcakes. Cupcakes can be stored up to 3 days at room temperature in airtight containers.

4. To finish, use an offset spatula to spread frosting over each cupcake, leaving a small well in the middle. Dollop about 1 teaspoon jam or jelly into each well. Frosted cupcakes can be refrigerated up to 1 day in airtight containers; bring to room temperature before serving.

dipped AND glazed

Where a heavier frosting might compete for attention with the cupcake underneath, a smooth, subtle glaze complements without being overpowering. Although these coolly elegant confections appear refined, the methods used to produce them are decidedly simple: Each cupcake is either dipped into a bowl of icing, or set to rest on a rack while the glaze is spooned, ladled, or poured over it. The result is a miniature cake with a supple, silky sheen that is sometimes topped with another decorative element, sometimes not. Many of the glazes and icings are not much more than a whisked concoction of confectioners' sugar and a liquid, such as milk or fresh citrus juice. Some are infused with a heady dose of rum or other spirits to match the grown-up flavors of the cakes themselves. All in all, the understated cupcakes in this chapter prove the old adage that less can indeed add up to more.

Brown Sugar Pound Cakes

Pound-cake batters bake into especially rich and dense cupcakes, and the traditional recipe can be adapted in many ways to vary the flavor and texture. In this version, brown sugar replaces granulated for a hint of caramel flavor, while buttermilk makes for a more tender crumb than when made with regular milk. Nutty brown-butter icing pairs especially well with these cupcakes, but many other toppings would also work, including brown-sugar cream-cheese frosting (page 310) or whipped cream (page 316). MAKES 28

3 cups sifted all-purpose flour

2 teaspoons baking powder

1/2 teaspoon salt

1 cup (2 sticks) unsalted butter, room temperature

2 1/4 cups packed light-brown sugar

4 large eggs, room temperature

3/4 cup buttermilk

Brown-Butter Icing (page 314)

1. Preheat oven to 325°F. Line standard muffin tins with paper liners. Whisk together flour, baking powder, and salt.

2. With an electric mixer on medium-high speed, cream butter and brown sugar until pale and fluffy. Add eggs, one at a time, beating until each is incorporated, scraping down sides of bowl as needed. Add flour mixture in three batches, alternating with two additions of buttermilk, and beating until combined after each.

3. Divide batter evenly among lined cups, filling each three-quarters full. Bake, rotating tins halfway through, until golden brown and a cake tester inserted in centers comes out clean, about 25 minutes. Transfer tins to wire racks to cool 10 minutes; turn out cupcakes onto racks and let cool completely. Cupcakes can be stored up to 3 days at room temperature, or frozen up to 2 months, in airtight containers.

4. To finish, place cupcakes on a wire rack set over a baking sheet; spoon icing over cupcakes, and let set. Cupcakes are best eaten the day they are glazed; keep at room temperature until ready to serve.

Streusel Cupcakes

All the features of a traditional coffee cake—tender cake base, crumbly streusel top, and simple milk-and-sugar glaze—are packed into portable, single-size portions. Try serving them for brunch, or as an after-school snack. MAKES 24

2½ cups all-purpose flour

½ teaspoon baking soda

1¼ teaspoons baking powder

½ teaspoon coarse salt

½ cup plus 2 tablespoons (1¼ sticks) unsalted butter, room temperature

1 cup sugar

3 large eggs

1½ teaspoons pure vanilla extract

1¼ cups sour cream

Streusel Topping (recipe follows)

Milk Glaze (recipe follows)

1. Preheat oven to 350°F. Line standard muffin tins with paper liners. Whisk together flour, baking soda, baking powder, and salt.

2. With an electric mixer on medium-high speed, cream butter and sugar until pale and fluffy. Add eggs, one at a time, beating until each is incorporated, scraping down sides of bowl as needed. Stir in vanilla by hand. Add flour mixture and sour cream; stir until just combined.

3. Divide batter evenly among lined cups. Sprinkle half the topping over cupcakes, gently pressing it into the batter. Sprinkle evenly with remaining topping. Bake, rotating tins halfway through, until golden brown and a cake tester inserted in centers comes out clean, about 20 minutes. Transfer tins to wire racks to cool completely before removing cupcakes.

4. To finish, place cupcakes on a wire rack set over a baking sheet; drizzle evenly with milk glaze. Glazed cupcakes can be stored up to 3 days at room temperature in airtight containers.

. . . .

STREUSEL TOPPING
MAKES ENOUGH FOR 24 CUPCAKES

2¼ cups all-purpose flour

¾ cup packed dark-brown sugar

2¼ teaspoons ground cinnamon

¾ teaspoon coarse salt

½ cup plus 2 tablespoons (1¼ sticks) unsalted butter, room temperature

Whisk together flour, brown sugar, cinnamon, and salt; cut in the butter using a pastry blender, your fingertips, or two table knives until combined but still crumbly. Refrigerate 30 minutes before using.

. . . .

MILK GLAZE
MAKES ENOUGH FOR 24 CUPCAKES

1½ cups confectioners' sugar, sifted

3 tablespoons milk

Whisk together ingredients until smooth. Use immediately.

Triple-Citrus Cupcakes

A trio of citrus zests brightens simple cupcakes. The ones pictured are finished with lime-flavored glaze and finely grated lime zest, but lemons or oranges could replace the lime. Or, for a particularly pretty display, divide the glaze into thirds and flavor each portion with a different citrus, with garnishes to match. MAKES 36

3⅓ cups all-purpose flour

2 teaspoons coarse salt

1 pound (4 sticks) unsalted butter, room temperature

2 cups sugar

3 tablespoons finely grated lemon zest (from 3 lemons)

3 tablespoons finely grated orange zest (from 2 oranges)

3 tablespoons finely grated lime zest, plus more for garnish (from about 3 limes)

1 teaspoon pure vanilla extract

9 large eggs, room temperature

Citrus Glaze (made with lime juice and zest; page 315)

1. Preheat oven to 325°F. Line standard muffin tins with paper liners. Whisk together flour and salt.

2. With an electric mixer on medium-high speed, cream butter and sugar until pale and fluffy, scraping down sides of bowl every few minutes. Add citrus zests. Reduce speed to medium, and add vanilla. Add eggs, three at a time, beating until incorporated, scraping down sides of bowl as needed. Reduce speed to low. Add flour mixture in four batches, beating until completely incorporated after each.

3. Divide batter evenly among lined cups, filling each three-quarters full; tap pans on countertop once to distribute batter. Bake, rotating tins halfway through, until a cake tester inserted in centers comes out clean, about 20 minutes. Transfer tins to wire racks to cool 10 minutes; turn out cupcakes onto racks and let cool completely. Cupcakes can be stored up to 2 days at room temperature, or frozen up to 2 months, in airtight containers.

4. To finish, dip tops of cupcakes in glaze, then turn over quickly and garnish with zest. Cupcakes are best eaten the day they are glazed; keep at room temperature until ready to serve.

Coconut-Pecan Cupcakes with Chocolate Ganache

The batter for these candy-bar-like cupcakes is laden with ground sweetened coconut and pecans; to further enhance their appeal, the cupcakes are dipped in a bittersweet chocolate glaze, then sprinkled with toasted coconut flakes. Creamed coconut, usually sold in jars at natural-food stores or online, differs from "cream of coconut," which has added sugar and is typically used in cocktails. If you can't locate creamed coconut, you can use another quarter cup of butter in its place. MAKES 36

1 cup firmly packed sweetened shredded coconut

$3/4$ cup pecans (about 3 ounces), toasted (see page 323) and cooled

2 cups sugar

$2^{1}/4$ cups all-purpose flour

1 tablespoon baking powder

$3/4$ teaspoon salt

$3/4$ cup ($1^{1}/2$ sticks) unsalted butter, room temperature

$1/4$ cup creamed coconut (or 4 tablespoons unsalted butter, room temperature)

1 tablespoon pure coconut extract

4 large eggs, room temperature

1 cup plus 2 tablespoons unsweetened coconut milk (9 ounces)

Chocolate Ganache Glaze (page 312)

2 cups unsweetened coconut flakes, toasted (see page 323), for garnish

1. Preheat oven to 350°F. Line standard muffin tins with paper liners. In a food processor, finely grind shredded coconut; transfer to a bowl. Process pecans with 2 tablespoons sugar until finely ground. Sift together flour, baking powder, and salt; stir in ground coconut and pecans.

2. With an electric mixer on medium-high speed, cream butter, creamed coconut, and remaining sugar until pale and fluffy. Add extract and then eggs, one at a time, beating until each is incorporated, scraping down sides of bowl as needed. Reduce speed to low. Add flour mixture in three batches, alternating with two additions of coconut milk, and beating until just combined after each.

3. Divide batter evenly among lined cups, filling each three-quarters full. Bake, rotating tins halfway through, until golden and a cake tester inserted in centers comes out clean, 20 to 22 minutes (cupcakes will not be domed). Turn out cupcakes onto wire racks and let cool completely. Cupcakes can be stored overnight at room temperature, or frozen up to 2 months, in airtight containers.

4. To finish, dip tops of cupcakes in chocolate glaze, then turn over quickly and garnish with toasted coconut. Cupcakes are best eaten the day they are glazed; keep at room temperature until ready to serve.

Iced Pistachio Cupcakes

These cupcakes are made with a triple dose of pistachio: Some nuts are ground to a paste and mixed into the batter; others are chopped and folded in at the end for added texture. Even more nuts are sprinkled on top as a colorful garnish. Slivered pistachios are available at specialty markets and baking-supply stores; if you can't find them, use chopped pistachios instead. **MAKES 34**

1 cup unsalted shelled pistachios

1$\frac{1}{4}$ cups (2$\frac{1}{2}$ sticks) unsalted butter, room temperature

6 ounces cream cheese, room temperature

3 cups sugar

6 large eggs, room temperature

2 teaspoons pure vanilla extract

3 cups all-purpose flour

1 tablespoon coarse salt

$\frac{3}{4}$ cup coarsely chopped salted pistachios

Drippy Icing (recipe follows)

1$\frac{1}{2}$ cups unsalted pistachio slivers (see Sources, page 342), for garnish

1. Preheat oven to 325°F. Line standard muffin tins with paper liners. In a food processor, grind shelled pistachios to a paste.

2. With an electric mixer on medium-high speed, beat butter, cream cheese, and pistachio paste until fluffy, about 3 minutes. Reduce speed to medium-low. Gradually add sugar; beat until smooth, scraping down sides of bowl as needed. Add eggs, one at a time, beating until each is incorporated. Beat in vanilla. Reduce speed to low. Add flour and salt, beating until just combined. Fold in chopped pistachios by hand.

3. Divide batter evenly among lined cups, filling each three-quarters full. Bake, rotating tins halfway through, until a cake tester inserted in centers comes out clean, about 30 minutes. Transfer tins to wire racks to cool completely before removing cupcakes. Cupcakes can be stored up to 1 day at room temperature, or frozen up to 2 months, in airtight containers.

4. To finish, place cupcakes on a wire rack set over a baking sheet; spoon icing onto each, and garnish with pistachio slivers. Cupcakes are best eaten the same day they are glazed; keep at room temperature until ready to serve.

. . . .

DRIPPY ICING
MAKES ENOUGH FOR 34 CUPCAKES

1 cup plus 3 tablespoons confectioners' sugar, sifted

$\frac{3}{4}$ cup heavy cream

1 teaspoon fresh lemon juice

Whisk all ingredients in a small bowl until smooth. Use immediately.

Pumpkin–Brown Butter Cupcakes

These cupcakes are made with a combination of ingredients commonly found in a beloved autumn pie—pumpkin, cinnamon, nutmeg, and cloves—and enhanced with brown butter and fresh sage. To cut sage into chiffonade, or very fine strips, stack the leaves, then roll up tightly before slicing thinly crosswise with a sharp knife. MAKES 15

¾ cup (1½ sticks) unsalted butter, room temperature, plus more for tins

1⅔ cups all-purpose flour, plus more for tins

¼ cup fresh sage leaves, cut into chiffonade (optional)

2 teaspoons baking powder

1 teaspoon salt

½ teaspoon ground cinnamon

¼ teaspoon freshly grated nutmeg

⅛ teaspoon ground cloves

1 cup canned pumpkin puree (not pie filling)

1 cup packed light-brown sugar

½ cup granulated sugar

2 large eggs

Brown-Butter Icing (page 314)

1. Preheat oven to 325°F. Brush standard muffin tins with butter; dust with flour, tapping out excess. In a saucepan, melt the butter over medium-low heat. Add the sage, if desired, and continue to cook, swirling occasionally, until butter turns golden brown. Skim foam from top, and remove from heat. Pour into a bowl to stop the cooking, leaving any burned sediment behind; let cool.

DIPPING CUPCAKES IN ICING

2. Whisk together flour, baking powder, salt, cinnamon, nutmeg, and cloves. In another bowl, whisk together the pumpkin puree, both sugars, eggs, and brown-butter mixture. Add flour mixture, and whisk until just combined.

3. Divide batter evenly among lined cups, filling each three-quarters full. Bake, rotating tins halfway through, until a cake tester inserted in centers comes out clean, about 20 minutes. Transfer tins to wire racks to cool completely before removing cupcakes. Cupcakes can be stored overnight at room temperature, or frozen up to 2 months, in airtight containers.

4. To finish, dip top of each cupcake in icing, then turn over quickly and let set. Cupcakes are best eaten the day they are glazed; keep at room temperature until ready to serve.

Apricot-Glazed Black and White Cheesecakes

With their cookie-crumb crust, creamy filling, and fruity topping, individual cheesecakes are a delightful spin on the full-size dessert. Glossy apricot jam gives the desserts a golden glow, while store-bought dark-chocolate-flavored biscuits provide a crisp, quick-to-assemble base. **MAKES 18**

FOR CRUST

- ³/₄ cup crumbled dark-chocolate-flavored biscuits (about 18)
- 1 tablespoon plus 1 teaspoon sugar
- 3 tablespoons unsalted butter, melted

FOR FILLING

- 1 pound cream cheese, room temperature
- ¹/₂ cup sugar
- ¹/₂ teaspoon pure vanilla extract
- 2 large eggs, lightly beaten
- ¹/₂ cup sour cream
  Pinch of salt
- ³/₄ cup apricot jam

1. Make crust: Preheat oven to 350°F. Line standard muffin tins with paper liners. Stir to combine chocolate biscuit crumbs and 1 tablespoon plus 1 teaspoon sugar, then stir in melted butter. Press 1 tablespoon crumb mixture firmly in the bottom of each lined cup to form crust. Bake, rotating tins halfway through, until set, about 7 minutes. Transfer tins to wire racks to cool. Reduce oven temperature to 275°F.

2. Make filling: With an electric mixer on medium-high speed, beat cream cheese until smooth. Gradually add ½ cup sugar, followed by the vanilla. Beat until well combined, about 3 minutes. Drizzle in eggs, a bit at a time, stopping often to scrape down sides of bowl. Beat in sour cream and salt until combined.

3. Pour batter into crust-lined cups, filling each almost to the very top. Bake, rotating tins halfway through, until filling is set around edges but centers appear soft, 20 to 22 minutes. Transfer tins to wire racks to cool completely. Refrigerate (in tins) at least 4 hours (or overnight).

4. To finish, bring cheesecakes to room temperature and remove from tins. Heat jam in a saucepan until loose. Strain through a fine sieve to remove lumps. Spoon warm jam (about 1 teaspoon) onto each cheesecake. Serve immediately.

Mrs. Kostyra's Spice Cupcakes

These glazed cupcakes are adapted from a recipe by Martha's late mother, Martha Kostyra, who was an avid baker. She especially enjoyed making spice cakes. The orange glaze is also hers, but the cupcakes would be equally delicious topped with cream-cheese frosting (page 303) or brown-butter icing (page 314). Don't skip the crucial step of sifting the dry ingredients three times, as it helps to fully distribute the spices for the best flavor. MAKES 24

½ cup (1 stick) unsalted butter, room temperature, plus more for tins

4 cups cake flour (not self-rising), sifted, plus more for tins

1 tablespoon plus 1 teaspoon baking powder

½ teaspoon salt

2 teaspoons ground cinnamon

1 teaspoon ground allspice

½ teaspoon freshly grated nutmeg

½ teaspoon ground mace

Pinch of ground cloves

1½ cups packed dark-brown sugar

4 large eggs, room temperature

1½ cups milk, room temperature

Citrus Glaze (made with orange juice and zest; page 315)

1. Preheat oven to 350°F. Brush standard muffin tins with butter; dust with flour, tapping out excess. Sift together cake flour, baking powder, salt, and spices three times.

2. With an electric mixer on medium-high speed, cream butter and brown sugar until pale and fluffy. Add eggs, one at a time, beating until each is incorporated, scraping down sides of bowl as needed. Reduce speed to low. Add flour mixture in two batches, alternating with two additions of milk, and beating until combined after each.

3. Divide batter evenly among prepared cups, filling each three-quarters full. Bake, rotating tins halfway through, until golden brown and a cake tester inserted in centers comes out clean, about 20 minutes. Transfer tins to wire racks to cool completely before removing cupcakes.

4. To finish, place cupcakes on a wire rack set over a baking sheet; spoon glaze over cupcakes, and let set. Cupcakes are best eaten the same day they are glazed; keep at room temperature until ready to serve.

Sticky Toffee Pudding Cupcakes

Unlike the creamy American dessert of the same name, puddings from Great Britain are dense and cakey. This small-scale version includes pureed dates and a splash of brandy; after baking, the puddings are coated with a delectable toffee glaze. MAKES 14

- ½ cup (1 stick) unsalted butter, room temperature, plus more for tins
- 2 cups all-purpose flour, plus more for tins
- ½ cup water
- ½ cup brandy
- 8 ounces plump, moist dates (preferably Medjool), halved and pitted
- ¼ teaspoon baking soda
- 1½ teaspoons baking powder
- ½ teaspoon coarse salt
- ½ teaspoon ground cinnamon
- 1 cup packed dark-brown sugar
- 2 large eggs, room temperature
- Toffee Glaze (recipe follows)

1. Preheat oven to 350°F. Brush standard muffin tins with butter; dust with flour, tapping out excess. Bring the water, brandy, and dates to a boil in a saucepan over medium-high heat. Reduce heat to medium-low; cover, and cook until dates are very soft, about 5 minutes. Transfer mixture to a food processor and puree until smooth. Let cool 15 minutes.

2. Whisk together flour, baking soda, baking powder, salt, and cinnamon. With an electric mixer on medium-high speed, cream butter and brown sugar until pale and fluffy. Add eggs, one at a time, beating until each is incorporated, scraping down sides of bowl as needed. Reduce speed to low. Add flour mixture in three batches, alternating with two additions of date puree, and beating until just combined after each.

3. Divide batter evenly among prepared cups. Bake, rotating tins halfway through, until a cake tester inserted in centers comes out clean, 23 to 25 minutes. (Toward the end of the baking time, make the glaze.)

4. As soon as they are removed from the oven, use a toothpick to lift one side of each cupcake so they are all slightly tilted; lifting a cupcake even more with your fingertips, pour 2 tablespoons glaze into each cup, then nudge cupcake back in place. Let cool 10 minutes.

5. To finish, invert cupcakes onto a wire rack set over a baking sheet; spoon 2 tablespoons glaze over each, and let set. Serve immediately.

. . . .

TOFFEE GLAZE
MAKES ENOUGH FOR 14 CUPCAKES

- 1 cup heavy cream
- 1 cup packed dark-brown sugar
- 4 tablespoons (½ stick) unsalted butter, cut into tablespoons, room temperature
- ¼ cup brandy
- ¼ teaspoon coarse salt

Bring cream, brown sugar, and butter to a boil over medium-high heat in a saucepan, stirring occasionally. Cook 3 minutes. Stir in brandy and salt, and cook 1 minute more. Use immediately.

Stout Cupcakes

Stout beer, which gets its dark color and bold flavor from roasted malt, is sometimes used in English and Irish recipes for spice cakes and quick breads. The cupcake versions make excellent hostess gifts or after-dinner treats; serve them with coffee or glasses of stout. MAKES 28

3³/₄ cups all-purpose flour

¹/₂ teaspoon plus ¹/₈ teaspoon baking soda

1³/₄ teaspoons baking powder

1¹/₄ teaspoons salt

1 tablespoon ground cinnamon

1¹/₄ teaspoons freshly grated nutmeg

1¹/₄ cups vegetable oil

1¹/₄ cups unsulfured molasses

¹/₂ cup plus 1 tablespoon packed light-brown sugar

2 large whole eggs plus 1 egg yolk

1 tablespoon plus 1 teaspoon finely grated orange zest

1¹/₄ cups (10 ounces) stout beer, such as Guinness, poured and settled

Stout Glaze (recipe follows)

1. Preheat oven to 350°F. Line standard muffin tins with paper liners. Whisk together flour, baking soda, baking powder, salt, cinnamon, and nutmeg.

2. With an electric mixer on medium-low speed, beat oil, molasses, brown sugar, whole eggs, yolk, zest, and stout until combined. Reduce speed to low. Gradually add flour mixture, beating until just combined.

3. Divide batter evenly among lined cups, filling each three-quarters full. Bake, rotating tins halfway through, until a cake tester inserted in centers comes out clean, about 20 minutes. Turn out cupcakes onto wire racks to cool completely. Cupcakes can be stored overnight at room temperature, or frozen up to 2 months, in airtight containers.

4. To finish, place cupcakes on a wire rack set over a baking sheet; spoon glaze over cupcakes, and let set. Cupcakes are best eaten the day they are glazed; keep at room temperature until ready to serve.

. . . .

STOUT GLAZE
MAKES ENOUGH FOR 28 CUPCAKES

2 cups confectioners' sugar, sifted

¹/₄ cup stout beer, such as Guinness, poured and settled

Whisk together ingredients until combined. Use immediately.

Chai-Tea Mini Cupcakes

These cupcakes get their flavor from a traditional Indian spiced tea, known as masala chai. The tea is often lightened (and sweetened) with condensed milk; here, condensed milk is used to make the glaze.

MAKES 46 MINI

- ¾ cup milk
- 2 bags black tea (such as Ceylon)
- 1 cup all-purpose flour
- 1 cup cake flour (not self-rising), sifted
- 1½ teaspoons baking powder
- ½ teaspoon coarse salt
- ¼ teaspoon freshly ground pepper
- ¼ teaspoon ground cinnamon
- ¼ teaspoon ground ginger
- ¼ teaspoon ground cardamom
- Pinch of ground cloves
- Pinch of freshly grated nutmeg
- 4 tablespoons (½ stick) unsalted butter, room temperature
- ¾ cup packed dark-brown sugar
- 2 large eggs, room temperature
- Condensed-Milk Icing (recipe follows)

1. Preheat oven to 350°F. Line mini muffin tins with paper liners. Bring milk to a simmer over medium heat. Remove from heat; add tea bags, and let steep, covered, 15 minutes. Remove tea bags, squeezing the bags over the pan, and discard. Allow milk to cool completely. Whisk together both flours, baking powder, salt, pepper, and spices.

2. With an electric mixer on medium-high speed, cream butter and brown sugar until pale and fluffy. Add eggs, one at a time, beating until each is incorporated, scraping sides of bowl as needed. Reduce speed to low. Add flour mixture in three batches, alternating with two additions of tea-infused milk, and beating until just combined after each.

3. Divide batter evenly among lined cups, filling each three-quarters full. Bake, rotating tins halfway through, until tops spring back when lightly touched and are pale golden, 10 to 12 minutes. Turn out onto wire racks to cool completely. Cupcakes can be frozen up to 1 month in airtight containers.

4. To finish, dip top of each cupcake in icing, then turn over quickly, and let set. Cupcakes are best eaten the day they are glazed; keep at room temperature until ready to serve.

· ·

CONDENSED-MILK ICING
MAKES ENOUGH FOR 46 MINI CUPCAKES

- 4 tablespoons (½ stick) unsalted butter, room temperature
- ½ cup plus 2 tablespoons sweetened condensed milk (7 ounces)
- Pinch of coarse salt
- ¾ cup confectioners' sugar, sifted

With an electric mixer on medium-high speed, whisk together butter, condensed milk, and salt until smooth. Whisk in confectioners' sugar, ¼ cup at a time, until combined, then whisk on high speed until thick and smooth. Use immediately.

Chocolate-Spice Cupcakes

Over the years some of the most popular recipes in *Martha Stewart Living* have featured the combination of chocolate, ginger, and other spices, including cookies, brownies, and spice cakes. These dapper upside-down cupcakes are the latest variation on the theme. **MAKES 12**

- 5 tablespoons unsalted butter, room temperature, plus more for tin
- ¼ cup unsweetened Dutch-process cocoa powder, plus more for tin
- 1 teaspoon baking soda
- ⅔ cup boiling water
- 1¼ cups all-purpose flour
- ¼ teaspoon salt
- 1 teaspoon ground ginger
- ¾ teaspoon ground cinnamon
- ¼ teaspoon freshly grated nutmeg
- ½ cup packed dark-brown sugar
- 1 large egg, room temperature
- ⅔ cup unsulfured molasses
- Chocolate Ganache Glaze (page 312)
- Candied ginger, finely diced, for garnish

1. Preheat oven to 350°F. Brush a standard muffin tin with butter; dust with cocoa powder, tapping out excess. Stir baking soda into the boiling water. In another bowl, whisk together the flour, cocoa, salt, ground ginger, cinnamon, and nutmeg.

2. With an electric mixer on medium-high speed, cream butter and brown sugar until pale and fluffy. Beat in the egg. Add molasses and baking-soda mixture, and beat until combined, scraping down sides of bowl as needed. Reduce speed to low. Add flour mixture, and beat until well combined (batter will look lumpy).

3. Divide batter evenly among prepared cups, filling each about halfway. Bake, rotating tin halfway through, until a cake tester inserted in centers comes out clean, about 20 minutes. Transfer tin to a wire rack to cool 15 minutes; invert cupcakes onto rack and let cool completely. Cupcakes can be stored up to 3 days at room temperature in airtight containers.

4. To finish, place inverted cupcakes on a wire rack set over a baking sheet; spoon glaze over cupcakes. Glazed cupcakes can be refrigerated up to 3 days in a single layer in airtight containers; bring to room temperature and garnish with candied ginger before serving.

Coconut Rum-Raisin Cupcakes

Drizzled with a liquor-spiked caramel glaze and filled with rum-soaked raisins, these cupcakes are reminiscent of a popular ice cream flavor. **MAKES 36**

1¼ cups (2½ sticks) unsalted butter, room temperature, plus more for tins

3 cups all-purpose flour, plus more for tins

½ cup dark rum

1 cup raisins

½ teaspoon baking powder

1 teaspoon salt

2¾ cups plus 2 tablespoons packed light-brown sugar

6 large eggs, room temperature

2 teaspoons pure vanilla extract

¾ cup heavy cream

1 cup sweetened flaked coconut

Rum-Caramel Glaze (recipe follows)

1. Preheat oven to 325°F. Brush standard muffin tins with butter; dust with flour, tapping out excess. In a bowl, pour rum over raisins, and let soak. In another bowl, whisk together flour, baking powder, and salt.

2. With an electric mixer on medium-high speed, cream butter and brown sugar until pale and fluffy. Add eggs, one at a time, beating until each is incorporated, scraping down sides of bowl as needed. Beat in vanilla. Reduce speed to low. Add flour mixture in three batches, alternating with two additions of heavy cream, and beating until combined after each. Mix in raisin mixture and coconut.

3. Divide batter evenly among prepared cups, filling each three-quarters full. Bake, rotating tins halfway through, until a cake tester inserted in centers comes out clean, about 30 minutes. Transfer tins to wire racks to cool 20 minutes. Run a small offset spatula or knife around edges; turn out cupcakes onto racks and let cool completely. Cupcakes can be stored up to 3 days at room temperature in airtight containers.

4. To serve, set cupcakes on dessert plates, and spoon glaze over each. Alternatively, finish by placing cupcakes on a wire rack set over a baking sheet; spoon glaze over cupcakes, and let set. Cupcakes are best eaten the day they are glazed; keep at room temperature until ready to serve.

. . . .

RUM-CARAMEL GLAZE
MAKES ENOUGH FOR 36 CUPCAKES

1 cup sugar

¼ cup water

¼ cup dark rum

¼ cup heavy cream

Heat sugar and the water in a heavy saucepan over medium, stirring occasionally, until sugar is dissolved and syrup is clear. Stop stirring, and cook until syrup comes to a boil, washing down sides of pan with a wet pastry brush to prevent crystals from forming. Continue to boil, gently swirling occasionally to color evenly, until mixture is medium amber. Remove from heat. Carefully stir in rum and cream (the mixture will spatter) with a wooden spoon until smooth. Let cool, stirring occasionally, until thickened, about 5 to 10 minutes.

Lavender-Iced Brownie Cupcakes

Appearances can be deceiving: These sugared flower–topped cupcakes look like dainty petits four, but the lavender-flavored and -colored icing hides a rich chocolate brownie cupcake. Look for dried lavender at specialty markets or online; edible pesticide-free flowers can be found at baking-supply stores. You can also make the icing without the lavender. MAKES 24

3/4 cup plus 2 tablespoons all-purpose flour

1/2 teaspoon baking powder

1/2 teaspoon salt

1/2 cup (1 stick) plus 2 1/2 tablespoons unsalted butter, cut into pieces, room temperature

3 1/2 ounces unsweetened chocolate, finely chopped

1 1/3 cups sugar

2 large eggs, room temperature

1 teaspoon pure vanilla extract

Lavender Icing (recipe follows)

Crystallized Flowers (page 322)

1. Preheat oven to 350°F. Line standard muffin tins with paper liners. Whisk together flour, baking powder, and salt. Melt butter and chocolate in a heatproof bowl set over (not in) a pan of simmering water; stir until smooth. Remove from heat, and let cool slightly.

2. With an electric mixer on medium speed, beat chocolate mixture and sugar until combined. Add eggs, one at a time, beating until each is incorporated, scraping down sides of bowl as needed. Beat in vanilla. Reduce speed to low. Add flour mixture, and beat until just combined.

3. Divide batter evenly among lined cups, filling each two-thirds full. Bake, rotating tins halfway through, until a cake tester inserted in centers comes out clean, about 17 minutes (cupcakes will not be domed). Transfer to wire racks to cool completely.

4. To finish, use a small spoon to coat cupcakes with icing, covering tops completely. Let set, about 1 hour. Top with crystallized flowers. Iced cupcakes can be stored up to 2 days at room temperature in airtight containers.

. . . .

LAVENDER ICING
MAKES ENOUGH FOR 24 CUPCAKES

1/3 cup milk

1/2 teaspoon dried lavender (see Sources, page 342)

3 cups confectioners' sugar, sifted

Violet gel-paste food color

Bring milk and lavender just to a boil in a saucepan. Remove from heat, and cover; let steep 10 minutes. Strain through a fine sieve into a bowl, and discard lavender. Whisk in confectioners' sugar until smooth. Strain again. Add food color, a little at a time, stirring until desired shade is achieved. Use immediately.

simple AND sweet

It's often not the "icing on the cake" that makes it memorable, but the cake itself (the icing is a mere bonus). The singular sensations in this chapter are flavorful enough to stand on their own—no frostings, fillings, glazes, or other embellishments required. Most are adorned with only a dusting of confectioners' sugar or cocoa powder—or, in one indulgent exception, a generous scoop of ice cream—just before serving. Admittedly, a few of the examples in this section—especially those laden with fresh berries or other fruit—straddle a fine line between so-called muffins and what we recognize as cupcakes. But no matter how you choose to classify them, the modest cupcakes in the pages that follow taste divine. Some keep for days, so you can bake a bunch on the weekend to enjoy the week through. And because there's no icing to smudge, most are perfect for packing, and travel quite nicely.

Marble Cupcakes

Bakers have long swirled dark and light batters together to make marble-ized cakes. This version, baked in cupcake tins, relies on equal parts milk and cream for richness. Creating the two-tone appearance is as easy as a few strokes with a knife or skewer. There's no need to be precise; each cupcake's unique pattern is part of its charm. They're pretty enough to leave unadorned, but if you prefer, drizzle the cupcakes with milk glaze (page 63) or top with dark chocolate frosting (page 302). MAKES 16

1¾ cups cake flour (not self-rising), sifted

2 teaspoons baking powder

½ teaspoon salt

⅓ cup milk, room temperature

⅓ cup heavy cream, room temperature

½ cup (1 stick) unsalted butter, room temperature

1 cup granulated sugar

3 large eggs, room temperature

1 teaspoon pure vanilla extract

⅓ cup unsweetened Dutch-process cocoa powder

¼ cup boiling water

Confectioners' sugar, for dusting

1. Preheat oven to 350°F. Line standard muffin tins with paper liners. Sift together cake flour, baking powder, and salt. Combine milk and cream.

2. With an electric mixer on medium-high speed, cream butter and granulated sugar until pale and fluffy. Add eggs, one at a time, beating until each is incorporated, scraping down sides of bowl as needed. Beat in vanilla. Add flour mixture in three batches, alternating with two additions of milk mixture, and beating until combined.

3. To make chocolate batter, measure out 1 cup batter, and transfer to another bowl. Combine cocoa and the boiling water in a bowl. Stir into reserved 1 cup batter.

4. Fill prepared cups with alternating spoonfuls of vanilla and chocolate batter, filling each three-quarters full. Run the tip of a paring knife or wooden skewer through batter in a figure-eight motion to make swirls. Bake, rotating tins halfway through, until tops are golden and a cake tester inserted in centers comes out clean, about 20 minutes. Transfer tins to wire racks to cool completely before removing cupcakes. Cupcakes can be stored overnight at room temperature, or frozen up to 2 months, in airtight containers.

5. To finish, dust with confectioners' sugar just before serving.

Tiny Cherry and Almond Tea Cakes

Make the most of fresh cherry season by baking the little stone fruits right into charming tea cakes. The cakes, made with ground almonds, brown butter, and egg whites, are similar to financiers, which are small, springy brick-shaped cakes named for their resemblance to gold bullion. These cakes are baked with the pits left inside the cherries (be sure to warn guests before serving). Or, if you prefer, remove the pits before baking, leaving the stems intact. **MAKES 30 MINI**

½ cup plus 2 tablespoons (1¼ sticks) unsalted butter, room temperature, plus more for tins

1 cup all-purpose flour, plus more for tins

1 cup unblanched almonds (5 ounces)

1 cup sugar

1 teaspoon coarse salt

5 large egg whites

1 tablespoon plus 1 teaspoon kirsch (cherry brandy)

30 sweet (Bing) cherries, stems intact

1. Preheat oven to 400°F. Brush mini muffin tins with butter; dust with flour, tapping out excess. In a small saucepan, melt the butter over medium heat. Cook, swirling pan occasionally, until butter is lightly browned and fragrant. Skim foam from top, and remove from heat.

2. In a food processor, finely grind almonds (you should have 1 cup), and transfer to a bowl; whisk in flour, sugar, and salt to combine. Add egg whites, and whisk until smooth. Stir in kirsch. Pour in browned butter, leaving any burned sediment behind, and whisk to combine. Let batter rest 20 minutes.

3. Fill each prepared cup with 1 tablespoon batter. Push a cherry into batter of each cup, keeping stem end up. With a small spoon, smooth batter over cherries to cover.

4. Bake, rotating tins halfway through, until golden brown and a cake tester inserted near cherries comes out clean, 12 to 15 minutes. Transfer tins to wire racks to cool 10 minutes. Run a small offset spatula or knife around edges to loosen; turn out cakes onto racks to cool completely. Cakes can be stored overnight at room temperature in airtight containers.

OATMEAL-RAISIN
CUPCAKES

PEANUT BUTTER
CUPCAKES

CHOCOLATE CHUNK
CUPCAKES

Cookie Cupcakes

Inspired by everyone's favorite cookies, these packable cupcakes were created with bake sales in mind. Chocolate chunk cookies are transformed into golden-brown cupcakes; peanut butter cakes get a layer of peanut butter and cream cheese frosting, crosshatched on top; and oatmeal cupcakes (made with oat bran) are topped with crumbly oats and coconut. Choose one recipe or bake a batch of each.

Chocolate Chunk Cupcakes MAKES ABOUT 24

1½ cups all-purpose flour

¾ teaspoon baking powder

½ teaspoon salt

1 cup (2 sticks) unsalted butter, room temperature

¾ cup granulated sugar

¾ cup packed light-brown sugar

3 large eggs

1 teaspoon pure vanilla extract

1 cup milk

8 ounces semisweet chocolate, cut into ½-inch chunks (or 8 ounces chocolate chips)

1. Preheat oven to 375°F. Line standard muffin tins with paper liners. Whisk together flour, baking powder, and salt.

2. With an electric mixer on medium-high speed, cream butter and both sugars until pale and fluffy. Add eggs, one at a time, beating until each is incorporated, scraping down sides of bowl as needed. Beat in vanilla. Reduce speed to low. Add flour mixture in two batches, alternating with the milk, and beating until combined after each. Stir in chocolate chunks by hand.

3. Fill each lined cup with ¼ cup batter. Bake, rotating tins halfway through, until pale golden and a cake tester inserted in centers comes out clean, about 20 minutes. Transfer tins to wire racks to cool completely before removing cupcakes. Cupcakes can be stored up to 3 days at room temperature in airtight containers.

CONTINUED >>

Cookie Cupcakes

Peanut Butter Cupcakes MAKES ABOUT 30

FOR CUPCAKES

- 1¾ cups all-purpose flour
- ¼ teaspoon baking soda
- ¾ teaspoon baking powder
- ½ teaspoon salt
- ¾ cup (1½ sticks) unsalted butter, room temperature
- 1⅓ cups granulated sugar
- ⅔ cup creamy peanut butter, preferably natural-style
- 3 large eggs
- ½ teaspoon pure vanilla extract
- ½ cup sour cream

FOR FROSTING

- 12 ounces cream cheese, room temperature
- 1½ cups confectioners' sugar, sifted, plus more for scoring
- 3 tablespoons unsalted butter, room temperature
- 1½ cups creamy peanut butter

1. Make cupcakes: Preheat oven to 375°F. Line standard muffin tins with paper liners. Whisk together flour, baking soda, baking powder, and salt.

2. With an electric mixer on medium-high speed, cream butter and granulated sugar until pale and fluffy. Reduce speed to low. Beat in peanut butter until combined. Add eggs, one at a time, beating until each is incorporated, scraping down sides of bowl as needed. Beat in vanilla. Add flour mixture, and mix until just combined. Beat in sour cream.

3. Fill each lined cup with 3 scant tablespoons batter. Bake, rotating tins halfway through, until pale golden and a cake tester inserted in centers comes out clean, about 13 minutes. Transfer tins to wire racks to cool completely before removing cupcakes.

4. Make frosting: With an electric mixer on medium-high speed, beat cream cheese, confectioners' sugar, and butter until pale and fluffy. Stir in peanut butter by hand.

5. To finish, use an offset spatula to spread 1 to 2 tablespoons frosting onto each cupcake. Refrigerate until frosting is firm, about 10 minutes. Score each top in a crosshatch pattern with the tines of a fork, dipping tines in confectioners' sugar each time to prevent sticking. Cupcakes can be refrigerated up to 2 days in airtight containers; bring to room temperature before serving.

Oatmeal-Raisin Cupcakes MAKES ABOUT 30

3¾ cups old-fashioned rolled oats (not instant)

2½ cups all-purpose flour

⅔ cup oat bran

½ teaspoon baking soda

1½ teaspoons baking powder

1 teaspoon salt

2 teaspoons ground cinnamon

1½ cups (3 sticks) unsalted butter, room temperature

1 cup granulated sugar

1 cup packed light-brown sugar

4 large eggs

2 teaspoons pure vanilla extract

1 cup sour cream

1½ cups raisins

1 cup sweetened flaked coconut

1. Preheat oven to 375°F. Line standard muffin tins with paper liners. Whisk 2 cups oats with the flour, oat bran, baking soda, baking powder, salt, and cinnamon to combine.

2. With an electric mixer on medium-high speed, cream butter and both sugars until pale and fluffy. Add eggs, one at a time, beating until each is incorporated, scraping down sides of bowl as needed. Beat in vanilla. Reduce speed to low. Add flour mixture, and beat until just combined. Beat in sour cream. Stir in raisins by hand. Transfer 2¾ cups batter to another bowl, and stir in remaining 1¾ cups oats and the coconut; reserve for topping.

3. Fill each lined cup with 2 to 3 tablespoons plain batter; top with 1 to 2 tablespoons reserved oat-coconut batter. Bake, rotating tins halfway through, until golden and a cake tester inserted in centers comes out clean, 18 to 20 minutes. Transfer tins to wire racks to cool completely before removing cupcakes. Cupcakes can be stored up to 3 days at room temperature in airtight containers.

Raspberry Marble Cheesecakes

Smaller adaptations of favorite desserts, such as raspberry-swirled cheese-cake, are always appealing. Everyone gets his or her own, with plenty of buttery graham-cracker crust in each bite. Drops of fresh raspberry puree are pulled through cream-cheese batter to give the cakes a marbleized look. Baking the cupcakes in a hot-water bath produces the creamiest results and prevents the batter from sinking in the oven. MAKES 32

1½ cups finely ground graham crackers (about 12 sheets; use a mini chopper or food processor)

3 tablespoons unsalted butter, melted

1½ cups plus 5 tablespoons sugar

1 container (6 ounces) fresh raspberries

2 pounds cream cheese, room temperature

Pinch of salt

1 teaspoon pure vanilla extract

4 large eggs, room temperature

1. Preheat oven to 325°F. Line standard muffin tins with paper liners. Stir together ground graham crackers, butter, and 3 tablespoons sugar. Press 1 tablespoon crust mixture firmly into bottom of each lined cup. Bake until set, about 5 minutes. Transfer tins to a wire rack to cool.

2. Process raspberries in a food processor until smooth, about 30 seconds. Pass puree through a fine sieve into a small bowl, pressing with a flexible spatula to remove as much liquid as possible; discard solids. Whisk in 2 tablespoons sugar.

3. With an electric mixer on medium-high speed, beat cream cheese until fluffy, scraping down sides of bowl as needed. With mixer on low speed, add remaining 1½ cups sugar in a steady stream. Add salt and vanilla; mix until well combined. Add eggs, one at a time, beating until just combined after each.

4. Spoon 3 tablespoons filling over crust in each cup. Dollop ½ teaspoon raspberry puree in a few dots over each. With a wooden skewer or toothpick, swirl sauce into filling. Place each tin in a roasting pan (bake in batches, if necessary); pour enough hot water into pan to come three-quarters of the way up sides of cups.

5. Bake, rotating pans halfway through, until filling is set, about 22 minutes. Carefully remove tins from water bath and transfer to wire racks to cool completely. Refrigerate (in tins) at least 4 hours (or out of tins up to 5 days in airtight containers). Remove from tins just before serving.

FILLING AND SWIRLING CHEESECAKES

Blondie Cupcakes

For those who like their baked goods chunky and nutty, these cupcakes, inspired by the popular bar cookies, are nearly bursting with cashews, butterscotch chips, and toffee bits. If you can't find toffee bits, chop a small chocolate-covered toffee bar, such as Skor or Heath, to use instead. **MAKES 12**

$1^2/_3$ cups all-purpose flour

1 teaspoon baking powder

$^3/_4$ teaspoon salt

$^1/_2$ cup (1 stick) plus 1 tablespoon unsalted butter, room temperature

1 cup packed light-brown sugar

2 large eggs, room temperature

1 teaspoon pure vanilla extract

$^1/_3$ cup butterscotch chips

$^1/_2$ cup unsalted cashews, coarsely chopped (3 ounces)

$^1/_4$ cup toffee bits

1. Preheat oven to 350°F. Line a standard muffin tin with paper liners. Whisk together flour, baking powder, and salt.

2. With an electric mixer on medium-high speed, cream butter and brown sugar until pale and fluffy. Add eggs and vanilla; beat until combined, scraping down sides of bowl as needed. Reduce speed to low. Add flour mixture, and beat until incorporated. Fold in butterscotch chips, cashews, and toffee bits by hand.

3. Divide batter evenly among lined cups, filling each three-quarters full. Bake, rotating tin halfway through, until golden brown and a cake tester inserted in centers comes out with only a few moist crumbs attached (but is not wet), about 30 minutes. Transfer tin to a wire rack to cool completely before removing cupcakes. Cupcakes can be stored up to 5 days at room temperature in airtight containers.

Blackberry-Cornmeal Cupcakes

Succulent blackberries, picked fresh from a farm or bought at a local market, are baked into golden cornmeal cupcakes for a delicious taste of summer. Serve the cakes warm from the oven or at room temperature, and pair with ice cream, if desired. Oven temperature is crucial here: If it's any cooler than 375 degrees, the berries will sink to the bottom. MAKES 16

1¼ cups all-purpose flour

½ cup fine-ground yellow cornmeal

2 teaspoons baking powder

1 teaspoon salt

1¼ cups sugar

½ cup buttermilk, room temperature

2 large eggs, room temperature

7 tablespoons unsalted butter, melted and cooled

1 to 2 containers (6 ounces each) fresh blackberries

1. Preheat oven to 375°F. Line standard muffin tins with paper liners. Whisk together flour, cornmeal, baking powder, salt, and 1 cup plus 2 tablespoons sugar. In another bowl, whisk together buttermilk, eggs, and melted butter; pour over flour mixture, whisking to combine.

2. Fill each lined cup with a scant ¼ cup batter. Top batter with blackberries (3 to 4 berries per cup), then sprinkle evenly with remaining 2 tablespoons sugar.

3. Bake, rotating tins halfway through, until evenly browned on top, 20 to 25 minutes. Transfer to a wire rack to cool completely before removing cupcakes. Cupcakes are best eaten the day they are baked, but will keep up to 2 days at room temperature in airtight containers.

Cookies and Cream Cheesecakes

These single-serving delights are a staff favorite—not only because they are delectable, but also since they are easy to prepare. Instead of a cookie-crumb crust, a whole sandwich cookie serves as the base for each cheesecake. In addition, chopped cookies are mixed into the filling. **MAKES 30**

42 cream-filled chocolate sandwich cookies, such as Oreos, 30 left whole and 12 coarsely chopped

2 pounds cream cheese, room temperature

1 cup sugar

1 teaspoon pure vanilla extract

4 large eggs, room temperature, lightly beaten

1 cup sour cream

Pinch of salt

1. Preheat oven to 275°F. Line standard muffin tins with paper liners. Place 1 whole cookie in the bottom of each lined cup.

2. With an electric mixer on medium-high speed, beat cream cheese until smooth, scraping down sides of bowl as needed. Gradually add sugar, and beat until combined. Beat in vanilla.

3. Drizzle in eggs, a bit at a time, beating to combine and scraping down sides of bowl as needed. Beat in sour cream and salt. Stir in chopped cookies by hand.

4. Divide batter evenly among cookie-filled cups, filling each almost to the top. Bake, rotating tins halfway through, until filling is set, about 22 minutes. Transfer tins to wire racks to cool completely. Refrigerate (in tins) at least 4 hours (or up to overnight). Remove from tins just before serving.

ASSEMBLING CHEESECAKES

Pistachio-Raspberry Tea Cakes

These brightly colored cupcakes are very simple to make—a food processor handles all the mixing. You'll find slivered pistachios at specialty stores or online retailers; you may substitute chopped pistachios instead.

MAKES 15 STANDARD OR 36 MINI

Nonstick cooking spray

1 cup unsalted shelled pistachios

1½ cups sugar

1 teaspoon salt

½ cup (1 stick) unsalted butter, room temperature, cut into pieces

2 teaspoons pure vanilla extract

4 large eggs

1 cup all-purpose flour

1 to 2 containers (6 ounces each) fresh raspberries

¼ cup slivered or chopped pistachios, for sprinkling

1. Preheat oven to 375°F. Line standard or mini muffin tins with paper liners; coat liners with cooking spray. In a food processor, finely grind shelled pistachios with the sugar and salt. Add butter, vanilla, and eggs; process until smooth. Add flour; pulse until just moistened and combined (do not overmix).

2. Divide batter evenly among lined cups, filling each three-quarters full. Drop raspberries into batter (4 to 6 per standard tea cake; 2 per mini) and sprinkle with slivered pistachios. Bake, rotating tins halfway through, until golden brown, about 28 minutes for standard cupcakes, 14 for minis. Transfer tins to wire racks to cool. Serve warm or at room temperature. Cakes can be stored up to 2 days at room temperature in airtight containers.

Flourless Chocolate Cupcakes

With their crackly, sunken tops, these chocolate cupcakes seem tailor-made for cradling scoops of ice cream. In place of flour and leaveners, whipped egg whites produce cakes with a light-as-air texture. MAKES 22

6 tablespoons (³/₄ stick) unsalted butter

8 ounces bittersweet chocolate, coarsely chopped (or 1¹/₂ cups semisweet chocolate chips)

6 large eggs, separated, room temperature

¹/₂ cup sugar

Ice cream, for serving (optional)

1. Preheat oven to 275°F. Line standard muffin tins with paper liners. Melt butter and chocolate in a large heatproof bowl set over (not in) a pan of simmering water. Stir to combine, then remove bowl from heat and let cool slightly. Whisk in egg yolks.

2. With an electric mixer on medium speed, whisk egg whites until soft peaks form. Gradually add sugar, beating until peaks are stiff and glossy but not dry (do not overbeat). Whisk one quarter of the beaten egg whites into chocolate mixture to lighten; gently fold mixture into remaining whites.

3. Divide batter evenly among lined cups, filling each three-quarters full. Bake, rotating tins halfway through, until cupcakes are just set in centers, about 25 minutes. Transfer tins to wire racks to cool completely before removing cupcakes (their centers will sink). Cupcakes are best eaten the same day they are baked; keep at room temperature until ready to serve, topped with scoops of ice cream, if desired.

Allergen-Free Chocolate Cupcakes

Anyone allergic to nuts, eggs, or dairy shouldn't miss out on all the fun. Whether someone in your family has dietary restrictions or you're making treats for a whole classroom of kids, these chocolate cupcakes should suit most needs. Divvies Bakery, which specializes in allergen-free sweets, kindly shared this recipe on *The Martha Stewart Show*. MAKES 12

1½ cups cake flour (not self-rising), sifted

¾ cup granulated sugar

¼ cup unsweetened cocoa powder, plus more for dusting

1 teaspoon baking soda

½ teaspoon salt

¼ cup plus 1 tablespoon vegetable oil

1 tablespoon distilled white vinegar

1 teaspoon pure vanilla extract

1¼ cups water

Confectioners' sugar, for dusting

1. Preheat oven to 350°F. Line a standard muffin tin with paper liners. Sift together cake flour, granulated sugar, cocoa, baking soda, and salt.

2. With an electric mixer on medium-high speed, mix together oil, vinegar, vanilla, and the water until well combined. Add flour mixture and mix until smooth, scraping down sides of bowl as needed (batter will be very thin).

3. Divide batter evenly among lined cups, filling each three-quarters full. Bake, rotating tin halfway through, until a cake tester inserted into centers comes out clean, 20 to 25 minutes. Turn out cupcakes onto a wire rack and let cool completely.

4. Cupcakes can be stored up to 3 days at room temperature, or frozen up to 1 month, in airtight containers. Dust cupcakes with cocoa and confectioners' sugar just before serving.

filled AND layered

One bite is all it takes to discover the true nature of filled and layered cupcakes. Each has something delicious—bracing lemon curd, rich pastry cream, a cool peppermint patty, or other unexpected ingredients—tucked inside. Although they're a bit more involved to prepare than more classic cupcakes, these little treats are well worth any extra effort. Many are constructed to resemble miniature versions of larger desserts, such as Boston cream pie and German chocolate cake, and this variation in scale renders them instantly enchanting. You can adapt the simple techniques used in this chapter to suit other cupcake recipes, or swap in other luscious fillings for those suggested. Whether piped through the bottom, spread between layers, or baked right inside, the filling introduces another enticing element—and adds the thrill of surprise.

Boston Cream Pie Cupcakes

Boston cream pie—which, of course, is not a pie at all—originated at the Parker House Hotel in Boston in the 1850s. When home cooks replicated the dessert, they baked the soft yellow sponge cake in pie tins (hence the name), which were more readily available than cake pans. This petite variation is at once familiar and novel. MAKES 20

6 tablespoons (¾ stick) unsalted butter, cut into pieces, plus more, room temperature, for tins

1½ cups all-purpose flour, plus more for tins

1½ teaspoons baking powder

½ teaspoon salt

½ cup milk

3 large eggs, room temperature

1 cup sugar

1 teaspoon pure vanilla extract

Pastry Cream (page 316)

Chocolate Ganache Glaze (page 312)

1. Preheat oven to 350°F. Brush standard muffin tins with butter; dust with flour, tapping out excess. Whisk together flour, baking powder, and salt. Combine milk and butter in a saucepan; set over very low heat.

2. With an electric mixer on high speed, whisk eggs and sugar until fluffy, pale yellow, and thick enough to hold a ribbon on the surface for several seconds when whisk is lifted, about 5 minutes. Reduce speed to medium. Gradually add flour mixture, whisking until just incorporated.

3. Bring milk and butter just to a boil. With mixer on low speed, add hot-milk mixture to batter in a slow, steady stream; mix until smooth (do not overmix). Beat in vanilla.

4. Divide batter evenly among prepared cups, filling each halfway. Bake, rotating tins halfway through, until cupcakes are golden and a cake tester inserted in centers comes out clean, about 15 minutes. Transfer tins to wire racks to cool 10 minutes. Run a small offset spatula or knife around the edges to loosen; turn out cupcakes onto racks and let cool completely. Cupcakes can be stored overnight at room temperature, or frozen up to 2 months, in airtight containers.

5. To finish, use a serrated knife (and a gentle sawing motion) to split cupcakes in half horizontally. Spread about 1 tablespoon pastry cream on the bottom half of each cupcake. Replace top halves. Spoon about 1 table-spoon glaze over each cupcake. Refrigerate 30 minutes before serving.

Strawberry-Jam Tea Cakes

You can use any variety of jam to fill these versatile little cakes, as well as vary the type of citrus used in the batter and in the glaze. You could also substitute milk glaze (page 63) for the citrus glaze used here. MAKES 16

1 cup (2 sticks) unsalted butter, room temperature, plus more for tins

3 cups all-purpose flour, plus more for tins

1 teaspoon baking powder

½ teaspoon salt

1½ cups sugar

2 teaspoons finely grated orange zest

4 large eggs, separated, room temperature

½ cup milk

1 cup strawberry jam or preserves

Citrus Glaze (made with orange juice and zest, page 315)

1. Preheat oven to 350°F. Brush standard muffin tins with butter; dust with flour, tapping out excess. Whisk together flour, baking powder, and salt.

2. With an electric mixer on medium-high speed, cream butter, sugar, and zest until pale and fluffy. Add egg yolks, one at a time, beating until each is incorporated, scraping down sides of bowl as needed. Reduce speed to low. Add flour mixture in three batches, alternating with two additions of milk, and beating until just combined after each.

3. In another bowl, with an electric mixer on medium speed, whisk egg whites to soft peaks; gently fold into batter. Spoon 2 tablespoons batter into each prepared cup. Make an indentation in the middle of each; fill with 1 tablespoon jam. Top with an additional 2 tablespoons batter, covering jam completely.

4. Bake, rotating tins halfway through, until a cake tester inserted in centers of top layers comes out clean, about 30 minutes. Remove from oven. Run a small offset spatula around the edges, and turn out cakes onto wire racks and let cool completely.

5. To finish, drizzle cakes evenly with glaze, and let set, about 30 minutes. Glazed cupcakes can be stored up to 2 days in a single layer at room temperature in airtight containers.

Peanut Butter–Filled Chocolate Cupcakes

An abundance of creamy peanut-butter filling renders these cupcakes extra-rich and irresistible. The batter and filling—each whisked together by hand—are layered, then swirled to create the marbleized pattern on top. MAKES 12

2/3 cup all-purpose flour

1/2 teaspoon baking powder

1/4 teaspoon salt

1/2 cup (1 stick) unsalted butter, cut into small pieces

4 ounces semisweet chocolate, coarsely chopped

2 ounces unsweetened chocolate, coarsely chopped

3/4 cup granulated sugar

3 large eggs

2 teaspoons pure vanilla extract

Peanut-Butter Filling (recipe follows)

1. Preheat oven to 325°F. Line a standard muffin tin with paper liners. Whisk together flour, baking powder, and salt. Put butter and chocolates in a heatproof bowl set over (not in) a pan of simmering water; stir until melted. Remove from heat, and let cool slightly.

2. Whisk granulated sugar into cooled chocolate mixture. Add eggs, and whisk until mixture is smooth. Stir in vanilla. Add flour mixture; stir until well incorporated.

3. Spoon 2 tablespoons chocolate batter into each lined cup, followed by 1 tablespoon peanut butter filling. Repeat with another tablespoon of batter, and top with 1 teaspoon filling. Swirl top of cupcake batter and filling with a wooden skewer or toothpick.

4. Bake, rotating tin halfway through, until a cake tester inserted in centers comes out with only a few moist crumbs attached, about 40 minutes. Transfer tin to a wire rack to cool completely before removing cupcakes. Cupcakes can be stored up to 3 days at room temperature in airtight containers.

. . . .

PEANUT-BUTTER FILLING
MAKES ENOUGH FOR 12 CUPCAKES

4 tablespoons (1/2 stick) unsalted butter, melted

1/2 cup confectioners' sugar, sifted

3/4 cup smooth peanut butter

1/4 teaspoon salt

1/2 teaspoon pure vanilla extract

Stir together all ingredients until smooth. Use immediately.

Martha's Meyer Lemon Cupcakes

The mild and sweet flavor of Meyer lemon is one of Martha's favorites; these zest-flecked cupcakes are filled with Meyer lemon curd, which peeks out from the tops. The fruit, which is actually a lemon-orange hybrid, is generally available at specialty stores in winter and early spring. If you can't find Meyer lemons, use regular lemons instead. The recipe yields a lot of cupcakes, so you may want to consider these for a bake sale or large gathering, such as a shower or special birthday celebration. MAKES 42

3½ cups all-purpose flour, sifted

2 tablespoons finely grated Meyer lemon zest, plus 2 tablespoons fresh Meyer lemon juice (from 1 to 2 Meyer lemons)

½ teaspoon baking powder

1½ teaspoons coarse salt

1¾ cups (3½ sticks) unsalted butter, room temperature

3 cups granulated sugar

8 ounces cream cheese, room temperature

7 large eggs, room temperature

1 teaspoon pure vanilla extract

Confectioners' sugar, for dusting

Lemon Curd (made with Meyer lemons; page 317)

1. Preheat oven to 325°F. Line standard muffin tins with paper liners. Whisk together flour, zest, baking powder, and salt.

2. With an electric mixer on medium-high speed, cream butter and granulated sugar until pale and fluffy. Beat in cream cheese. Reduce speed to low. Add eggs, one at a time, beating until each is incorporated, scraping down sides of bowl as needed. Beat in lemon juice and vanilla. Add flour mixture in three batches, beating until just combined after each.

3. Divide batter evenly among lined cups, filling each three-quarters full. Bake, rotating tins halfway through, until a cake tester inserted in centers comes out clean, about 28 minutes. Transfer tins to wire racks to cool completely before removing cupcakes. Cupcakes can be stored overnight at room temperature, or frozen up to 2 months, in airtight containers.

4. To finish, dust cupcakes with confectioners' sugar. Fill a pastry bag fitted with a coupler and a medium round tip (#8) with curd. Insert tip into top of each cupcake, and squeeze some curd below top to fill the inside, then lift the tip and squeeze more curd in a pool on top. Filled cupcakes can be kept at room temperature up to 1 hour (or refrigerated a few hours more) before serving.

FILLING CUPCAKES WITH LEMON CURD

Mint-Filled Brownie Cupcakes

Each of these chewy brownie cupcakes has a secret center: a chocolate-covered peppermint fondant. To ensure they have a dense, fudgy texture, be careful not to overbake (start checking at thirty minutes). **MAKES 12**

8 ounces semisweet or bittersweet chocolate, coarsely chopped

½ cup (1 stick) unsalted butter, cut into pieces, room temperature

1 cup sugar

¾ teaspoon salt

3 large eggs

½ cup all-purpose flour

¼ cup unsweetened Dutch-process cocoa powder, sifted

12 small (1½-inch) chocolate-covered peppermint fondants, such as After Eight Mints

1. Preheat oven to 350°F. Line a standard muffin tin with paper liners. Place chocolate and butter in a heatproof bowl set over (not in) a pan of simmering water. Stir occasionally just until melted, 4 to 5 minutes.

2. Remove bowl from heat. Whisk in sugar and salt until mixture is smooth; whisk in eggs to combine. Gently whisk in flour and cocoa just until smooth (do not overmix).

3. Spoon 1 heaping tablespoon of batter into each lined cup. Place 1 peppermint fondant on top, gently pressing into batter. Top with 2 tablespoons batter, covering the fondant completely. Bake, rotating tin halfway through, until a cake tester inserted halfway in centers (above mint fondant) comes out with only a few moist crumbs attached, about 35 minutes. Transfer tin to a wire rack to cool completely before removing cupcakes. Cupcakes can be stored up to 3 days at room temperature in airtight containers.

Lemon-Yogurt Cupcakes with Raspberry Jam

Stripes of sweet crimson jam give otherwise ordinary-looking cupcakes a striking finish. The cupcakes are tender (thanks to yogurt in the batter) but slice easily into even layers. Serve these cheerful treats at an afternoon tea, or box them up for gift giving. MAKES 24

1½ cups (3 sticks) unsalted butter, room temperature, plus more for tins

2¾ cups all-purpose flour, plus more for tins

½ teaspoon baking soda

2 teaspoons baking powder

¾ teaspoon salt

3 large eggs, separated, room temperature

1¼ cups granulated sugar

1 tablespoon finely grated lemon zest, plus 4½ teaspoons fresh lemon juice

1½ teaspoons pure vanilla extract

¾ cup plain whole-milk yogurt

1 cup seedless raspberry jam or preserves

Confectioners' sugar, for dusting

1. Preheat oven to 350°F. Brush standard muffin tins with butter; dust with flour, tapping out excess. Whisk together flour, baking soda, baking powder, and salt.

2. With an electric mixer on medium speed, whisk egg whites until soft peaks form. Add ½ cup granulated sugar; whisk until peaks are stiff and glossy but not dry (do not overbeat). Transfer mixture to a large bowl.

3. In another bowl, with an electric mixer on medium-high speed, cream butter until smooth. Add remaining ¾ cup granulated sugar and the zest; beat until pale and fluffy. Add yolks, one at a time, beating until each is incorporated, scraping down sides of bowl as needed. Mix in lemon juice and vanilla. Reduce speed to low. Add flour mixture in three batches, alternating with two additions of yogurt, and beating until just combined after each. Whisk one third of the egg-white mixture into batter to lighten, then gently fold in remaining whites.

4. Divide batter evenly among prepared cups, filling each three-quarters full. Bake, rotating tins halfway through, until a cake tester inserted in centers comes out clean, about 20 minutes. Transfer tins to wire racks to cool completely before removing cupcakes.

5. To finish, use a serrated knife (and a gentle sawing motion) to slice each cupcake twice horizontally to make three even layers. Spread a thin layer of jam (about 1 teaspoon) on each bottom layer, then top with middle layers. Spread another layer of jam on each middle layer. Top with third cupcake layer, pressing gently on top so layers adhere. Filled cupcakes can be stored up to 3 days at room temperature in airtight containers. Dust with confectioners' sugar just before serving.

German Chocolate Cupcakes

Although you might think these cakes have a German pedigree, they're actually named for German's chocolate, a sweet baking chocolate developed in the nineteenth century for an American company called Baker's Chocolate. Modern versions call for semisweet chocolate instead, which gives the cupcakes a well-rounded flavor, perfectly complemented by the traditional sticky-sweet coconut-pecan filling and frosting. MAKES 24

3/4 cup (1 1/2 sticks) unsalted butter, room temperature, plus more for tins

2 cups cake flour (not self-rising), sifted, plus more for tins

1 teaspoon baking soda

3/4 teaspoon salt

1 1/3 cups sugar

3 large eggs, room temperature

1 1/2 teaspoons pure vanilla extract

1 cup buttermilk

5 ounces semisweet chocolate, melted and cooled (see page 323)

Coconut-Pecan Frosting (page 311)

1. Preheat oven to 350°F. Brush standard muffin tins with butter; dust with cake flour, tapping out excess. Whisk together cake flour, baking soda, and salt.

2. With an electric mixer on medium-high speed, cream butter and sugar until pale and fluffy. Add eggs, one at a time, beating until each is incorporated, scraping down sides of bowl as needed. Beat in vanilla. Reduce speed to low. Add flour mixture in three batches, alternating with two additions of buttermilk, and beating until combined after each. Beat in chocolate until combined.

3. Divide batter evenly among prepared cups, filling each three-quarters full. Bake, rotating tins halfway through, until a cake tester inserted in centers comes out clean, 20 minutes. Transfer tins to wire racks to cool 10 minutes. Run a small offset spatula or knife around the edges to loosen; turn out cupcakes onto racks and let cool completely. Cupcakes can be stored up to 3 days at room temperature in airtight containers.

4. To finish, use a serrated knife (and a gentle sawing motion) to split cupcakes in half horizontally. Spread a heaping tablespoon of frosting on top of each bottom half; replace top halves. Spread more frosting on top of each cupcake. Serve immediately.

Meringue Cupcakes with Berry Compote

It's no secret that nearly everyone at *Martha Stewart Living*—especially Martha—loves meringue, and these billowy puffs, with their distinctive peaks and berries-and-cream filling, illustrate why. The cupcakes need to bake for about three hours, so plan accordingly. And avoid making meringues on a humid day, as they will never become crisp. MAKES 12

Nonstick cooking spray

6 large egg whites, room temperature

½ teaspoon salt

1 teaspoon distilled white vinegar

1 teaspoon pure vanilla extract

1¾ cups sugar

1 cup crème fraîche

½ cup heavy cream

Strawberry and Raspberry Compote (recipe follows), chilled

PIPING THE MERINGUE TO FORM CUPCAKES

1. Preheat oven to 225°F. Line every other cup of two standard muffin tins with paper liners (so meringues cook evenly); coat liners with cooking spray. With an electric mixer on medium-high speed, whisk egg whites, salt, vinegar, and vanilla until frothy. Add sugar, 1 tablespoon at a time, beating 2 minutes and scraping down sides of bowl after each addition. Continue whisking until stiff, glossy (but not dry) peaks form.

2. Transfer meringue to a pastry bag fitted with a plain coupler (no tip), and pipe equally into lined cups so meringue is about 2 inches above rims, swirling the tops into a peak. Clean around edges so meringue is not touching the tins. Bake until meringues are just beginning to color and are completely dry on the outside but still soft in the middle (a toothpick inserted at base of top, through the side, should have moist but cooked crumbs attached), 3 to 3¼ hours, rotating tins after 1½ hours of baking. Remove from oven. Immediately remove meringues from tins; gently peel off liners. Let cool completely on a wire rack.

3. To finish, whisk together crème fraîche and heavy cream until soft peaks form. Using a serrated knife (and a gentle sawing motion), gently slice off tops (don't worry if they crack); reserve. Spoon some compote onto bottom of each cupcake, then spoon whipped-cream mixture over compote. Replace tops and serve immediately.

STRAWBERRY AND RASPBERRY COMPOTE
MAKES ENOUGH FOR 12 CUPCAKES

1 container (10 ounces) fresh strawberries, rinsed, hulled, and coarsely chopped

½ cup sugar

1 tablespoon fresh lemon juice

1 container (6 ounces) fresh raspberries

Bring strawberries, sugar, and lemon juice to a simmer in a nonreactive saucepan over medium heat. Cook, stirring occasionally, until reduced to ¾ cup. Let cool completely before stirring in raspberries. Refrigerate up to 1 day in an airtight container.

Amaretto-Pineapple Cupcakes

These tropical cupcakes, scaled-down versions of the most well-known upside-down cake, have a retro appeal thanks to the flambéed fruit filling.

MAKES 15

½ cup (1 stick) unsalted butter, room temperature, plus more for tins

1½ cups all-purpose flour, plus more for tins

⅓ cup unblanched almonds, finely ground in a food processor

1 teaspoon baking powder

1 teaspoon salt

1¼ cups sugar

3 large eggs, room temperature

1 teaspoon pure vanilla extract

½ teaspoon pure almond extract

½ cup milk

½ cup amaretto (almond-flavored liqueur)

1 cup heavy cream

Flambéed Pineapple (recipe follows)

1. Preheat oven to 325°F. Brush standard muffin tins with butter; dust with flour, tapping out excess. Whisk together flour, ground almonds, baking powder, and salt.

2. With an electric mixer on medium-high speed, cream butter and sugar until pale and fluffy. Add eggs, one at a time, beating until each is incorporated, scraping down sides of bowl as needed. Mix in extracts. Reduce speed to low. Add flour mixture in three batches, alternating with two additions of milk, and mixing until just combined.

3. Divide batter among prepared cups, filling each three-quarters full. Bake, rotating tins halfway through, until a cake tester inserted in centers comes out clean, about 30 minutes. Transfer tins to wire racks; immediately poke holes all over tops of cupcakes with a toothpick. Pour amaretto evenly on top; let cool completely before removing from tins.

4. To finish, whip cream to soft peaks. Using a serrated knife (and a gentle sawing motion), slice off tops; reserve. Spoon 1 tablespoon flambéed pineapple on each cupcake bottom; replace tops. Dollop cupcakes with whipped cream; spoon more pineapple on top. Serve immediately.

FLAMBÉED PINEAPPLE

MAKES ENOUGH FOR 15 CUPCAKES

8 rounds (each ¼ inch thick) peeled pineapple

½ cup sugar

½ cup amaretto

½ cup heavy cream

2 tablespoons fresh orange juice

1 vanilla bean, halved lengthwise, seeds scraped and reserved

Pinch of salt

1. Stack pineapple rounds; cut into quarters. Trim core from each wedge, and discard. Cut pineapple into small dice. Heat sugar in a large skillet over medium-high, stirring, until sugar melts and turns golden brown. Add pineapple; toss.

2. Carefully pour in amaretto; immediately tilt skillet slightly to ignite alcohol. (If using an electric stove, use a long match to ignite alcohol.) When flames subside and caramel melts, carefully stir in cream, orange juice, and vanilla-bean seeds (reserve pod for another use). Reduce heat to medium; boil, stirring occasionally, until thickened, about 5 minutes. Let cool completely before using or storing. Refrigerate up to 3 days in an airtight container; bring to room temperature before using.

Jumbo Cream-Filled Chocolate Cupcakes

Store-bought snack cakes can't compare to these homemade versions: Dark chocolate cupcakes are filled with fluffy marshmallow cream, which is also used to pipe decorations on the tops. Take care not to overfill the hollowed-out cupcakes, or the cream may seep out. **MAKES 12 JUMBO**

1 cup (2 sticks) unsalted butter, room temperature, plus more for tins

$3/4$ cup unsweetened cocoa powder, plus more for tins

2 cups all-purpose flour

$1/2$ teaspoon baking soda

2 teaspoons baking powder

$1/2$ teaspoon salt

2 cups sugar

3 large eggs, room temperature

1 cup sour cream, room temperature

Marshmallow Cream Filling (recipe follows)

1. Preheat oven to 350°F. Brush jumbo muffin tins with butter; dust with cocoa powder, tapping out excess. Whisk together flour, cocoa, baking soda, baking powder, and salt.

2. With an electric mixer on medium-high speed, cream butter and sugar until pale and fluffy. Add eggs, one at a time, beating until each is incorporated, scraping down sides of bowl as needed. With mixer on low speed, add flour mixture in two batches, alternating with the sour cream, and mixing until just incorporated after each.

3. Divide batter evenly among prepared cups, filling each with about $1/2$ cup. Bake, rotating tins halfway through, until a cake tester inserted in centers comes out clean, about 25 minutes. Transfer tins to wire racks to cool 5 minutes. Run a small offset spatula or knife around the edges to loosen; turn out cupcakes onto racks and let cool completely.

4. Transfer filling to a large heavy-duty resealable plastic bag, and twist bag to remove excess air before sealing. Snip off one corner of the bag to make a $1/4$-inch opening. (Alternatively, use a pastry bag fitted with a medium round tip, such as #8.)

5. Using a small melon baller, scoop out center of each cupcake from the bottom, and reserve (to reseal cupcake after filling). Hollow out each cupcake a bit more, discarding crumbs. Insert snipped corner of bag (or pastry tip) into each cavity, and squeeze just to fill; replace reserved cake pieces. Decorate tops with remaining filling. Filled cupcakes can be stored up to 2 days at room temperature in airtight containers.

. . . .

MARSHMALLOW CREAM FILLING
MAKES ENOUGH FOR 12 JUMBO CUPCAKES

$1^{1}/2$ cups marshmallow cream, such as Marshmallow Fluff

$1/2$ cup (1 stick) unsalted butter, cut into pieces, room temperature

Whisk marshmallow cream and butter until smooth. Cover with plastic wrap, and chill until slightly firm, 15 to 30 minutes, before using.

Black Forest Cupcakes

Chocolate and cherries are a match made in heaven—or, in this case—the Black Forest region of Germany, where the original layer cake was created (and cherries are abundant). These miniature versions of the classic German dessert are saturated with cherry liqueur, layered with sweet pastry cream and preserved cherries, and drizzled with rich chocolate ganache. **MAKES 32**

- 1 cup plus 2 tablespoons (2¼ sticks) unsalted butter, room temperature, plus more for tins
- 1 cup plus 2 tablespoons unsweetened Dutch-process cocoa powder, plus more for tins
- 2½ cups plus 2 tablespoons all-purpose flour
- 2 teaspoons baking soda
- ⅛ teaspoon salt
- 1 cup granulated sugar
- 1 cup packed dark-brown sugar
- 3 large eggs, room temperature
- ¾ cup sour cream
- 1½ cups buttermilk
- 1 jar (12 ounces) preserved cherries in light syrup
- 2 tablespoons kirsch (cherry-flavored brandy)
- Pastry Cream (page 316)
- Chocolate Ganache Glaze (page 312)

1. Preheat oven to 350°F. Brush standard muffin tins with butter; dust with cocoa powder, tapping out excess. Whisk together flour, cocoa, baking soda, and salt.

2. With an electric mixer on medium-high speed, cream butter and granulated sugar until pale and fluffy. Add brown sugar, and beat until fluffy. Add eggs, one at a time, beating until well incorporated and scraping down sides of bowl as needed. Mix in sour cream. Reduce speed to low. Add flour mixture in three batches, alternating with two additions of buttermilk, and mixing until just combined after each.

3. Divide batter evenly among prepared cups, filling each three-quarters full. Bake, rotating tins halfway through, until tops are firm to the touch and a cake tester inserted in centers comes out clean, about 20 minutes. Transfer tins to wire racks to cool completely before removing cupcakes. Cupcakes can be stored overnight at room temperature, or frozen up to 2 months, in airtight containers.

4. To finish, drain cherries, reserving ¼ cup plus 2 tablespoons syrup. Cut each cherry in half. Combine reserved syrup and kirsch in a small bowl. Using a serrated knife (and a gentle sawing motion), split cupcakes in half horizontally. Brush both cut sides with kirsch mixture. Arrange halved cherries over cupcake bottoms; spoon about 1 heaping tablespoon pastry cream evenly over cherries. Replace top halves. Spoon 2 tablespoons glaze over tops. Refrigerate 30 minutes before serving.

piped AND topped

Don't be intimidated by the fanciful designs of the cupcakes in this section; anyone can add flourishes that are impressive, yet not necessarily time-consuming. A pastry bag and a large tip make deceptively quick work of finishing dozens of cupcakes at a time (which is why so many bakeries rely on this trick). Just a squeeze—and, in some cases, a twist of the wrist—and your cupcake is covered. The versatility of the tips allows for some improvisation; a big star tip creates a ridged peak of frosting, while a plain round tip (or even just a coupler) produces a topping more seamless and sleek. And once you get the hang of piping, you can switch to other pastry tips to make cupcakes that feature a series of piped designs, such as dots or shells. After piping, feel free to garnish with simple accents, such as fresh strawberry or banana slices, gumdrop candies, or anything else that hints at the flavor underneath.

Snickerdoodle Cupcakes

Capped with "kisses" of seven-minute frosting and dusted with cinnamon-sugar, these cupcakes are a play on the cookie of the same name, also finished with cinnamon-sugar. The crackled cookies are thought to be of German origin, and their whimsical name a mispronunciation of *schneckennudeln* (crinkly noodles). **MAKES 28**

1½ cups all-purpose flour

1½ cups cake flour (not self-rising), sifted

1 tablespoon baking powder

½ teaspoon salt

1 tablespoon ground cinnamon, plus ½ teaspoon for dusting

1 cup (2 sticks) unsalted butter, room temperature

1¾ cups sugar, plus 2 tablespoons for dusting

4 large eggs, room temperature

2 teaspoons pure vanilla extract

1¼ cups milk

Seven-Minute Frosting (page 303)

1. Preheat oven to 350°F. Line standard muffin tins with paper liners. Sift together both flours, baking powder, salt, and 1 tablespoon cinnamon.

2. With an electric mixer on medium-high speed, cream butter and sugar until pale and fluffy. Add eggs, one at a time, beating until each is incorporated, scraping down sides of bowl as needed. Beat in vanilla. Reduce speed to low. Add flour mixture in three batches, alternating with two additions of milk, and beating until combined after each.

3. Divide batter evenly among lined cups, filling each three-quarters full. Bake, rotating tins halfway through, until a cake tester inserted in centers comes out clean, about 20 minutes. Transfer tins to wire racks to cool completely before removing cupcakes. Cupcakes can be stored up to 2 days at room temperature, or frozen up to 2 months, in airtight containers.

4. To finish, combine remaining ½ teaspoon cinnamon and 2 tablespoons sugar. Using a pastry bag fitted with a large plain tip (Ateco #809 or Wilton #1A), pipe frosting on each cupcake: Hold bag over cupcake with tip just above top, and squeeze to create a dome of frosting, then release pressure and pull up to form a peak. Using a small, fine sieve, dust peaks with cinnamon-sugar. Cupcakes are best eaten the day they are frosted; keep at room temperature until ready to serve.

Roasted Banana Cupcakes

Roasting the fruit before folding it into the batter gives these cupcakes a pronounced banana flavor and keeps them very moist. Honey, often paired with bananas, is added to the frosting. **MAKES 16**

3 ripe bananas, plus 1 to 2 more for garnish

2 cups cake flour (not self-rising), sifted

1/2 teaspoon baking soda

1/2 teaspoon baking powder

3/4 teaspoon salt

1/2 cup (1 stick) unsalted butter, room temperature

3/4 cup sugar

3 large eggs, separated

1/2 cup sour cream

1 teaspoon pure vanilla extract

Honey-Cinnamon Frosting (recipe follows)

1. Preheat oven to 400°F. Line standard muffin tins with paper liners. Place 3 whole unpeeled bananas on a baking sheet and roast 15 minutes (the peels will darken). Meanwhile, sift together cake flour, baking soda, baking powder, and salt. Remove bananas from oven and let cool before peeling. Reduce oven temperature to 350°F.

2. With an electric mixer on medium-high speed, cream butter and sugar until pale and fluffy. Add egg yolks, one at a time, beating until each is incorporated, scraping down sides of bowl as needed. Add roasted bananas, and beat to combine. Add flour mixture in three batches, alternating with two additions of sour cream, and beating until just combined after each. Beat in vanilla.

3. In another mixing bowl, with electric mixer on medium speed, whisk egg whites to soft peaks; fold one-third whites into batter to lighten. Gently fold in remaining whites in two batches.

4. Divide batter evenly among lined cups, filling each three-quarters full. Bake, rotating tins halfway through, until a cake tester inserted in centers comes out clean, about 20 minutes. Transfer tins to wire racks to cool completely. Cupcakes can be stored up to 3 days at room temperature, or frozen up to 2 months, in airtight containers.

5. To finish, fill a pastry bag fitted with a medium French-star tip (Ateco #863 or Wilton #363) with frosting. Pipe seven scallops around perimeter of cupcake, and pipe a large starburst in the center. Just before serving, thinly slice remaining bananas, and place 2 pieces on top of each cupcake.

. . . .

HONEY-CINNAMON FROSTING
MAKES ENOUGH FOR 16 CUPCAKES

2 1/2 cups confectioners' sugar, sifted

1 cup (2 sticks) unsalted butter, room temperature

2 tablespoons honey

1/4 teaspoon ground cinnamon

With an electric mixer on medium speed, beat all ingredients until smooth. Use immediately, or refrigerate up to 5 days in an airtight container; before using, bring to room temperature and beat until smooth.

Lemon Meringue Cupcakes

Tender lemon buttermilk cake, tart lemon curd, and a lightly browned peak of seven-minute frosting combine in cupcakes inspired by Martha's mile-high lemon meringue pie—one of her signature desserts. **MAKES 24**

3 cups all-purpose flour

1 tablespoon baking powder

½ teaspoon salt

1 cup (2 sticks) unsalted butter, room temperature

2 cups sugar

4 large eggs, room temperature

Finely grated zest of 3 lemons (about 3 tablespoons), plus 2 tablespoons fresh lemon juice

1 teaspoon pure vanilla extract

1 cup buttermilk

Lemon Curd (page 317)

Seven-Minute Frosting (page 303)

1. Preheat oven to 325°F. Line standard muffin tins with paper liners. Whisk together flour, baking powder, and salt.

2. With an electric mixer on medium-high speed, cream butter and sugar until pale and fluffy. Add eggs, one at a time, beating until each is incorporated, scraping down sides of bowl as needed. Beat in zest and vanilla. Add flour mixture in three batches, alternating with two additions of buttermilk and lemon juice, and beating until just combined after each.

3. Divide batter evenly among lined cups, filling each three-quarters full. Bake, rotating tins halfway through, until golden brown and a cake tester inserted in centers comes out clean, about 25 minutes. Transfer tins to wire racks to cool completely before removing cupcakes. Cupcakes can be stored overnight at room temperature, or frozen up to 2 months, in airtight containers.

4. To finish, spread 1 tablespoon lemon curd onto middle of each cupcake. Fill a pastry bag fitted with a large open-star tip (Ateco #828 or Wilton #8B) with frosting. Pipe frosting onto each cupcake, swirling tip slightly and releasing as you pull up to form a peak. Hold a small kitchen torch (see Sources, page 342) 3 to 4 inches from surface of frosting, and wave it back and forth until frosting is lightly browned all over. Serve immediately.

Orange–Vanilla Bean Cupcakes

Candied orange slices top fragrant vanilla-orange cupcakes; a circle of tiny piped buttercream dots frames each slice. Feel free to garnish with other candied citrus, such as lemons or blood oranges. MAKES 12

- 2 cups all-purpose flour
- 1/4 teaspoon baking soda
- 1/4 teaspoon baking powder
- 1/4 teaspoon salt
- 3/4 cup heavy cream
- 1 tablespoon finely grated orange zest, plus 1/4 cup fresh orange juice (from 1 orange)
- 1 tablespoon pure vanilla extract
- 1/2 cup (1 stick) unsalted butter, room temperature
- 1 cup sugar
- 2 vanilla beans, halved lengthwise, seeds scraped and reserved
- 2 large eggs
- Swiss Meringue Buttercream (page 304)
- Candied Orange Slices, for garnish (recipe follows)

1. Preheat oven to 350°F. Line standard muffin tins with paper liners. Sift together flour, baking soda, baking powder, and salt. In another bowl, combine cream, orange juice, and vanilla extract.

2. With an electric mixer on medium-high speed, cream butter, sugar, vanilla-bean seeds, and zest until pale and fluffy. Add eggs, one at a time, beating until each is incorporated, scraping down sides of bowl as needed. Reduce speed to low. Add flour mixture in three batches, alternating with two additions of the cream mixture, and beating until just combined.

3. Divide batter evenly among lined cups, filling each three-quarters full. Bake, rotating tins halfway through, until a cake tester inserted in centers comes out clean, about 25 minutes. Transfer tins to wire racks to cool completely before removing cupcakes. Cupcakes can be stored overnight at room temperature, or frozen up to 2 months, in airtight containers.

4. To finish, use a serrated knife to trim tops of cupcakes to make level. Using an offset spatula, spread buttercream over cupcakes in a smooth, even layer. Place a candied orange slice on each cupcake. Fill a pastry bag fitted with a small plain tip (#5) with buttercream, and pipe dots around edge of each orange. Cupcakes can be refrigerated up to 1 day in airtight containers; bring to room temperature before serving.

CANDIED ORANGE SLICES
MAKES ENOUGH FOR 12 CUPCAKES

- 2 small navel oranges
- 1 cup sugar
- 1 cup water

1. Wash the oranges, trim off tops and bottoms, and cut oranges into 1/8-inch-thick slices (12 total). Remove seeds.

2. Bring sugar and the water to a boil in a large saucepan over medium heat; boil, stirring, until clear, about 5 minutes. Add enough orange slices to fit in one layer; simmer, turning slices occasionally, 20 to 40 minutes (depending on toughness of rinds), or until translucent but still orange in color. Using a slotted spoon, transfer slices to a heatproof container. Repeat with remaining slices. Pour the syrup into container with slices; let cool completely. Orange slices can be refrigerated up to 1 week in airtight containers.

Strawberry Cupcakes

Chopped fresh strawberries are folded into the cupcake batter, and thin slices are added as a garnish for a pretty-in-pink treat. Strawberry buttercream (made with jam) ups the fruit-flavor ante, but sweetened whipped cream (page 316) is an easy and delicious alternative. MAKES 34

2¾ cups all-purpose flour

½ cup cake flour (not self-rising)

1 tablespoon baking powder

1 teaspoon salt

1 cup (2 sticks) unsalted butter, room temperature

2¼ cups sugar

1½ teaspoons pure vanilla extract

3 large whole eggs plus 1 egg white

1 cup milk

2 cups finely chopped fresh strawberries (about 20), plus about 10 more for garnish

Strawberry Meringue Buttercream (page 306)

1. Preheat oven to 350°F. Line standard muffin tins with paper liners. Sift together both flours, baking powder, and salt.

2. With an electric mixer on medium-high speed, cream butter, sugar, and vanilla until pale and fluffy. Add whole eggs and the white, one at a time, beating until each is incorporated, scraping down sides of bowl as needed. Reduce speed to low. Add flour mixture in two batches, alternating with the milk, and beating until well combined. Fold in chopped strawberries by hand.

3. Divide batter evenly among lined cups, filling each three-quarters full. Bake, rotating tins halfway through, until golden and a cake tester inserted in centers comes out clean, 25 to 30 minutes. Transfer tins to wire racks to cool 15 minutes; turn out cupcakes onto rack and let cool completely. Cupcakes can be stored up to 1 day at room temperature in airtight containers.

4. To finish, fill a pastry bag fitted with a large open-star tip (Ateco #826 or Wilton #8B) with buttercream. Pipe buttercream onto each cupcake, swirling tip and releasing as you pull up to form a peak. Just before serving, thinly slice remaining strawberries, and tuck a few pieces into buttercream.

Chocolate Salted-Caramel Mini Cupcakes

Salted caramels, including chocolate varieties, have become quite popular in recent years; a touch of salt draws out caramel's buttery taste and highlights the sweetness. This cupcake, created with the candy's popularity in mind, serves as an excellent incentive to try your hand at making caramel at home. The soft caramel centers hide under a piped peak of satiny chocolate frosting. Fleur de sel, a type of sea salt prized for its distinctive flavor, is available at specialty stores; if you can't find it, you may substitute another sea salt, such as Maldon. MAKES ABOUT 56 MINI

1½ cups all-purpose flour

¾ cup unsweetened Dutch-process cocoa powder

1½ cups sugar

1½ teaspoons baking soda

¾ teaspoon baking powder

¾ teaspoon salt

2 large eggs

¾ cup buttermilk

3 tablespoons vegetable oil

1 teaspoon pure vanilla extract

¾ cup warm water

Salted Caramel Filling (page 322; keep warm)

Sea salt, preferably fleur de sel, for garnish

Dark Chocolate Frosting (page 302)

1. Preheat oven to 350°F. Line mini muffin tins with paper liners. In a mixing bowl, whisk together flour, cocoa, sugar, baking soda, baking powder, and salt. Add eggs, buttermilk, oil, vanilla, and the water. With an electric mixer on low speed, beat until smooth and combined, scraping down sides of bowl as needed.

2. Divide batter evenly among lined cups, filling each about two-thirds full. Bake, rotating tins halfway through, until a cake tester inserted in centers comes out clean, about 15 minutes. Transfer tins to wire racks to cool 10 minutes; turn out cupcakes onto racks and let cool completely. Cupcakes can be stored overnight at room temperature, or frozen up to 1 month, in airtight containers.

3. To finish, use a paring knife to cut a cone-shaped piece (about ½ inch deep) from the center of each cupcake (discard pieces). Spoon 1 to 2 teaspoons warm filling into each hollowed-out cupcake. Sprinkle a pinch of sea salt over filling.

4. Fill a pastry bag fitted with a medium open-star tip (Ateco #821 or Wilton #18) with frosting. Pipe frosting onto each cupcake, swirling tip and releasing as you pull up to form a peak. Garnish each cupcake with a pinch of sea salt. Cupcakes are best eaten the day they are filled and frosted; store at room temperature in airtight containers (do not refrigerate) until ready to serve.

Campfire Cupcakes

The old campfire classic takes on a new identity as a charming cupcake. Graham flour, available at health-food stores and specialty markets, flavors the cupcake base, which is topped with chocolate glaze and piled high with piped sticky marshmallow frosting, browned to mimic the effects of toasting over a fire. MAKES 24

1½ cups all-purpose flour

1⅓ cups graham flour

2 teaspoons baking powder

1½ teaspoons salt

1½ teaspoons ground cinnamon

1¼ cups (2½ sticks) unsalted butter, room temperature

2 cups packed light-brown sugar

¼ cup honey

6 large eggs

2 teaspoons pure vanilla extract

Chocolate Ganache Glaze (page 312)

Marshmallow Frosting (recipe follows)

BROWNING THE FROSTING

1. Preheat oven to 350°F. Line standard muffin tins with paper liners. Whisk together both flours, baking powder, salt, and cinnamon.

2. With an electric mixer on medium-high speed, cream butter, brown sugar, and honey until pale and fluffy. Reduce speed to medium; beat in eggs and vanilla, scraping down sides of bowl as needed. Add flour mixture; mix until just combined.

3. Divide batter evenly among lined cups, filling each about three-quarters full. Bake, rotating tins halfway through, until golden brown and a cake tester inserted in centers comes out with only a few moist crumbs attached, about 25 minutes. Transfer tins to wire racks to cool 10 minutes; turn out cupcakes onto racks and let cool completely. Cupcakes can be stored up to 1 day at room temperature, or frozen up to 1 month, in airtight containers.

4. To finish, spoon 2 teaspoons chocolate glaze onto each cupcake. Fill a pastry bag fitted with a large plain tip (Ateco #806 or Wilton #2A) with frosting; pipe frosting onto each cupcake, swirling tip and releasing as you pull up to form a peak. Hold a small kitchen torch (see Sources, page 342) 3 to 4 inches from surface of frosting, and wave it back and forth until frosting is lightly browned all over. Serve immediately.

. . . .

MARSHMALLOW FROSTING

MAKES ENOUGH FOR 24 CUPCAKES

1 envelope unflavored gelatin (1 scant tablespoon)

⅓ cup plus ¼ cup cold water

1 cup sugar

1. In a mixing bowl, sprinkle gelatin over ⅓ cup cold water. Allow gelatin to soften, about 5 minutes.

2. Heat remaining ¼ cup water and the sugar in a saucepan over medium-high, stirring until sugar is dissolved. Stop stirring; clip a candy thermometer onto side of pan. Boil syrup until temperature reaches the soft-ball stage (238°F), brushing down sides of pan with a wet pastry brush to prevent sugar crystals from forming. Remove from heat; add syrup to softened gelatin. Whisk mixture by hand to cool, about 1 minute, then use an electric mixer to whisk on medium-high speed until soft, glossy (but not dry) peaks form, 8 to 10 minutes. Use immediately (frosting will harden).

One-Bowl Chocolate Cupcakes with Gumdrops

Piped buttercream starbursts and chewy gumdrops make playful toppings for these ever-popular chocolate cupcakes. As the name of the recipe implies, all the ingredients come together in one bowl. Using vegetable oil instead of butter makes an exceptionally moist cake; good-quality cocoa powder, such as Valrhona, produces a deep, dark color and the best flavor. White icing and clear gumdrops combine in this elegant monochromatic motif; use multi-colored gumdrops for a more whimsical effect. You can customize the cake flavor by using a different extract in place of the vanilla; for example, anise would complement the clear gumdrops used here (increase amount of extract to 1½ teaspoons). MAKES 18

1½ cups all-purpose flour

¾   cup unsweetened Dutch-process cocoa powder

1½ cups sugar

1½ teaspoons baking soda

¾   teaspoon baking powder

¾   teaspoon salt

2   large eggs

¾   cup buttermilk

3   tablespoons vegetable oil

1   teaspoon pure vanilla extract

¾   cup warm water

    Swiss Meringue Buttercream (page 304)

¾   pound gumdrops, for garnish

1. Preheat oven to 350°F. Line standard muffin tins with paper liners. With an electric mixer on medium speed, whisk together flour, cocoa, sugar, baking soda, baking powder, and salt. Reduce speed to low. Add eggs, buttermilk, oil, extract, and the water; beat until smooth and combined, scraping down sides of bowl as needed.

PIPING STARBURSTS AND TOPPING WITH GUMDROPS

2. Divide batter evenly among lined cups, filling each about two-thirds full. Bake, rotating tins halfway through, until a cake tester inserted in centers comes out clean, about 20 minutes. Transfer tins to wire racks to cool 10 minutes; turn out cupcakes onto racks and let cool completely. Cupcakes can be stored overnight at room temperature, or frozen up to 2 months, in airtight containers.

3. To finish, fill a pastry bag fitted with a medium French-star tip (Ateco #863 or Wilton #363) with buttercream. Pipe 5 starbursts around perimeter of cupcake, then pipe another starburst in the center. Cupcakes can be stored up to 1 day at room temperature, or refrigerated up to 3 days, in airtight containers. Bring to room temperature and place a gumdrop in the center of each starburst before serving.

White Cupcakes with Pastel Buttercream Peaks

Fanciful peaks in a spectrum of shades crown cupcakes with a motif inspired by a vintage Russian cookbook. You could also opt to use just one color of frosting, or leave it untinted. White cupcakes, made with egg whites only (instead of whole eggs), are very light and delicate. For a stronger vanilla flavor, scrape the seeds of one vanilla bean (halved lengthwise) into the milk in step one, and omit vanilla extract. MAKES 24

3¼ cups sifted cake flour (not self-rising)

1½ tablespoons baking powder

¼ teaspoon salt

1 tablespoon pure vanilla extract

1 cup plus 2 tablespoons milk

½ cup plus 6 tablespoons (1¾ sticks) unsalted butter, room temperature

1¾ cups sugar

5 large egg whites, room temperature

Swiss Meringue Buttercream (page 304)

Gel-paste food colors (pink, violet, and yellow are pictured)

1. Preheat oven to 350°F. Line standard muffin tins with paper liners. Sift together cake flour, baking powder, and salt. Stir vanilla into milk.

2. With an electric mixer on medium-high speed, cream butter until smooth. Gradually add sugar, beating until pale and fluffy. Reduce speed to low. Add flour mixture in three batches, alternating with two additions of milk, and beating until just combined after each.

3. In another bowl, with electric mixer on medium speed, whisk the egg whites until stiff peaks form (do not overmix). Fold one third of the egg whites into batter to lighten. Gently fold in remaining whites in two batches.

4. Divide batter evenly among lined cups, filling each three-quarters full. Firmly tap the tins once on countertop to release any air bubbles. Bake, rotating tins halfway through, until a cake tester inserted in centers comes out clean, 18 to 20 minutes. Transfer tins to wire racks to cool 10 minutes; turn out cupcakes onto racks and let cool completely. Cupcakes can be stored overnight at room temperature, or frozen up to 2 months, in airtight containers.

5. Divide buttercream into four portions; leave one untinted and tint remaining three to desired colors. Place each portion in a pastry bag fitted with a coupler. Using a small open-star tip (#20), pipe peaks: Squeeze gently while lifting the tip, then release at the halfway point, and draw up tip until icing forms a point. Starting with untinted buttercream, pipe a single peak in the center of each cupcake, then pipe more peaks in a ring around it. Switch to tinted buttercream; pipe rings of peaks around the plain, until you reach the edge. Refrigerate 30 minutes to allow frosting to set. Cupcakes can be refrigerated up to 3 days in airtight containers; bring to room temperature before serving.

Mint Chocolate Cupcakes

Mint-infused milk, along with mint extract, adds flavor (but not color) to pale buttercream; the dark chocolate cupcakes are also flavored with mint. A cluster of chocolate mint leaves on top suggests the primary flavor component of the finished treat. The leaves may admittedly not be an "any day" endeavor, but they can be prepared a day or so in advance. You can, of course, serve the cupcakes without any topping other than the frosting, or garnish them with a few chocolate curls (see page 323) shaved from a mint-flavored bar. **MAKES 18**

1½ cups all-purpose flour

¾ cup unsweetened Dutch-process cocoa powder

1½ cups sugar

1½ teaspoons baking soda

¾ teaspoon baking powder

¾ teaspoon salt

2 large eggs

¾ cup buttermilk

3 tablespoons vegetable oil

1 teaspoon pure peppermint extract

¾ cup warm water

Mint Buttercream (page 308)

Chocolate Mint Leaves, for garnish (page 321)

1. Preheat oven to 350°F. Line standard muffin tins with paper liners. With an electric mixer on medium speed, whisk together flour, cocoa, sugar, baking soda, baking powder, and salt. Add eggs, buttermilk, oil, extract, and the water; beat on low speed until smooth and combined, scraping down sides of bowl as needed.

2. Divide batter evenly among lined cups, filling each about two-thirds full. Bake, rotating tins halfway through, until a cake tester inserted in centers comes out clean, about 20 minutes. Transfer tins to wire racks to cool 10 minutes; turn out cupcakes onto racks to cool completely. Cupcakes can be stored overnight at room temperature, or frozen up to 2 months, in airtight containers.

3. To finish, fill a pastry bag fitted with a large plain tip (Ateco #809 or Wilton #1A) with buttercream and pipe small mounds onto cupcakes; flatten top slightly with an offset spatula. Cupcakes can be stored up to 1 day at room temperature or 3 days in the refrigerator. Bring to room temperature and garnish with chocolate mint leaves before serving.

CUPCAKES FOR

special days

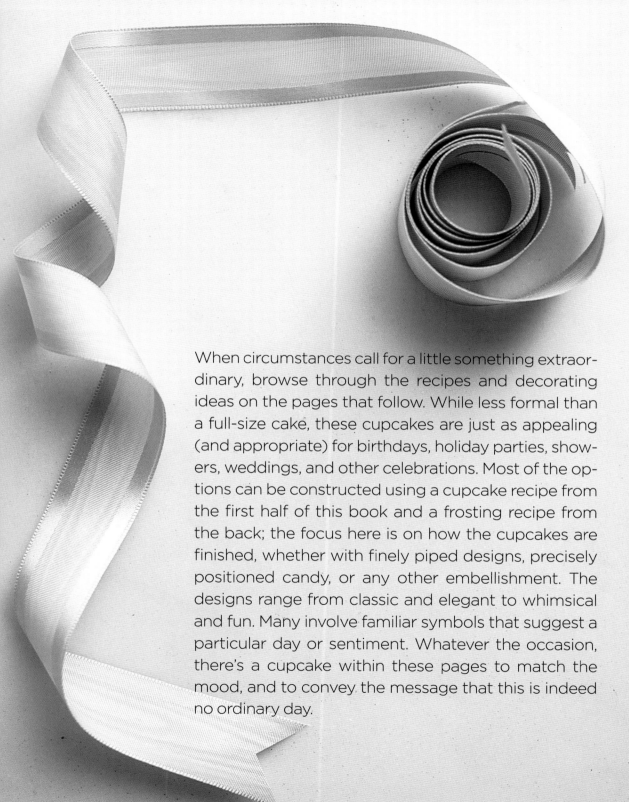

When circumstances call for a little something extraordinary, browse through the recipes and decorating ideas on the pages that follow. While less formal than a full-size cake, these cupcakes are just as appealing (and appropriate) for birthdays, holiday parties, showers, weddings, and other celebrations. Most of the options can be constructed using a cupcake recipe from the first half of this book and a frosting recipe from the back; the focus here is on how the cupcakes are finished, whether with finely piped designs, precisely positioned candy, or any other embellishment. The designs range from classic and elegant to whimsical and fun. Many involve familiar symbols that suggest a particular day or sentiment. Whatever the occasion, there's a cupcake within these pages to match the mood, and to convey the message that this is indeed no ordinary day.

birthdays

A significant part of the joy of celebrating a birthday is creating unforgettable memories for the guest of honor, no matter what age. A young nephew may delight in baseball cupcakes, while a mother-in-law is sure to swoon over those adorned with buttercream sweet peas and pansies. Anyone would appreciate the good fortune of receiving cupcakes topped with ladybugs "crawling" through plush piped "grass." With more than three dozen inspired cupcakes to choose from, there's sure to be one in this section to fulfill each and every birthday wish. Follow the instructions step by step, or use the techniques and your imagination to produce creations all your own. There are also plenty of opportunities for mixing and matching: Make a whole menagerie of animal-themed cupcakes, or pick just one and produce it en masse. And, most importantly, remember to have fun with the ideas on these pages.

Dotted-Letter Cupcakes

Spell out a birthday wish—or whatever your celebration calls for—with homemade dot letters on a big bunch of cupcakes. The colorful letters (and numbers) are made of tinted royal icing piped onto parchment paper and allowed to harden before they're placed atop the cupcakes. To save time on the day of the party, pipe the decorations the day before. **MAKES 36**

36 cupcakes, such as Yellow Buttermilk (page 26) or One-Bowl Chocolate (page 152)

+

2 recipes Cream-Cheese Frosting (page 303) or Fluffy Vanilla Frosting (page 302)

2 recipes Royal Icing (page 315)

+

Gel-paste food color (orange, pink, red, and blue are pictured)

1. Divide royal icing among four bowls. Tint each portion a different color (see page 304 for instructions; keep icing covered while working to prevent it from drying). Transfer to four separate piping bags fitted with small plain tips (#3), pressing to remove air and sealing tops of bags with rubber bands. Rest tips of pastry bags in glasses with damp paper towels in the bottoms.

PIPING LETTERS AND NUMBERS

2. You will need to create a template with your message printed on it; be sure the numbers and letters are spaced well apart (for easy piping). Tape template to a work surface. Tape a sheet of parchment or waxed paper over the template. Pipe solid lines of icing to follow the shape of a letter or number, tracing the template, then pipe dots close together over the piped solid lines. Continue for all the letters or numbers, piping with different colors as desired. Let dry at least 3 hours or overnight.

3. Using an offset spatula, spread cupcakes generously with a smooth layer of frosting. Using a clean offset spatula, gently lift a royal icing letter or number from paper and place on each cupcake. Decorate extra cupcakes with one or several dots, using tinted royal icing and plain tips in different sizes. Decorated cupcakes will keep up to 1 day in the refrigerator in airtight containers; bring to room temperature before serving.

Gelato-Topped Mini Cupcakes

Pastel-colored gelato is used to top mini cupcakes, but you can substitute sorbet or ice cream. The one-bowl vanilla cupcakes are baked in paper nut cups, available at craft-supply stores (see Sources, page 342), or you can use mini muffin tins lined with paper liners. For an authentic Italian touch, serve with small plastic ice-cream spoons. **MAKES 48 MINI**

$1\frac{1}{2}$ cups plus 2 tablespoons all-purpose flour

$1\frac{1}{4}$ cups sugar

$\frac{3}{4}$ teaspoon baking soda

$\frac{1}{2}$ teaspoon baking powder

$\frac{3}{4}$ teaspoon salt

1 large whole egg plus 1 egg yolk

$\frac{1}{2}$ cup plus 2 tablespoons warm water

$\frac{1}{2}$ cup plus 2 tablespoons buttermilk

$\frac{1}{4}$ cup plus 1 tablespoon vegetable oil

1 teaspoon pure vanilla extract

Gelato in assorted flavors, for topping

1. Preheat oven to 350°F. Arrange 48 paper nut cups on large rimmed baking sheets. Into a mixing bowl, sift together flour, sugar, baking soda, baking powder, and salt. Add whole egg and yolk, the warm water, buttermilk, oil, and vanilla. With an electric mixer on low speed, beat until well combined and smooth.

2. Divide batter evenly among cups, filling each about two-thirds full. Bake, rotating sheets halfway through, until golden brown and a cake tester inserted in centers comes out clean, about 17 minutes. Transfer sheets to wire racks to cool completely. (If using muffin tins, let cupcakes cool 30 minutes before turning out onto rack to cool completely.) Cupcakes can be stored up to 3 days at room temperature in airtight containers.

3. Wrap a rimmed baking sheet with plastic, pulling taut over top of sheet. Scoop gelato using a 2-inch ice-cream scoop (or a $1\frac{1}{2}$-inch scoop for cupcakes baked in mini muffin tins), gently dropping scoops onto the plastic wrap as you work. Freeze until set, about 30 minutes. To finish, place a scoop of gelato on each cupcake, and serve immediately.

By the Sea Cupcakes

If you're planning a party at the shore (or are at least inspired to), decorate cupcakes with sand dollars, tiny fish swimming in buttercream waves, or starfish sunning themselves on graham cracker crumb "sand." All three types of sea creatures are fashioned from marzipan, so you could decorate some cupcakes with each for a beach-themed summer party. The cut-paper shark fin cupcakes that follow are a quick and easy alternative. You will need one batch of Swiss meringue buttercream (page 304) to frost two dozen cupcakes. The marzipan creatures can be made a day ahead and stored at room temperature in airtight containers. Use a food processor or mini chopper to grind graham crackers into crumbs. MAKES 24 PER RECIPE

Sand Dollar Cupcakes

MAKE SAND DOLLARS: You will need 12 ounces of marzipan to make 24 sand dollars. On a work surface lightly dusted with cornstarch, roll out marzipan to ¼ inch thick. Using a cookie cutter, cut out 2½- to 2¾-inch rounds. Arrange 5 almond slivers in a star pattern on each round, attaching with a dab of frosting. Use a toothpick to make impressions between almonds and on edges.

DECORATE CUPCAKES: Using an offset spatula, spread a smooth layer of buttercream over each cupcake. Place sand dollar on top, pressing gently to adhere to frosting. Cupcakes are best served the same day they are decorated; keep at room temperature.

Starfish Cupcakes

MAKE STARFISH: You will need 9 ounces of marzipan to make 24 starfish. Pinch off a small piece of marzipan; roll into a 1¼-inch ball, then flatten slightly with the palm of your hand. Mold into a star shape. Press top of starfish against the small holes of a box grater, repeating to cover entire surface, for texture. Repeat until you have one for each cupcake.

DECORATE CUPCAKES: Using an offset spatula, spread buttercream over cupcake, smoothing into a dome. Place graham-cracker crumbs in a small bowl. Dip cupcake into crumbs, coating completely. Sprinkle with more crumbs. Place starfish on top, pressing gently to adhere, and mold to top of cupcakes. Cupcakes are best served the same day they are decorated; keep at room temperature.

FORMING MARZIPAN STARFISH

CONTINUED >>

By the Sea Cupcakes

Fish Cupcakes

MAKE FISH: You will need 9 ounces of marzipan to make 48 fish. Tint marzipan with green gel-paste food color (see page 299 for instructions). Pinch off a small piece of marzipan and roll into a ¾-inch ball, then mold into a fish, forming a head on the larger end and then tapering down to a forked tail. Make two tiny marzipan fins and attach to the sides of the fish, pinching the pieces together to adhere. For the eyes, dab the tip of a toothpick in blue gel-paste food color, then poke into two sides of the head. Repeat until you have two fish for each cupcake.

DECORATE CUPCAKES: Tint buttercream pale blue with gel-paste food color. Using an offset spatula, spread butercream generously over each cupcake, swirling and swooping into small peaks to resemble waves. Place two fish on top, curving bodies as desired and nestling them gently into the frosting. Cupcakes are best served the same day they are decorated; keep at room temperature.

FORMING MARZIPAN FISH

Shark and Sand Dune Cupcakes

There's nothing to fear from these stealthy sharks, whose paper fins peek out from waves of blue buttercream. Alongside is a cupcake made to resemble a sandy dune, with graham-cracker crumbs and a paper parasol.

MAKE SHARKS: Cut out fin shapes from blue construction paper or card stock (one for each cupcake). Tint half of the Swiss meringue buttercream (page 304) blue with gel-paste food color. Using a small offset spatula, frost a dozen cupcakes, swirling and swooping into small peaks to resemble waves. Just before serving, press paper fins into frosting.

MAKE SAND DUNES: Frost the remaining dozen cupcakes with untinted buttercream, smoothing into dome shapes. Place graham-cracker crumbs in a small bowl. Dip each cupcake into crumbs, coating completely. Just before serving, insert a paper drink umbrella into each cupcake.

Ladybird Cupcakes

Cheery marzipan ladybirds nestled in a piped buttercream lawn make adorable cupcakes. Once you get the hang of piping the frosting into blades of grass, the work moves very quickly; meanwhile, you can enlist children to help form the ladybirds. MAKES 24

24 Yellow Buttermilk
Cupcakes
(page 26)

+

Swiss Meringue
Buttercream
(page 304)

+

Green, red, and
black gel-paste
food colors

7 ounces marzipan

Cornstarch, for
work surface

1. Tint buttercream green with gel-paste food color. Transfer to a pastry bag fitted with a small multi-opening tip (#233). Starting at the center and moving outward, pipe rows of grass on top of cupcakes: With tip on surface of cupcake, squeeze bag, then release while quickly pulling up to form ¼-inch-long blades, making some slightly longer than others.

2. Form ladybirds: Divide marzipan in half. Working on a surface lightly dusted with cornstarch, tint one portion red and the other black with gel-paste food colors. Form a ½-inch ball of red marzipan for each ladybird body, and a ¼-inch ball of black marzipan for each head. Flatten the red ball slightly into an oval shape, and press the head onto the body. Pinch off black marzipan to make tiny balls for the spots, and press onto the body. Repeat to make additional ladybirds with remaining marzipan. Place one or two ladybirds on top of each frosted cupcake, gently pressing them into the buttercream grass. Refrigerate 30 minutes to allow frosting to set. Cupcakes are best served the same day they are decorated; keep at room temperature.

PIPING BUTTERCREAM GRASS

FORMING MARZIPAN LADYBIRDS

Buttercream-Blossom Cupcakes

These beautiful piped-flower cupcakes seem to have been just been picked from a spring garden. They may look intimidating, but with a bit of practice (on parchment paper), you should be able to produce the piped designs with relative ease. Stems can be trickier than they appear, so be sure to also try out a few of these; pipe too quickly and the stems break, too slowly, and they won't be straight. (Any breaks may be filled in with more buttercream.) Before piping onto cupcakes, lightly mark the pattern on the frosting with a skewer or toothpick. When piping, use your writing hand to hold and squeeze the bag near the top and your other hand to steady and steer the tip. MAKES 24 PER RECIPE

Cherry Blossom Cupcakes

24 Yellow Buttermilk
Cupcakes
(page 26)

+

Swiss Meringue
Buttercream
(page 304)

+

Chocolate-brown,
peach, lemon-
yellow, leaf-green,
and pink gel-paste
food colors

1. Using a serrated knife, trim top of each cupcake to make level. Tint ¼ cup buttercream brown with gel-paste food color. Tint 2 cups buttercream peach. Tint ¼ cup each yellow and green. Transfer tinted buttercreams to pastry bags fitted only with couplers. Tint remaining buttercream pale pink. Using an offset spatula, spread a smooth layer of pink buttercream over each cupcake.

PIPING CHERRY BLOSSOMS

2. Using brown buttercream and a fine plain tip (#1), pipe thin branches on cupcake. With peach buttercream (shown opposite; pink is shown below) and a small petal tip (#103), pipe basic petals: Hold the bag at a 45-degree angle to the cupcake, with the tip's wide end down and narrow end pointed away and slightly to the left. Move the tip forward ⅛ inch and back again while you pivot the narrow end to the right. Make five or six petals, turning the cupcake as you go. Then, if desired, pipe a small petal on stem to make the bud shown at left. With yellow buttercream and a small plain tip (#2), pipe three or four dots in center of flower. Pipe tiny leaves with green buttercream and a small V-leaf tip (#349). Repeat for remaining cupcakes. Refrigerate 30 minutes to allow frosting to set. Cupcakes can be refrigerated up to 3 days in airtight containers; bring to room temperature before serving.

CONTINUED >>

CHERRY
BLOSSOM

SWEET PEA

PANSY

Buttercream-Blossom Cupcakes

Pansy Cupcakes

24 Yellow Buttermilk
Cupcakes
(page 26)

+

Swiss Meringue
Buttercream
(page 304)

+

Leaf-green,
lemon-yellow,
violet, and pink
gel-paste food
colors

1. Using a serrated knife, trim top of each cupcake to make level. Tint ½ cup buttercream green and ¼ cup pale yellow with gel-paste food colors. Divide 2 cups buttercream among two bowls; tint one portion light violet and the other a darker shade. Transfer tinted frostings to pastry bags fitted only with couplers. Tint remaining buttercream pale pink. Using an offset spatula, spread a smooth layer of pink buttercream over cupcakes.

PIPING PANSIES

2. With green buttercream and a small plain tip (#2), pipe stems on cupcake. Using dark violet buttercream and a small petal tip (#103), pipe two large, basic petals (similar to cherry blossom petals, page 172) side by side. Then make two smaller petals, one on top of each of the first ones, using the same petal technique; apply less pressure and make a smaller arc than you did for larger petals. Using light violet buttercream and same petal tip, pipe a ruffle for the flower's base, pivoting tip as with petals, and turning the cupcake while connecting the petals. To finish the ruffle neatly, pull bag toward center of flower as you release pressure. Pipe a dot in center of each blossom with yellow buttercream and the #2 tip. If desired, use green buttercream and another small petal tip (#60) to pipe the leaf shown at left. Repeat for remaining cupcakes. Refrigerate 30 minutes to allow frosting to set. Cupcakes can be refrigerated up to 3 days in airtight containers; bring to room temperature before serving.

Sweet Pea Cupcakes

24 Yellow Buttermilk
Cupcakes
(page 26)

+

Swiss Meringue
Buttercream
(page 304)

+

Leaf-green and
pink gel-paste
food colors

1. Using a serrated knife, trim top of each cupcake to make level. Tint ½ cup buttercream green and 1 cup pink with gel-paste food colors. Transfer to pastry bags fitted only with couplers. Tint remaining buttercream a paler shade of pink. Using a small offset spatula, spread a smooth layer of pale pink buttercream over cupcakes.

PIPING SWEET PEAS

2. Pipe stems using green buttercream and a small plain tip (#2) on a cupcake. Then, using pink buttercream and a small petal tip (#103), form two basic petals (similar to cherry blossom petals, page 172) side by side. Pipe two smaller petals overlapping each other on top of the first two, then hold bag 90 degrees to the flower with wide end facing forward, and pipe a center, pulling down slightly. With green buttercream and a small V-leaf tip (#352), pipe small leaves: Start at the base of the bloom with the tip's pointed end facing up, and then pull tip toward flower as you release pressure. Switch to the #2 tip, and add curlicues. Refrigerate 30 minutes to allow frosting to set. Cupcakes can be refrigerated up to 3 days in airtight containers; bring to room temperature before serving.

Flower Power Cupcakes

Make your own sweet garden with an array of cupcakes in bloom. One batch of Swiss meringue buttercream (page 304) is enough to decorate two dozen cupcakes, including the piped flower versions. See Sources, page 342, for where to find the tools and candies used below.

MAKES 24 PER RECIPE

LOLLIPOP GARDEN CUPCAKES Using an offset spatula, spread buttercream on cupcakes, smoothing into dome shapes. Place sprinkles in a small bowl. Gently press each frosted cupcake into sprinkles, rolling it around so entire surface is coated. Insert a lollipop into the center of each cupcake. Using a paring knife or kitchen shears, cut leaf shapes out of green taffy strips. Press one leaf into each cupcake, next to the lollipop. Refrigerate 30 minutes to allow frosting to set.

JELLIED-CANDY FLOWER CUPCAKES Using an offset spatula, spread cupcakes with a smooth layer of buttercream (if desired, tint half green with gel-paste food color). Fill one bowl with cream-colored sprinkles and another with green sprinkles. Gently press each frosted cupcake into sprinkles, rolling it around so entire surface is coated. For flowers, use 1- to 1½-inch aspic cutters (or a paring knife) to cut petals from jellied citrus slices. Use scissors or a sharp knife to cut off lower third from gumdrops; discard. Arrange 6 jellied petals on each cupcake in a flower shape; gently press gumdrop into center, cut side down.

PIPED FLOWER CUPCAKES Using a pastry bag fitted with a small petal tip (#104), pipe plain or tinted buttercream petals: Keeping the wide edge of the tip in the center of the cupcake, pipe a petal by making a half-moon motion with the outer, thinner edge of the tip. Repeat until you have five or six slightly overlapping petals that cover the top of the cupcake. Place a round colored candy, such as a pastel lentil, M&M, or Skittle, in the center of the flower. Repeat to decorate remaining cupcakes. Refrigerate 30 minutes to allow frosting to set.

SUGAR-COOKIE FLOWER CUPCAKES
Make sugar cookie cutouts (page 319), using a 2- to 3-inch flower cookie cutter (see Sources, page 342) to cut out 24 shapes; place a rolled-paper lollipop stick under each flower (press lightly to adhere) before chilling and baking as directed. Divide 1 cup buttercream into thirds; tint pink, yellow, and light blue. Tint remaining buttercream green; use a small open-star tip (#22) to pipe "grass" on cupcakes. Use a small plain tip (#4) to outline each flower and dot the center. Insert a lollipop cookie into center of each cupcake. Cut candy spearmint leaves in half; place on either side of lollipop. Refrigerate 30 minutes to allow frosting to set.

Cookie Monogram Cupcakes

Celebrating the guest of honor is as easy as A-B-C with these letter-cookie cupcake toppers. To create the cookies, cut rounds from sugar cookie cutouts (two different sizes are shown, but just one will do), then cut a letter from the inside of each round with a mini cookie cutter (see Sources, page 342). Instead of a single letter, you can make a set of cookies featuring the entire alphabet (you will need a couple more cupcakes to show them off), a great idea for a party full of preschoolers just learning their letters. MAKES 24

24 Yellow Buttermilk
   Cupcakes
   (page 26)

   +

   Swiss Meringue
   Buttercream
   (page 304)

   +

   Sugar Cookie
   Cutouts
   (page 319)

   +

   Royal Icing
   (page 315)

   Gel-paste
   food color (blue
   is pictured)

1. Make cookies, using 2-inch cookie cutters to cut out 12 rounds and 1½-inch cutters to cut out another 12 rounds. Use mini letter-shaped cookie cutters to cut out letters from centers of rounds. Gather together and reroll scraps; cut out more rounds and letters, as needed.

2. Tint royal icing with gel-paste food color (see page 304 for instructions). Transfer icing to a pastry bag fitted with a small plain tip (#3), pressing out air and sealing top of bag with a rubber band to keep icing from drying out. Pipe icing to outline each cookie and then outline letter cut out. Fill in with a thin layer of icing, using a toothpick to spread evenly. Let stand until icing is set, at least 3 hours (or overnight).

3. Fill a pastry bag fitted with a large plain tip (Ateco #806 or Wilton #2A) with buttercream, and pipe in a spiral pattern onto each cupcake, starting at the edges and ending with a peak in the center. Cupcakes can be refrigerated up to 3 days in airtight containers; bring to room temperature, and place one iced letter cookie upright in the buttercream on each cupcake, before serving.

Mini Menagerie Cupcakes

Decorate a batch (or two) of cupcakes with pig, mouse, monkey, or lion faces, or make a few of each animal for a sweet set. You can use most any cupcake flavor for these creatures; try banana-pecan cupcakes (page 41; nuts can be omitted) or roasted banana cupcakes (page 141) for the monkeys. Before adding the facial features, lightly mark the placement in the frosting with a round cookie cutter (or use a skewer or toothpick).

MAKES 24 PER RECIPE

Pig Cupcakes

24 Yellow Buttermilk Cupcakes (page 26) or One-Bowl Chocolate Cupcakes (page 152)

+

Swiss Meringue Buttercream (page 304)

+

Pink gel-paste food color

48 mini brown candy-coated choco-lates, such as mini M&M's

Bubblegum tape

FORMING FACIAL FEATURES FOR THE PIG

1. Tint 1½ cups buttercream pale pink with gel-paste food color. Transfer to a pastry bag fitted with only a coupler. Tint another 2 cups buttercream a deeper shade of pink. Transfer ½ cup to a pastry bag fitted with only a coupler, and reserve the rest.

2. Using an offset spatula, spread each cupcake with reserved deep pink buttercream in a smooth, even layer. For the snout, use a small plain tip (#6) to pipe a pale pink circle just off center, in the lower part of the cupcake, then pipe lines to almost fill in the circle; smooth with an offset spatula. Then, using the deep pink frosting and #6 tip, pipe two pink dots in the center of the pale pink circle.

3. For the eyes, place two candy-coated chocolates above the pale pink circle. Cut bubblegum tape into small triangles, and press two into the top of each cupcake to resemble ears, bending tips forward. Refrigerate 30 minutes to allow frosting to set. Cupcakes are best served the same day they are decorated; keep at room temperature.

CONTINUED >>

Mini Menagerie

Mouse Cupcakes

24 Yellow Buttermilk Cupcakes (page 26) or One-Bowl Chocolate Cupcakes (page 152)

+

Swiss Meringue Buttercream (page 304)

+

4 ounces semisweet chocolate, melted and cooled (see page 323)

24 black licorice buttons (or brown candy-coated chocolates, such as M&M's)

1 small bag (about 5 ounces) black licorice laces, cut into 2-inch pieces

48 chocolate-covered sunflower seeds (see Sources, page 342)

48 chocolate candy wafers, such as Necco

1. Measure out ¾ cup buttercream and combine with melted and cooled chocolate, stirring until smooth with a flexible spatula. Transfer to a pastry bag fitted with a small plain tip (#6).

CREATING MOUSE FACIAL FEATURES

2. Using an offset spatula, spread plain buttercream in a smooth, even layer over cupcakes. Pipe chocolate buttercream in a 2-inch oval in lower part of each cupcake. Place a licorice button in the center of the piped oval for the nose. Arrange three licorice pieces in the buttercream on each side of the nose for whiskers. Place two chocolate-coated sunflower seeds above the piped chocolate oval for the eyes.

3. Using a paring knife, make two small slits, about an inch apart, in top of cupcake, just above the liner. Insert two candy wafers into slits for ears, securing with dabs of buttercream, if necessary. Refrigerate 30 minutes to allow frosting to set. Cupcakes are best served the same day they are decorated; keep at room temperature.

Monkey Cupcakes

24 Banana-Pecan Cupcakes (page 41)

+

Swiss Meringue Buttercream (chocolate variation; page 305)

+

48 chocolate candy wafers, such as Necco

12 ounces rolled fondant

Yellow gel-paste food color

Cornstarch, for work surface

1. Using a paring knife, make a small slit in opposite sides of cupcake, just above the liner. Insert two candy wafers into slits for ears, securing with dabs of buttercream, if necessary. Using an offset spatula, spread top of cupcake and wafers with frosting in a smooth, even layer. Repeat with remaining cupcakes.

2. Tint the fondant pale yellow with gel-paste food color (see page 299 for instructions) and roll out to ⅛ inch thick on a work surface lightly dusted with cornstarch. To create the mouth, cut out a round of fondant using a 2-inch cookie cutter. Cut out a second piece of fondant using a 3-inch fluted flower cookie cutter; slice off two petal portions from the flower for the eyes. Make the ear pieces by cutting two ⅞-inch rounds from the remaining flower petals; trim circles with a knife to create one straight edge on each.

3. Arrange fondant shapes on cupcakes, starting with the eyes and then slightly overlapping the round mouth piece over the eyes, and facing the straight edge of each ear piece inward. Fill a pastry bag fitted with a small plain tip (#3) with buttercream; pipe eyes, nose, and mouth details on fondant. Refrigerate 30 minutes to allow frosting to set. Cupcakes are best served the same day they are decorated; keep at room temperature.

COVERING MONKEY FACES AND EARS WITH BUTTERCREAM

CREATING MONKEY FACES

CONTINUED >>

Mini Menagerie

Lion Cupcakes

24 Yellow Buttermilk
   Cupcakes
   (page 26)

   +

   Swiss Meringue
   Buttercream
   (page 304)

   +

   Pink gel-paste
   food color

 2 ounces semisweet
   chocolate, melted
   and cooled (see
   page 323)

48 mini brown
   candy-coated
   chocolates, such
   as M&M's

24 white gumdrops,
   halved crosswise

 1 small bag (about
   5 ounces) black
   licorice laces, cut
   into 1-inch long
   pieces

 1 package (7
   ounces) sweet-
   ened shredded
   coconut, toasted
   (see page 323)

1. Tint ½ cup buttercream pale pink with gel-paste food color. Transfer to a pastry bag fitted with a small plain tip (#4). Add melted and cooled chocolate to remaining buttercream, and stir until combined with a flexible spatula.

CREATING LION FACES

2. Using an offset spatula, spread cupcakes with chocolate buttercream in a smooth, even layer. Attach two candy-coated chocolates for the eyes and two gumdrop halves, cut sides down, for the cheeks. Arrange three licorice pieces in the buttercream on each side of gumdrop cheeks for whiskers. To make the nose, pipe a dot in the center with pink buttercream. Gently press toasted coconut around the edge of cupcake to resemble a mane. Refrigerate 30 minutes to allow frosting to set. Cupcakes are best served the same day they are decorated; keep at room temperature.

SINGLE FLOWER

FUNNY FACE

DIAMONDS AND DOTS

Fun Piping Ideas for Kids

With just a basic few piping tips and a little imagination, kids (and their grown-ups) can learn to embellish cupcakes with all sorts of fanciful designs. It's a great activity for a birthday party—mix up batches of frosting in several colors, and fit pastry bags with couplers and set out a few tips for sharing. Beginners can practice on parchment paper, then scoop the frosting back into the pastry bag.

SINGLE FLOWER: Use a small plain tip (#4) and green frosting to pipe the stem; switch to a small V-leaf tip (#352) to pipe the leaf. Using #352 tip and red frosting, pipe the petals. Use the #4 tip and brown frosting to add the flower's center.

FUNNY FACE: Use a large plain tip (#12) to pipe the nose and the #4 tip for eyes and mouth. Use a small open-star tip (#14) and brown (or yellow or red) frosting to pipe rosettes for curly hair; use other tips for different hairstyles.

DIAMONDS AND DOTS: Use the #4 tip to draw lines and dots, each made with a different color frosting. To pipe lines, hold tip just above cupcake's surface; squeeze, and let icing fall into place across cupcake. Add dots where lines intersect.

Dinosaur Cupcakes

Treat a class full of budding paleontologists to a bunch of cupcakes topped with colossal brachiosaurus cookies and dinosaur eggs. The gingerbread cookie that adorns each cupcake is cut out with a large dinosaur-shaped cutter, then pressed onto a lollipop stick before it's baked. (See Sources, page 342, for where to find the necessary tools.) You could also use any other animal or insect cookie cutters (they come in all shapes and sizes), and omit the candy eggs. MAKES 24

24 One-Bowl
   Chocolate
   Cupcakes
   (page 152)

+

   Swiss Meringue
   Buttercream
   (page 304)

+

   Gingerbread
   Cookie Cutouts
   (page 320)

24 rolled-paper
   lollipop sticks
   (4-inch)

   Orange and
   brown gel-paste
   food colors

   Green gummy
   candy, such as
   Swedish fish

72 candy-coated
   chocolate eggs

1. Make gingerbread cookie cutouts, using a 5- to 7-inch dinosaur-shaped cookie cutter to cut out shapes, and placing a lollipop stick under each shape, in the center (press lightly to adhere), before chilling and baking as directed.

2. Using gel-paste food colors, tint 1 cup buttercream pale orange, ½ cup deep orange, and the remaining pale brown. Transfer pale orange buttercream to a pastry bag fitted with a small plain tip (#7), and dark orange to a pastry bag fitted with another small plain tip (#3). Using an offset spatula, spread pale brown buttercream over each cupcake. Insert the stick of a cookie into each cupcake. Pipe small pale orange spikes along the top ridge of each dinosaur cookie (squeeze out a dot of frosting, then release while pulling up to end with a pointed peak), and pipe tiny deep orange spikes alongside, at the point where the larger ones meet. With a paring knife, cut "grass" from green gummy candy, with some spears longer than others. Arrange 3 candy eggs beside each dinosaur cookie, and stick a few pieces of candy grass in among the eggs. Refrigerate 30 minutes to allow frosting to set. Cupcakes are best served the same day they are decorated; keep at room temperature.

Sports Day Cupcakes

Go team! Root for your favorite sport with a triple play of easy-to-decorate cupcakes. Colorful sprinkles are used to simulate the bumpy or fuzzy textures of sports balls, on top of which the "seams" are either piped with buttercream or drawn with licorice laces. Make one type of ball or all three; you will need one batch of Swiss meringue buttercream (page 304) to decorate two dozen cupcakes in any design. Once decorated, cupcakes can be stored up to one day at room temperature in airtight containers.

MAKES 24 PER RECIPE

Home Run Cupcakes

Tint 1 cup buttercream dark red with gel-paste food color, and transfer to a pastry bag fitted with a small plain tip (#3). Place white round candy sprinkles (nonpareils) in a small bowl. Using an offset spatula, spread a smooth layer of untinted buttercream over each cupcake. Dip each frosted cupcake in sprinkles, rolling it around to coat completely. Pipe two red curved lines on each cupcake for the seams, then pipe short lines angled off both sides of curved lines to mimic small stitches. Refrigerate 30 minutes to allow frosting to set.

Match Point Cupcakes

Transfer 1 cup untinted buttercream to a pastry bag fitted with a small plain tip (#6). Place long yellow candy sprinkles in a small bowl. Using an offset spatula, spread a smooth layer of buttercream over each cupcake. Dip each frosted cupcake in sprinkles, rolling it around to coat completely. Pipe two white curved lines on each cupcake for the seams. Refrigerate 30 minutes to allow frosting to set.

Slam Dunk Cupcakes

Place orange round candy sprinkles (nonpareils) in a small bowl. Using an offset spatula, spread a smooth layer of untinted buttercream over each cupcake. Dip each frosted cupcake in sprinkles, rolling it around to coat completely. Cut 96 lengths (each about 3 inches) from licorice laces. Arrange three laces parallel to each other on each cupcake, one straight across the middle and the outer laces curved toward the edge. Lay a fourth piece in crosswise fashion over the other laces. Gently press licorice into frosting to adhere. Refrigerate 30 minutes to allow frosting to set.

Pretzel-Topped Cupcakes

Sometimes everyday snacks can do double duty as decorative touches, such as the pretzel sticks and twists in these delightful dog, butterfly, apple, and owl cupcakes. You'll need one recipe Swiss meringue buttercream (page 304) for two dozen cupcakes. See Sources, page 342, for where to find the candies used below. Refrigerate decorated cupcakes for thirty minutes; serve at room temperature the same day. MAKES 24 PER RECIPE

PLAYFUL PUPPY Using an offset spatula, spread a smooth layer of buttercream (plain or tinted, as desired) on cupcakes. Using a paring knife, cut red sour belt candy into rounded strips to resemble tongues; place on lower part of cupcake, in the center, bending tip slightly forward. Break small pretzel twists in half; press two small curved pieces into each cupcake for ears. Break the long W-shaped curve off additional pretzel twists; place rounded sections just above tongue, overlapping it slightly. Use black licorice buttons to create noses and brown mini chocolate-coated candies for eyes.

BUTTERFLIES IN FLIGHT Tint ½ cup buttercream pale blue with gel-paste food color; tint remaining 4½ cups pale green. Using an offset spatula, spread a smooth layer of green buttercream on cupcakes. Press 2 small pretzel twists, curved ends down, into center of each cupcake for wings. Place a candy-coated chocolate between wings at one end for the head. Snip black licorice laces into ½-inch pieces; slide 2 pieces under candy head for antennae. Starting at head, pipe dots in descending sizes between pretzels with blue buttercream and a small plain tip (#4) to resemble bodies.

RED-DELICIOUS APPLE Tint buttercream red with gel-paste food color. Using an offset spatula, spread buttercream on cupcakes (the applesauce-spice cupcakes on page 55 are a good choice), smoothing to form domed shapes. Use a paring knife to cut 24 leaf shapes from green-apple sour belt candy. Break 12 small pretzel sticks in half; insert a pretzel half into each cupcake for a stem; arrange a candy leaf shape alongside.

WISE OWLS Tint half of buttercream brown with gel-paste food color. Using an offset spatula, spread a thin layer of untinted buttercream on cupcakes. Break long curves off tiny pretzel twists; reserve for beaks. Place remaining pretzel portion in middle of cupcake. Fill a pastry bag fitted with a small leaf tip (#66) with untinted and brown buttercream, placing them side by side in bag. Starting around pretzel and working outward, pipe "feathers" all over cupcakes. Insert reserved beaks, broken ends down. Melt 1 ounce semisweet chocolate and place in a paper cornet (see page 298); pipe eyes inside pretzel outlines.

Beetle and Butterfly Cupcakes

Indulge a child's natural curiosity for the insect world with cupcakes smartly fashioned into beetles and butterflies. MAKES 24

24 One-Bowl Chocolate Cupcakes (page 152)

+

Swiss Meringue Buttercream (page 304)

+

Gel-paste food color (pink, blue, yellow, and green are pictured)

1 small bag (about 5 ounces) black licorice laces

24 gumdrops

1. Divide buttercream evenly among five small bowls; leave one portion untinted, and tint each of the others a different color with gel-paste food color. Using a serrated knife (and a gentle sawing motion), cut the domed tops off each cooled cupcake. Cut each top in half for the wings.

2. Using an offset spatula, spread untinted or tinted buttercream on each flat cupcake top. Position wings on frosted cupcakes, pressing gently to adhere. To make beetles, attach wings, domed sides up, with points meeting just inside edge of cupcake and extending off opposite side. To create butterflies, attach wings, cut sides up, with rounded edges in center of cupcake. Refrigerate until frosting is firm, about 30 minutes. Cupcakes

can be refrigerated up to 2 days in airtight containers; bring to room temperature before proceeding.

3. Snip licorice strings diagonally into 1½-inch lengths (48 pieces). Use a toothpick to make two holes in the top of each gumdrop on opposite sides. Insert the pointed end of one licorice strip into each hole to create antennae. Use a dab of buttercream to attach a gumdrop head to each cupcake.

4. Decorate wings as desired: Spread buttercream over wings (or leave unfrosted). Using pastry bags fitted with couplers and plain tips in various sizes (such as #2, #7, and #11), pipe dots on wings. Cupcakes are best served the same day they are decorated; keep at room temperature.

ATTACHING INSECT "WINGS"

ADDING DECORATIVE DETAILS

Coconut Chick Cupcakes

Cupcakes disguised as baby chicks are equally appropriate for a birthday party or an Easter celebration. To decorate them, the cupcakes are first inverted, then coated with generous layers of frosting and toasted coconut; features made of candy and almonds complete the disguise. Frosting anchors each cupcake onto a shallow dish to make it easier to keep the dessert in place while you finish it. If you don't have vanilla beans, increase the amount of pure vanilla extract by one tablespoon. MAKES 20

FOR CUPCAKES

Nonstick cooking spray

3 cups all-purpose flour

1 tablespoon baking powder

1/2 teaspoon salt

3/4 cup (1 1/2 sticks) unsalted butter, room temperature

1 1/2 cups sugar

2 vanilla beans, halved lengthwise, seeds scraped and reserved

Finely grated zest of 2 lemons (about 2 tablespoons)

3 large eggs, room temperature

1 cup buttermilk

2 teaspoons pure vanilla extract

FOR DECORATING

Swiss Meringue Buttercream (page 304)

28 ounces (four 7-ounce packages) sweetened shredded coconut, lightly toasted (see page 323)

1 piece black licorice lace (10 inches), cut into forty 1/4-inch pieces

20 whole unblanched almonds

1/3 cup red candy-coated licorice pastels (about 140 pieces) or 1/2- to 3/4-inch pieces of snipped red licorice laces

1. Make cupcakes: Preheat oven to 350°F. Line standard muffin tins with paper liners, and coat liners with cooking spray. Whisk together flour, baking powder, and salt. With an electric mixer on medium-high speed, beat butter, sugar, vanilla-bean seeds, and zest until pale and fluffy. Reduce speed to medium; add eggs, one at a time, beating until each is incorporated, scraping down sides of bowl as needed. Reduce speed to low; add flour mixture in three batches, alternating with two additions of buttermilk. Beat in vanilla extract.

FROSTING INVERTED CUPCAKES

2. Divide batter evenly among lined cups, filling each three-quarters full. Bake, rotating tins halfway through, until a cake tester inserted in centers comes out clean, about 20 minutes. Transfer tins to wire racks to cool 10 minutes; turn out cupcakes onto racks and let cool completely.

3. Decorate cupcakes: Gently peel liners off cooled cupcakes. Spread buttercream on top of a cupcake; invert onto a small dish. Using an offset spatula, spread buttercream over sides of cupcake, then generously spread more over inverted bottom to create a dome shape.

4. Place toasted coconut in a bowl. Holding cupcake dish at an angle over the bowl, press coconut into frosted top and sides of cupcake, letting excess fall back into bowl.

5. With kitchen tweezers, press 2 black licorice pieces into each cupcake for eyes. Insert an almond for a beak. Arrange 3 red licorice pastels on top for the comb and 2 at either side of base for feet. Cupcakes are best served the same day they are decorated; keep at room temperature.

Clown Cupcakes

Encourage a bit of clowning around with these crowd-pleasing cupcakes, brought to life with features fashioned from colorful sprinkles and candy. Cone-shaped pieces of cake cut from the centers become pointed hats that rest atop heads (and hidden bellies) piped with creamy frosting. **MAKES 24**

24 Yellow Buttermilk
   Cupcakes
   (page 26)

+

   Swiss Meringue
   Buttercream
   (page 304)

+

   Multicolored
   round candy
   sprinkles
   (nonpareils)

3 pounds mini
   uncoated
   gumdrops,
   such as Dots

24 small cinnamon
   candies, such as
   Red Hots

   Long chocolate
   sprinkles

1. For the hat, use a paring knife to score a circle in center of each cupcake. Holding knife at a slight angle, cut out a cone shape, rotating cupcake as you go.

2. Using a pastry bag fitted with only a plain coupler, pipe untinted buttercream into the cavity of each cupcake and in a mound on top for the head. Refrigerate 30 minutes to allow frosting to set.

FORMING CLOWN SHAPES

3. Using a small plain tip (#7), pipe a pompom of frosting on top of each cone-shaped piece; dip pompom in a bowl filled with multicolored sprinkles to coat completely. Place the cones on top of buttercream heads, pointed sides up. Arrange gumdrops around the base of each head to resemble a ruffled collar; press a cinnamon candy nose into each face. With kitchen tweezers, insert two chocolate sprinkles into each head for eyes. Serve immediately.

Ice-Cream Cone Cupcakes

Baked inside sugar cones, these cupcakes-in-hiding combine the best aspects of an ice cream sundae (all those great toppings!) in a no-melt treat. The cones are adorned with buttercream and topped with the usual fixings—whipped cream, colorful sprinkles, chopped nuts, melted chocolate, and even a cherry on top. Any leftover batter can be baked in mini muffin tins. An old-fashioned ice-cream-cone stand is a charming (and convenient) way to serve the cupcakes. MAKES 12

FOR CUPCAKES

- 12 sugar cones
- 1½ cups all-purpose flour
- 1 teaspoon baking powder
- ½ teaspoon salt
- ½ cup (1 stick) unsalted butter, room temperature
- 1 cup sugar
- 3 large eggs
- 1½ teaspoons pure vanilla extract
- ¾ cup milk

FOR DECORATING

Swiss Meringue Buttercream (page 304), plus ½ recipe chocolate variation (optional; page 305)

Gel-paste food color (optional; pink is pictured)

Melted chocolate (see page 323)

Chopped roasted salted peanuts

Maraschino cherries

Assorted candy sprinkles

PREPARING CONES FOR BAKING UPRIGHT

1. Preheat oven to 350°F. Remove center of a 12-inch tube pan and cover pan with a double layer of heavy-duty foil. Use a skewer or paring knife to poke 12 small holes in the foil, 2½ inches apart. Gently place a cone in each hole, pushing it down until only about 1 inch of cone is showing.

2. Make cupcakes: Sift together flour, baking powder, and salt. With an electric mixer on medium-high speed, cream butter and sugar until light and fluffy. Add eggs, one at a time, beating until each is incorporated, scraping down sides of bowl as needed. Beat in vanilla. Add flour mixture in three batches, alternating with two additions of milk, and beating until combined after each. Fill each cone with 2 to 3 tablespoons batter. Bake, rotating pan halfway through, until a cake tester inserted in centers comes out clean, 18 to 20 minutes. Transfer pan to a wire rack to cool completely.

3. Decorate cupcakes: Tint some of the buttercream pink with gel-paste food color, if desired. Use an ice-cream scoop to place buttercream (untinted or pink) on top of cupcake, then top with sprinkles. For "soft-serve" cones, use a pastry bag fitted with only a coupler (or a large plain tip) to pipe buttercream in a swirl over cone, then top with multicolored sprinkles; or, for "sundae" cones, drizzle melted chocolate over buttercream, then sprinkle with peanuts and top with a cherry. For soft-serve "twist" cones, fill a pastry bag fitted with an open-star tip (Ateco #828) with untinted and chocolate buttercreams, placing them side by side in bag; pipe two-tone swirls. Serve immediately.

Flock of Sheep Cupcakes

Counting sheep was never this much fun. The mini-marshmallow sheep are darling on their own, but for an extra-special presentation, you can herd them into a fondant-covered pasture bordered by a wooden fence constructed from coffee stirrers (see box below). **MAKES 12**

12 White Cupcakes
(page 154)

+

Swiss Meringue
Buttercream
(page 304)

+

Pink and black
gel-paste food
colors

2 cups (about 4
ounces) miniature
marshmallows,
each cut in half

1. Using gel-paste food colors, tint ¼ cup buttercream pale pink and ¼ cup black. Transfer tinted buttercreams to pastry bags fitted with only couplers. Using an offset spatula, spread each cupcake with a smooth layer of untinted buttercream. Transfer remaining untinted buttercream to a pastry bag fitted with only a coupler.

2. Starting in center of each cupcake, pipe a pear-shaped head with untinted buttercream, increasing pressure as you pull back. Switch to a small V-leaf tip (#352), and pipe ears. Pipe black eyes and a pale-pink nose and mouth using a fine plain tip (#1).

3. Place 3 marshmallow pieces on each sheep head, cut sides down. Working from the base of the head out, continue to cover each cupcake with halved marshmallows, cut sides down. Refrigerate 30 minutes to allow frosting to set. Cupcakes can be refrigerated up to 4 hours in airtight containers; bring to room temperature before serving.

PASTURE HOW-TO

Lightly dampen a 9-by-12-by-1-inch Styrofoam board; shake off excess water. Roll out 1 pound plain fondant (see page 299) to an 11-by-14-inch rectangle. Lift fondant, and place on board. Smooth surface; trim excess with a pizza wheel. To form posts, cut coffee stirrers in half and hot-glue around perimeter of base. For rail, weave whole coffee stirrers in and out along top half of each post; secure with hot glue. Attach wide grosgrain ribbon around the bottom of fence with hot glue.

PIPING THE SHEEP'S HEAD
AND EARS

ATTACHING MARSHMALLOW
"FLEECE"

Maple-Sweetened Carrot Cupcakes

This recipe was developed as a more healthy option to serve at a baby's or young child's birthday party. Sweetened only with a combination of maple syrup and molasses, the moist carrot cupcakes are sure to entice children and adults alike (which is helpful, since parents and other older guests often outnumber little ones at early birthday celebrations). Paired with a tangy, mildly sweet frosting—just cream cheese and maple syrup—the cupcakes are also a better choice than most for anyone watching his or her refined sugar intake. Mini cupcakes get only a dab of frosting and a candied carrot chip, while standard cupcakes are dotted with a generous amount of frosting. MAKES 12 STANDARD AND 24 MINI

2½ cups unbleached all-purpose flour

2 teaspoons baking soda

½ teaspoon baking powder

½ teaspoon salt

1 tablespoon ground cinnamon

1 cup pure maple syrup, preferably grade B

⅓ cup unsulfured molasses

1 cup safflower or canola oil

1 teaspoon apple-cider vinegar

5 large egg yolks

2 cups peeled, grated carrots (4 to 5 medium)

Maple Cream-Cheese Frosting (recipe follows)

Candied Carrot Chips (page 322)

1. Preheat oven to 375°F. Line standard and mini muffin tins with paper liners. In a large bowl, whisk together flour, baking soda, baking powder, salt, and cinnamon. In another bowl, whisk together maple syrup, molasses, oil, vinegar, and egg yolks until smooth. Add to flour mixture, and whisk until combined. Stir in carrots.

2. Divide batter evenly among lined cups, filling each three-quarters full. Bake, rotating tins halfway through, until dark golden brown and a cake tester inserted in centers comes out clean, 10 to 12 minutes for mini, about 18 minutes for standard. Transfer tins to wire racks to cool completely before removing cupcakes. Cupcakes can be stored up to 3 days at room temperature, or frozen up to 1 month, in airtight containers.

3. To finish, fill a pastry bag fitted with a small plain tip (#7) with frosting. Starting in the center and working out in circles, pipe dots all over larger cupcakes to cover. Pipe a dot in center of each mini cupcake, then top with a carrot chip. Serve immediately.

. . . .

MAPLE CREAM-CHEESE FROSTING
MAKES ENOUGH FOR 12 STANDARD AND 24 MINI CUPCAKES

1 pound cream cheese, room temperature

¼ cup pure maple syrup, preferably Grade B

With an electric mixer on medium-high speed, beat cream cheese until fluffy. Add maple syrup, and beat until combined. Use immediately, or refrigerate up to 3 days in an airtight container; bring to room temperature and stir until smooth before using.

Cupcake Caterpillar

This oh-so-cute caterpillar, made by arranging fondant-covered cupcakes in a curved line, makes a memorable arrangement for a baby's first birthday party. Here, one jumbo cupcake is used for the head and a dozen standard cupcakes make up the body; the remaining standard cupcakes can be frosted for serving alongside or decorated as instructed below and added to the caterpillar to accommodate more guests. Or you can make two caterpillars by baking the batter in two jumbo and 26 standard cups.

MAKES 1 JUMBO AND 28 STANDARD

FOR CUPCAKES

- 2½ cups plus 2 tablespoons all-purpose flour
- 1 cup plus 2 tablespoons unsweetened Dutch-process cocoa powder
- 2 teaspoons baking soda
- ⅛ teaspoon salt
- 1 cup plus 2 tablespoons (2¼ sticks) unsalted butter, room temperature
- 1 cup granulated sugar
- 1 cup packed dark-brown sugar
- 3 large eggs, room temperature
- ¾ cup sour cream
- 1½ cups buttermilk

FOR DECORATING

- 15 ounces fondant

  Gel-paste food colors (green, yellow, light blue, and red are pictured)

  Cornstarch, for dusting

  Swiss Meringue Buttercream (page 304)

- 2 mini candy canes (or substitute licorice sticks or pretzel sticks)

1. Make cupcakes: Preheat oven to 350°F. Line 28 cups of standard muffin tins and 1 cup of a jumbo muffin tin with paper liners. Whisk together flour, cocoa, baking soda, and salt.

2. With an electric mixer on medium-high speed, cream butter and granulated sugar until pale and fluffy. Add brown sugar, and beat until fluffy. Add eggs, one at a time, beating until well incorporated, scraping down sides of bowl as needed. Mix in sour cream. Reduce speed to low. Add flour mixture in three batches, alternating with two additions of buttermilk, and mixing until just combined after each.

3. Divide batter evenly among prepared cups, filling each three-quarters full. Bake, rotating tins halfway through, until tops are firm to the touch and a cake tester inserted in centers comes out clean, 25 to 30 minutes. Transfer tins to wire racks to cool completely before removing cupcakes. Cupcakes can be stored overnight at room temperature, or frozen up to 2 months, in airtight containers.

4. Decorate cupcakes: Tint fondant with green gel-paste food color (see page 299 for instructions), and roll out to ⅛ inch thick on a work surface lightly dusted with cornstarch. Using cookie cutters, cut out one 4½-inch round and twelve 3¾-inch rounds. Divide 2 cups buttercream into two bowls; tint half yellow and half pale blue with gel-paste food colors. Transfer to pastry bags fitted with small plain tips (#3). Tint ¼ cup buttercream red; transfer to a pastry bag fitted with a fine plain tip (#1). Spread cupcakes with a thin layer of plain buttercream, and transfer remaining untinted buttercream to a pastry bag fitted with another small plain tip (#2). Place a fondant round on top of each cupcake, pressing gently to adhere, and mold to fit smoothly.

CONTINUED >>

5. To make the head, pipe two yellow dots for the eyes on top of jumbo cupcake, then pipe tiny white dots for pupils. Using a skewer or toothpick, poke two holes above eyes, and insert mini candy canes into holes for antennae. Use red buttercream to pipe the mouth. Pipe dots all over other half of cupcake, alternating between yellow and pale blue buttercreams. Continue to pipe yellow and blue dots all over remaining cupcakes, then pipe tiny white dots on top of each. Refrigerate 30 minutes to allow frosting to set. Cupcakes can be stored up to 1 day at room temperature in airtight containers.

6. Arrange 12 standard cupcakes side by side in a curving line, with the jumbo cupcake at the front. Serve remaining cupcakes as desired.

CUTTING OUT AND ATTACHING
FONDANT ROUNDS

PIPING DECORATIVE DETAILS
ON FONDANT

Toy Toppers

Finding great cupcake toppers can be as easy as visiting a toy store. Here, a collection of tiny dinosaurs tromping through fields of green buttercream will entertain birthday boys and girls, but you can replicate this idea with other small decorative objects. Plus, the toppers can serve as take-home favors (make sure to remove and rinse off toys before serving the cupcakes). To decorate, tint Swiss meringue buttercream (page 304) green with gel-paste food color. Using an offset spatula, spread buttercream generously over cupcakes; insert toy toppers.

holidays

Nothing says "happy" like a bunch of festive cupcakes dressed up in holiday finery. In this section you'll find a year's worth of artfully themed cupcakes for the young—and young at heart. Some appear effortless, with just a bit of creatively placed sprinkles; others require a little more technique. All are a joy to make— kids especially will relish decorating cupcakes with seasonal symbols made out of frosting, marzipan, and even candies. There are cup- cakes to carry you throughout the year, from a New Year's "clock" to a marshmallow snow- man, and plenty in between. So you can give that special someone a Valentine's Day sweet, top cupcakes with "stars and stripes" for the Fourth of July, or share cupcakes disguised as goblins and ghouls with eager trick-or-treaters. As the year draws to a close, gingerbread boys and girls atop snow-capped cupcakes spread seasonal cheer to one and all.

New Year's Clock Cupcakes

Count down to the new year with twelve cupcakes, each with a designated hour, arranged to suggest a clock. The hands of the clock are made from a clip-art design easily copied onto paper and cut out (see page 340). This clock has a timeless look thanks to the Roman numerals, but you can alter the style of the numbers as you please. You may also want to try your hand at piping a different letter of "Happy New Year" on another dozen cupcakes (or simply frost and serve alongside); in this case, you will need to make a full batch of buttercream. **MAKES 12**

12 cupcakes, such as Yellow Buttermilk (page 26) or One-Bowl Chocolate (page 152)

+

½ recipe Swiss Meringue Buttercream (page 304)

+

2 ounces bittersweet chocolate, melted and cooled (see page 323)

1. Using an offset spatula, spread a generous layer of buttercream over each cupcake, then smooth around the edge and flatten the tops.

2. Place melted bittersweet chocolate in a paper cornet (see page 298), and pipe a different Roman numeral on each cupcake. (You may want to practice piping the numbers on a piece of parchment paper before decorating the cupcakes. Return the chocolate to the cornet when you are finished.) Refrigerate 30 minutes to allow frosting and chocolate to set. Cupcakes can be refrigerated up to 3 days in airtight containers; bring to room temperature before serving.

3. To serve, arrange cupcakes on a large tray or platter (lined with parchment or other paper, as desired) to resemble a clock, and place clip-art paper hands in the center.

Valentine Cupcakes

Homemade cupcakes are a more thoughtful token of love or friendship on February 14 than any mass-produced sweet. The cupcakes below are all easy to decorate and (save for the brownie cupcake) can be made with two dozen cupcakes in any flavor. Prepare a batch for your sweetheart, box them up for a child's classroom party, or hand-deliver them one by one to neighbors and office mates. MAKES 24 PER RECIPE

HANDWRITTEN VALENTINES Inspired by the popular supermarket-variety cream-filled chocolate treats, these cupcakes are both playful and sophisticated. Make chocolate ganache glaze (page 312). Dip each cupcake into glaze, letting excess drip off; invert and let set, 30 minutes. Fill a paper cornet (see page 298) with 2 ounces melted, cooled white chocolate; write messages on cupcakes, working from left to right edges without stopping (practice on parchment paper). Cupcakes can be stored up to 2 days at room temperature in airtight containers.

HUGS AND KISSES These cupcakes look particularly charming when arranged in an alternating pattern. Using an offset spatula, spread cupcakes with a smooth layer of Swiss meringue buttercream (page 304). Press small cinnamon red-hot candies (you'll need about ¾ cup) into the frosting to form Xs, Os, and heart shapes. Frosted cupcakes can be refrigerated up to 3 days in airtight containers; bring to room temperature and adorn with candies just before serving.

BROWNIE CUT-OUT HEARTS What better gift for a chocolate lover than heart-shaped brownies stacked atop frosted brownie cupcakes? Prepare the brownie recipe on page 322; it yields 2 dozen cupcakes and an 8-inch square for cutting out hearts. Using an offset spatula, spread cupcakes with fluffy vanilla frosting (page 302) tinted pink with gel-paste food color. Cut out hearts from the brownie square using a 1½-inch cookie cutter. Place hearts on frosted cupcakes, pressing gently to adhere. Decorated cupcakes can be refrigerated up to 3 days in airtight containers; bring to room temperature before serving.

CANDY SPRINKLE HEARTS If you're short on time, or baking for a large crowd, you can rely on these easy-to-decorate cupcakes. Using an offset spatula, spread cupcakes with fluffy vanilla frosting (page 302) and sprinkle the tops with tiny candy hearts (see Sources, page 342). Frosted cupcakes can be refrigerated up to 3 days in airtight containers; bring to room temperature and sprinkle with heart candies just before serving.

St. Patrick's Day Cupcakes

Share the luck of the Irish with cupcakes coated in frosting flavored with Baileys Irish Cream—a liqueur made from a blend of cream, cocoa, and Irish whiskey—and decorated with a sprig or two of real three-leaf clovers. The clovers should be removed before eating (be sure to use only pesticide-free clovers from a reliable source or your garden). You could also decorate the tops with a shamrock stencil, available at craft-supply stores (see Sources, page 342), and green sanding sugar. MAKES 24

24 Brown Sugar
   Pound Cakes
   (page 60)

+

   Baileys Irish Cream
   Frosting (recipe
   follows)

+

24 to 48 three-leaf
   clover sprigs,
   crystallized
   (optional; see
   Crystallized
   Flowers, page 322)

Using an offset spatula, spread each cupcake with a smooth layer of frosting. Cupcakes can be refrigerated up to 3 days in airtight containers; bring to room temperature and top each with 1 or 2 clover sprigs just before serving.

BAILEYS IRISH CREAM FROSTING
MAKES ENOUGH FOR 24 CUPCAKES

1½ cups (3 sticks) unsalted butter, room temperature
 1 pound (4 cups) confectioners' sugar, sifted
 3 tablespoons Baileys Irish Cream liqueur
½ teaspoon pure vanilla extract

1. With an electric mixer on medium-high speed, cream butter until smooth. Reduce speed to medium. Add the confectioners' sugar, ½ cup at a time, beating well after each addition and scraping down sides of bowl as needed, about 5 minutes total; after every two additions, raise speed to high and beat 10 seconds (to aerate frosting).

2. Add Baileys and vanilla, and beat until combined and smooth. Use immediately, or refrigerate up to 5 days in an airtight container; bring to room temperature and beat on low speed until smooth before using.

Springerle Easter Bunny Cupcakes

Springerle molds, originally from Germany, are used to form the pure white, spice-laden Christmas cookies of the same name. Yet the wooden molds are also useful for shaping rolled fondant into cupcake toppers in dozens of finely detailed designs, including Easter bunnies. You'll need to use a springerle mold with a design that is three inches or smaller. Look for the molds from specialty retailers online, or see Sources, page 342. Fondant mimics the color of traditional springerle cookies, but if you can't find it, use marzipan instead; although it is not white, you can tint it a desired shade with gel-paste food color (see instructions on page 299). MAKES 24

24 Carrot Cupcakes
   (page 25)

   +

½ recipe Cream-
   Cheese Frosting
   (page 303)

   +

12 ounces
   fondant

   Cornstarch, for
   dusting

1. Make fondant bunnies: Using a small rolling pin, and working in batches, roll out fondant to ⅛ inch thick on a work surface lightly dusted with cornstarch. Use a pastry brush to lightly dust the springerle mold with cornstarch; place fondant over mold. Using your fingers, gently but firmly press fondant into mold to fully imprint. Remove mold. Invert fondant with image facing up. If the design has flaws, knead the fondant again and remold. Use a 3-inch round cookie cutter to cut around the design. Repeat with remaining fondant, dusting mold with cornstarch between uses, until you have 24 rounds.

2. Decorate cupcakes: Using an offset spatula, spread a thin layer of frosting over each cupcake. Place a fondant round on top of each, very gently pressing around edge to adhere. Decorated cupcakes can be refrigerated up to 2 days in airtight containers; bring to room temperature before serving.

FORMING FONDANT TOPPERS

Easter-Egg Cupcakes

Consider making decorative cupcakes instead of (or to go along with) traditional dyed eggs for Easter this year. The patterns are very simple to produce: Various pastel colors of royal icing are piped onto a cupcake, then quickly swirled or dragged with a toothpick. Modify the color scheme to make cupcakes for other holidays—red and green for Christmas, for example, or black and orange for Halloween. **MAKES 24**

24 One-Bowl
   Chocolate
   Cupcakes
   (page 152)

+

   Royal Icing
   (page 315)

+

   Pink, lavender, and
   yellow gel-paste
   food colors

1. Using a serrated knife, trim top of each cupcake to make level. Divide royal icing among bowls; tint each portion a different color using gel-paste food color (see page 304 for instructions). Transfer to paper cornets (see page 298).

2. For drawn lines (below, left): Outline the top of a cupcake with one color of icing, and then pipe more icing to flood (or fill) the inside. Working quickly, pipe four to five parallel lines with one or two different colors of icing over the first color. Use a toothpick to draw lines perpendicular to the piped ones, alternating between dragging downward and upward.

3. For a swirled effect (below, right): Outline cupcake with one color, and pipe squiggly lines inside the outline. Working quickly, fill in spaces with another color of icing to cover completely; use a toothpick to swirl the colors.

4. Allow icing to set, about 30 minutes. Iced cupcakes can be stored up to 1 day at room temperature in airtight containers (do not refrigerate).

CREATING DRAWN LINES AND SWIRLED DESIGNS

Chocolate-Walnut Cupcakes for Passover

During Passover, the proscription of any sort of leavening (including wheat flour) can greatly limit a baker's possibilities. Yet these cupcakes, inspired by Eastern European tortes, rely on egg whites for leavening and use ground walnuts in place of regular flour, making them a wonderful option for a seder or other gathering. They are also a good choice any time of year for those with gluten intolerance. **MAKES 26**

6 large eggs, separated

1/4 cup plus 3 tablespoons granulated sugar

1 3/4 cups finely ground toasted walnuts (6 ounces; see page 323)

3 ounces bittersweet chocolate, kosher if desired, finely chopped or grated

1 tablespoon finely grated orange zest

1/4 teaspoon salt

Confectioners' sugar, for dusting

1. Preheat oven to 300°F. Line standard muffin tins with paper liners. With an electric mixer on medium-high speed, whisk egg yolks and 1/4 cup granulated sugar until pale and thick. In another bowl, toss together ground walnuts, chocolate, zest, and salt. Sprinkle over yolk mixture; do not mix in.

2. Place egg whites in a heatproof bowl set over a pan of simmering water, and whisk until whites are warm to the touch. Remove from heat. With an electric mixer on high speed, whisk until soft peaks form. Add remaining 3 tablespoons granulated sugar, and whisk until stiff and glossy (but not dry) peaks form. Fold one third of egg-white mixture into egg-yolk mixture to lighten. Gently fold in remaining egg whites.

3. Divide batter evenly among lined cups, filling each three-quarters full. Bake, rotating tins halfway through, until springy to the touch, about 30 minutes. Transfer tins to wire racks to cool 10 minutes; turn out cupcakes onto racks and let cool completely. Cupcakes can be stored up to 2 days at room temperature in airtight containers. Dust with confectioners' sugar just before serving.

Mother's Day Hummingbird Cupcakes

Some say the hummingbird cake, a Southern specialty replete with pine-apple chunks, bananas, coconut, and walnuts, earned its name because each otherworldly bite makes you hum with delight. Others hold that the cake is as sweet as the sugared water used to attract the tiny birds. Adorned with dried-pineapple "flowers," the cupcake variation makes a beautiful presentation for Mother's Day. To give the flowers a cupped shape (shown opposite), cool them in muffin tins as described on page 323 (instead of on a wire rack, shown below). MAKES 40

3 cups all-purpose flour

3/4 teaspoon baking soda

1 teaspoon salt

1 teaspoon ground cinnamon

1 cup (2 sticks) unsalted butter, melted and cooled

2 teaspoons pure vanilla extract

2 cups sugar

3 large eggs

2 cups mashed ripe banana (about 3 large bananas)

2 cans (8 ounces each) crushed pineapple, drained

1 cup walnuts (about 3 ounces), toasted (see page 323) and coarsely chopped

1 cup unsweetened desiccated coconut (see Sources, page 342)

Cream-Cheese Frosting (page 303)

Dried Pineapple Flowers (see page 323)

1. Preheat oven to 350°F. Line standard muffin tins with paper liners. Whisk together flour, baking soda, salt, and cinnamon.

2. With an electric mixer on medium-high speed, beat butter, vanilla, and sugar until combined. Add eggs, one at a time, beating until each is incorporated, scraping down sides of bowl as needed. Continue beating until mixture is pale and fluffy.

3. In another bowl, stir together banana, pineapple, walnuts, and coconut. Add to egg mixture, beating until combined. Stir in flour mixture with a flexible spatula.

4. Divide batter evenly among lined cups, filling each three-quarters full. Bake, rotating tins halfway through, until golden brown and a cake tester inserted in centers comes out clean, 25 to 28 minutes. Transfer tins to wire racks to cool completely before removing cupcakes. Cupcakes can be stored up to 3 days at room temperature in airtight containers.

5. To finish, use a small offset spatula to spread frosting over each cupcake. Top each with a dried-pineapple flower.

MAKING DRIED PINEAPPLE FLOWERS

Father's Day Tee-Time Cupcakes

Present Dad with a bunch of golf-themed cupcakes, complete with putting greens and sand traps, on his special day. The mini greens are adorned with colored sanding sugar, a candy golf ball, and a ribbon flag; graham-cracker crumbs stand in for sand. You could create an entire course by decorating eighteen cupcakes with different numbered flags, and the remaining six with sand traps. **MAKES 24**

24 Yellow Buttermilk Cupcakes (page 26) or One-Bowl Chocolate Cupcakes (page 152)

+

Swiss Meringue Buttercream (page 304)

+

1 to 2 cups green sanding sugar

18 round white candies, such as candy-coated mint balls (see Sources, page 342)

½ cup graham cracker crumbs (3 to 4 sheets finely ground in a food processor)

1. Using an offset spatula, spread each cupcake with a smooth layer of buttercream. Pour green sanding sugar into a small bowl. Dip tops of frosted cupcakes in the sugar, then sprinkle more on top to coat completely.

2. To create putting greens, make flags (you will need 18): Cut out lengths (3 to 4 inches) from white grosgrain ribbon. Fold each length around one end of a wooden skewer, and adhere folded sides together with hot glue or double-sided tape. Cut ribbon into a triangle shape, and plant the skewer into a cupcake. Place a small white candy "ball" near the flag.

3. To create sand traps, spoon about 1 teaspoon graham-cracker crumbs in the center of each of 6 cupcakes. With your thumb, make an indentation in the middle of each pile of crumbs, shifting it to one side to form a steeper side or an irregularly shaped trap. Refrigerate 30 minutes to allow frosting to set.

Flag Day Cupcakes

Tiny blue buttercream stars and red-licorice stripes create a patriotic batch of cupcakes to celebrate Independence Day. Festive cupcake liners carry out the theme; see Sources, page 342. **MAKES 24**

24 Yellow Buttermilk
    Cupcakes
    (page 26) or One-
    Bowl Chocolate
    Cupcakes
    (page 152)

+

    Swiss Meringue
    Buttercream
    (page 304)

+

    Blue gel-paste
    food color

 1 small bag (about
    5 ounces) red
    licorice laces

1. Tint 1 cup buttercream bright blue with gel-paste food color. Transfer to a pastry bag fitted with a small plain tip (#4). Using an offset spatula, spread each cupcake with a smooth layer of untinted buttercream. Cupcakes can be refrigerated up to 3 days in airtight containers; bring to room temperature before decorating.

2. To finish, cut licorice laces into seventy-two 1½-inch-long pieces and seventy-two ¾-inch-long pieces. Arrange three longer pieces and three shorter pieces to form a flag pattern on each cupcake. With blue frosting, pipe nine dots in each open corner to form "stars."

Creepcakes

For Halloween, create silly and scary-looking faces with buttercream, candy, marshmallows, and, of course, cupcakes. Decorating the cakes is a great activity for kids and parents to do together: Set out cupcakes and bowls of colored frostings and assorted candies and let everyone create his or her own aliens, monsters, and beasts. **MAKES 12 STANDARD AND 12 MINI**

12 each standard and mini cupcakes, such as Yellow Buttermilk (page 26) or One-Bowl Chocolate (page 152)

+

Swiss Meringue Buttercream (page 304)

+

Leaf-green, lemon-yellow, forest-green, and black gel-paste food colors

Assorted candies (see page 230)

½ cup semisweet chocolate chips, melted (optional; see page 323)

1. Tint buttercream desired color with gel-paste food color. For the bright green used on some of the cupcakes (opposite), use a mixture of leaf-green and lemon-yellow. Use forest-green for others. For a few of the creatures on page 231, mix in a small amount of black food color to make a gray color; leave some buttercream untinted for white.

2. Make the candy features as shown on page 230. Using an offset spatula, spread cupcakes with plain or tinted buttercreams, as desired. To create the split and filled aliens (opposite), use a serrated knife (and a gentle sawing motion) to slice off the top of the cupcake (reserve top), then spread buttercream generously over bottom part and replace tops (leave unfrosted).

3. To finish, attach candy features to frosted (or filled) cupcakes. Cupcakes are best eaten the day they are decorated; keep at room temperature until ready to serve.

CONTINUED >>

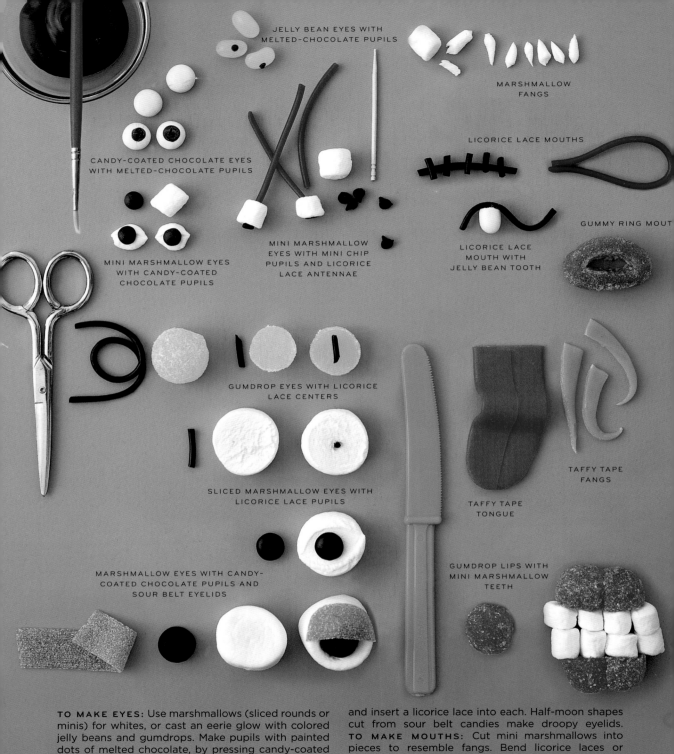

JELLY BEAN EYES WITH MELTED-CHOCOLATE PUPILS

MARSHMALLOW FANGS

CANDY-COATED CHOCOLATE EYES WITH MELTED-CHOCOLATE PUPILS

LICORICE LACE MOUTHS

MINI MARSHMALLOW EYES WITH CANDY-COATED CHOCOLATE PUPILS

MINI MARSHMALLOW EYES WITH MINI CHIP PUPILS AND LICORICE LACE ANTENNAE

LICORICE LACE MOUTH WITH JELLY BEAN TOOTH

GUMMY RING MOUT

GUMDROP EYES WITH LICORICE LACE CENTERS

SLICED MARSHMALLOW EYES WITH LICORICE LACE PUPILS

TAFFY TAPE FANGS

TAFFY TAPE TONGUE

MARSHMALLOW EYES WITH CANDY-COATED CHOCOLATE PUPILS AND SOUR BELT EYELIDS

GUMDROP LIPS WITH MINI MARSHMALLOW TEETH

TO MAKE EYES: Use marshmallows (sliced rounds or minis) for whites, or cast an eerie glow with colored jelly beans and gumdrops. Make pupils with painted dots of melted chocolate, by pressing candy-coated chocolates to the sticky sides of marshmallows, or with licorice lace pieces. For antennae eyes, push mini chocolate chips, tips down, into mini marshmallows, then make holes underneath (with a toothpick) and insert a licorice lace into each. Half-moon shapes cut from sour belt candies make droopy eyelids.
TO MAKE MOUTHS: Cut mini marshmallows into pieces to resemble fangs. Bend licorice laces or gummy rings into mouths; use mini marshmallows or white jelly beans (whole or cut) for teeth. Cut taffy tape into tongues, fangs, or tentacles. Halve red gumdrops and turn on their sides for lips.

Wicked Witch Cupcakes

Green-faced, straggly-haired witches may look mean, but they are actually sweet chocolate cupcakes dressed up for Halloween. Inverted chocolate ice-cream cones make perfectly pointed hats. Bake a coven's worth and set them out on display to greet—and treat—Halloween party guests. MAKES 24

24 One-Bowl Chocolate Cupcakes (page 152) or Devil's Food Cupcakes (page 34)

+

Swiss Meringue Buttercream (page 304)

+

Green gel-paste food color

24 chocolate sugar cones

24 candy corn pieces

48 brown mini candy-coated chocolates, such as mini M&M's

1 small bag (about 5 ounces) black licorice laces

1. Tint buttercream green with gel-paste food color. Spoon a generous mound of buttercream onto each cupcake; using an offset spatula, smooth into a dome shape. (Or use an ice-cream scoop to place a mound of buttercream atop each cupcake.)

2. Place an inverted sugar cone on top of each cupcake, tilting cones slightly backward. Press two candy-coated chocolates and one piece of candy corn into buttercream to make the eyes and nose.

3. With a paring knife or kitchen shears, snip licorice laces into pieces—longer ones (about 2½ inches) for hair, and shorter (about ½ inch) for eyebrows and bangs. Insert longer licorice pieces into frosting, just below the sugar cones, to make hair, and press two short licorice pieces over eyes, slanting them slightly to make eyebrows. Decorated cupcakes can be stored up to 1 day at room temperature.

Candy Ghoul Cupcake Toppers

This collection of edible Halloween toppers is assembled with gumdrops for bodies and assorted candies (see Sources, page 342) for features. Cutting gumdrops, or scraping away patches of sugar, creates sticky parts for easy adhering. Spread Swiss meringue buttercream (regular or chocolate variation; pages 304–305) over cupcakes, then decorate as instructed below.

BLACK CAT For one topper, you will need 2 black gumdrops, a length of black licorice lace, 1 black licorice wheel, 1 black licorice drop, and 2 red round candy sprinkles (nonpareils). Trim gumdrops and stick them together for the head and body. Snip licorice lace for arms, legs, tail, and whiskers. Cut 2 small triangles from licorice wheel for ears. Poke holes in gumdrops with a toothpick and insert sprinkle eyes (use kitchen tweezers), licorice drop nose, and licorice-lace arms, legs, and tail. Scrape away sugar around nose and attach licorice whiskers. Place black cat on frosted cupcake.

WITCH FACE For one topper, you will need 1 flat green gumdrop, 1 red spice drop, 2 long chocolate sprinkles, 2 long white sprinkles, black licorice lace, 1 black licorice stick, 1 black licorice gummy candy (such as Chuckles), and 1 green sour candy (such as Nerds). Cut gummy candy into a triangle hat; cut licorice stick into the brim. Snip licorice lace into a piece for hair. Poke holes in gumdrop with a toothpick; insert chocolate sprinkle eyes (use kitchen tweezers). Scrape away sugar from gumdrop; attach green candy nose. Snip off top of red spice drop; poke hole in middle and insert white sprinkle teeth. Place face on frosted cupcake. Curve hair around top; attach candy brim and hat.

LITTLE DEVIL For one topper, you will need 2 red gumdrops, a length of red licorice lace, and 1 black licorice wheel. Trim both gumdrops and stick together to form the head and body. Cut 2 small triangles from licorice wheel for the ears and a longer triangle for the nose; cut 2 tiny pieces for the eyes. Snip licorice lace for arms and tail. Poke holes in gumdrops with a toothpick and insert licorice eyes (use kitchen tweezers), ears, nose, arms, and tail. Place red devil on frosted cupcake (the one shown is sprinkled with red, orange, and yellow sanding sugar to resemble flames), and add a candle "pitchfork," if desired.

VAMPIRE BAT For one topper, you will need 1 black licorice wheel, 1 black gumdrop, and 2 red round candy sprinkles (nonpareils). Cut black licorice wheel in half and then into two wing shapes; cut two small triangles from remaining licorice pieces for the ears. Poke holes in gumdrop with a toothpick, and insert licorice ears and red sprinkle eyes (use kitchen tweezers). Place face on frosted cupcake, then insert wings into buttercream on either side.

Pumpkin Patch Cupcakes

Pumpkin spice cupcakes topped with tiny marzipan pumpkins are an un-expected alternative (or addition) to pie for Thanksgiving, but these treats would also be welcome at a Halloween party or any other fall occasion.

MAKES 32

FOR CUPCAKES

- 4 cups cake flour (not self-rising), sifted
- 1 teaspoon baking soda
- 1 tablespoon plus 1 teaspoon baking powder
- 1 teaspoon salt
- 2 teaspoons ground cinnamon
- 1 tablespoon ground ginger
- 1 teaspoon freshly grated nutmeg
- 1/4 teaspoon ground cloves
- 1 cup (2 sticks) unsalted butter, room temperature
- 2 1/2 cups packed light-brown sugar
- 4 large eggs
- 1 cup buttermilk
- 1 1/2 cups canned pumpkin puree (not pie filling)

FOR DECORATING

Cream-Cheese Frosting (page 303)

Marzipan Pumpkins (instructions follow)

1. Preheat oven to 350°F. Line standard muffin tins with paper liners. Sift together flour, baking soda, baking powder, salt, and spices.

2. With an electric mixer on medium-high speed, cream butter and brown sugar until pale and fluffy. Add eggs, one at a time, beating until each is incorporated, scraping down sides of bowl as needed. Reduce speed to low. Add flour mixture in three batches, alternating with two additions of buttermilk, and beating until just combined. Add pumpkin puree; beat until just combined.

FORMING MARZIPAN PUMPKINS

3. Divide batter evenly among lined cups, filling each three-quarters full. Bake, rotating tins halfway through, until golden brown, 15 to 18 minutes. Transfer tins to wire racks to cool 10 minutes; turn out cupcakes onto racks and let cool completely. Cupcakes can be refrigerated up to 3 days in airtight containers.

4. To finish, use an offset spatula to spread cupcakes with frosting. Top each with a marzipan pumpkin.

MARZIPAN PUMPKINS

You'll need a total of 14 ounces of marzipan to make 32 pumpkins. Tint two thirds marzipan orange with gel-paste food color (see page 299 for instructions). Tint remaining marzipan green. Using a small rolling pin, roll out green marzipan to about 1/8 inch thick on a work surface lightly dusted with cornstarch; use a mini leaf cutter (see Sources, page 342) to cut out leaf shapes. With the palms of your hands, roll bits of orange and green marzipan together into small ropes; cut and shape into stems. Shape pieces of orange marzipan into 3/4-inch balls. Use a toothpick to poke holes in tops of balls and press creases along outer edges from top to bottom. Attach leaves and stems to tops.

Marshmallow Turkey Cupcakes

Gobble, gobble! Gummy candies, marshmallows, and toasted coconut flakes make excellent facial features and feathers for tiny Thanksgiving "turkeys." Coconut marshmallows are available at specialty stores and online; if you can't find them, make your own: Coat marshmallows with buttercream and then dip them in ground, toasted coconut. MAKES 24

24 One-Bowl Chocolate Cupcakes (page 152)

+

Swiss Meringue Buttercream (page 304)

+

5 tablespoons semi-sweet chocolate chips, melted and cooled (see page 323)

24 coconut marsh-mallows, such as Kraft Jet-Puffed Toasted Coconut Marshmallows

48 long chocolate sprinkles

1 pound mini gummy fish (144 pieces)

12 ounces sweet-ened shredded coconut, lightly toasted (4 cups; see page 323)

1. Using a flexible spatula, fold melted and cooled chocolate into buttercream. Use an offset spatula to spread buttercream over cupcakes in a smooth layer.

2. With a wet toothpick, poke two holes in each coconut marshmallow; using kitchen tweezers, insert chocolate sprinkles for eyes. Cut 12 orange gummy fish in half; push one half into each marshmallow for a beak. Press marshmallow heads onto cupcakes. Press 5 more gummy fish into each cupcake to make tail feathers. Sprinkle toasted coconut over cupcakes to cover completely. Decorated cupcakes can be stored up to 1 day at room temperature in airtight containers.

Maple Cupcakes

The maple is among the most prized trees in the American Northeast, beloved for its bright fall foliage as well as the syrup made from its sap in the spring. Here the crimson autumn leaves are cast in marzipan and placed atop maple-flavored cupcakes and frosting. Keep these cupcakes in mind for Thanksgiving or a leaf-peeping picnic in the country. Unfrosted cupcakes, still warm from the oven, are great for breakfast. For where to find the leaf cutters, see Sources, page 342. MAKES 24 STANDARD OR 66 MINI

FOR CUPCAKES

2 3/4 cups all-purpose flour, sifted

1 tablespoon baking powder

1 teaspoon salt

1/2 cup (1 stick) unsalted butter, room temperature

2 cups pure maple syrup, preferably Grade B

3 large eggs, room temperature

1 cup milk

1 teaspoon pure vanilla extract

FOR DECORATING

Maple Buttercream (page 309)

Marzipan Maple Leaves (instructions follow)

1. Preheat oven to 350°F. Line standard or mini muffin tins with paper liners. Sift together flour, baking powder, and salt.

2. With an electric mixer on medium-high speed, cream butter until smooth. Add the maple syrup, and beat until combined. Add eggs, one at a time, beating until each is incorporated, scraping down sides of bowl as needed. Add flour mixture, and beat well to combine. Beat in milk and vanilla until combined.

3. Divide batter evenly among lined cups, filling each three-quarters full. Bake, rotating tins halfway through, until golden and a cake tester inserted in centers comes out clean, about 20 minutes for standard, 10 to 13 minutes for minis. Transfer tins to wire racks to cool completely before removing cupcakes.

4. To finish, use an offset spatula to spread each cupcake with maple buttercream. Top with marzipan leaves. Decorated cupcakes can be stored up to 1 day at room temperature in airtight containers.

. . . .

MARZIPAN MAPLE LEAVES

Divide 5 ounces marzipan into thirds, and tint with red, orange, and brown gel-paste food colors (see page 299 for instructions). Knead all pieces together briefly until colors are streaky. Using a rolling pin, roll out marzipan to 1/8 inch thick on a work surface lightly dusted with cornstarch. Cut out 24 leaves using a 2 1/4-inch leaf-shaped cookie cutter for standard cupcakes or 66 leaves using a 1 3/4-inch cutter for minis. Marzipan leaves can be stored up to 1 day at room temperature in an airtight container, between layers of parchment paper.

Candied Sweet Potato Cupcakes

Although the flavor might seem unusual for a cupcake, sweet potatoes have long been pureed and baked into desserts, such as sweet potato pie. This playful rendition of a traditional Thanksgiving side dish—complete with mini marshmallows and candied pecans on top—will appeal to anyone who loves the sweet, earthy flavors of root vegetables. Serve the cupcakes as one component of a holiday dessert buffet. If you like, bake and mash the sweet potatoes the day before you make the cupcakes; let cool completely and refrigerate, covered. MAKES 24

FOR CUPCAKES

- 2 pounds (about 3 medium) sweet potatoes, scrubbed
- 2 cups all-purpose flour
- 2 teaspoons baking powder
- 1 teaspoon coarse salt
- 2 teaspoons ground cinnamon
- 1/2 teaspoon freshly grated nutmeg
- 1 cup (2 sticks) unsalted butter, room temperature
- 1 cup granulated sugar
- 1 cup packed dark-brown sugar
- 4 large eggs, room temperature
- 2 teaspoons pure vanilla extract

FOR TOPPING

- 2 cups miniature marshmallows
- Candied Pecan Pieces (page 323)

1. Make cupcakes: Preheat oven to 400°F. Pierce sweet potatoes with a fork and place on a parchment-lined rimmed baking sheet. Bake until completely soft and juices begin to seep from the potatoes and caramelize, about 1 hour. Remove from oven. Reduce oven to 325°F.

2. When cool enough to handle, slice potatoes in half lengthwise and use a fork to scrape the flesh from the skin into a bowl, discarding skins. Mash potato with fork until smooth. (You should have about 2 cups.)

3. Line standard muffin tins with paper liners. Whisk together flour, baking powder, salt, cinnamon, and nutmeg. With an electric mixer on medium-high speed, cream butter and both sugars until pale and fluffy. Add eggs, one at a time, beating until each is incorporated, scraping down sides of bowl as needed. Beat in mashed sweet potatoes and vanilla. Reduce speed to low. Add the flour mixture in three batches, beating until completely incorporated after each.

4. Divide batter evenly among lined cups, filling each three-quarters full. Bake, rotating tins halfway through, until cupcakes are set and a cake tester inserted in centers comes out clean, about 28 minutes. Transfer tins to wire racks to cool completely before removing cupcakes. Cupcakes can be stored up to 3 days at room temperature, or frozen up to 3 months, in airtight containers.

5. Make topping: Dividing evenly into 24 mounds, place marshmallows on a large baking sheet or nonstick baking mat. Using a small kitchen torch, brown marshmallows all over (or heat under the broiler). With an offset spatula, transfer mounds to cupcakes, and top with candied pecans, dividing evenly. Cupcakes are best served the day they are topped; keep at room temperature.

Sparkly Star of David Cupcakes

This festive dessert was created for a Hanukkah celebration. To make the design, place a star-shaped cookie cutter on a frosted cupcake, then fill in with vibrant blue nonpareils. You could, of course, modify this idea with other cookie cutter shapes—just make sure they're no larger than three inches wide, so they'll fit atop a cupcake. MAKES 24

24 One-Bowl Chocolate Cupcakes (page 152) or White Cupcakes (page 154)

+

Swiss Meringue Buttercream (page 304)

+

2 cups blue round candy sprinkles (nonpareils)

1. Use a serrated knife to trim top of each cupcake to make level. Using an offset spatula, spread each cupcake with a smooth layer of buttercream.

2. When ready to serve, lay a six-sided star cookie cutter on top of a cupcake. Using a small spoon, fill inside cutter completely with sprinkles in an even layer. (For best results, do not overfill, as the star may lose its shape once the cutter is removed.) Carefully lift cookie cutter, and repeat with remaining cupcakes.

FORMING STARS

Gingerbread Cupcakes with Cookie Cutouts

Gingerbread is the most recognizable Christmastime flavor; the scent of its signature spices baking in the oven fills a home with holiday cheer. These cupcakes are made with the same mixture of spices—nutmeg, clove, cinnamon, and ginger—as the tiny gingerbread-cookie boys and girls they are topped with. The recipe for the cookie dough will yield more cutouts than you need to decorate twenty-two cupcakes; serve extra cookies alongside. MAKES 22

FOR CUPCAKES

- 1½ cups all-purpose flour
- 2 tablespoons ground ginger
- 2 teaspoons ground cinnamon
- ¼ teaspoon freshly grated nutmeg
- ¼ teaspoon ground cloves
- 1½ cups (3 sticks) unsalted butter, room temperature
- 1½ cups sugar
- 3 tablespoons unsulfured molasses
- 4 large eggs, room temperature
- 1 teaspoon pure vanilla extract

FOR DECORATING

- Gingerbread Cookie Cutouts (page 320; use 2-inch gingerbread boy and girl cutters)
- ½ recipe Royal Icing (page 315)
- Blue and pink gel-paste food colors
- Fluffy Vanilla Frosting (page 302)

1. Preheat oven to 350°F. Line standard muffin tins with paper liners. Sift together flour and spices.

2. With an electric mixer on medium-high speed, cream butter and sugar until pale and fluffy. Add the molasses, and beat until combined. Add eggs, one at a time, beating until each is incorporated, scraping down sides of bowl as needed. Beat in vanilla. Reduce speed to low. Gradually add flour mixture, beating until just combined.

3. Divide batter evenly among lined cups, filling each three-quarters full. Bake, rotating tins halfway through, until a cake tester inserted in centers comes out clean, about 25 minutes. Transfer tins to wire racks to cool 10 minutes; turn out cupcakes onto racks and let cool completely. Cupcakes can be stored up to 2 days at room temperature, or frozen up to 3 months, in airtight containers.

4. Tint ¼ cup icing pale pink with gel-paste food color; tint remaining icing pale blue. Transfer tinted icings to pastry bags fitted with small plain tips (#2). Pipe three blue dots on the front of each gingerbread cookie boy; pipe two pink dots on gingerbread girls.

5. To finish, use an offset spatula to spread each cupcake with a smooth layer of frosting. Place a gingerbread boy or girl upright on each cupcake before serving.

Fruitcakes with Meringue Mushrooms

Inspired by the time-honored specialty cakes of Christmas, these down-scaled versions are studded with mixed dried fruits and nuts and flavored with spirits. Once baked, they are blanketed with billowy frosting and topped with another familiar holiday treat, meringue mushrooms. In place of the apricots, figs, and dates used here, you may substitute other fruits, such as dried pineapple or candied citrus peel. Just be sure to purchase good-quality fruits from a store with a high turnover (avoid supermarket varieties sold as "mixed candied fruit") and use kitchen shears to cut the fruit into uniform pieces. MAKES 12

FOR CUPCAKES

- 4 ounces dried apricots, cut into 1/4-inch pieces (1/2 cup plus 2 tablespoons)
- 4 ounces dried figs, stemmed and cut into 1/4-inch pieces (1/2 cup plus 2 tablespoons)
- 4 ounces plump, moist dates, preferably Medjool, pitted and cut into 1/4-inch pieces (scant 1 cup)
- 1/4 cup hazelnut-flavored liqueur, such as Frangelico, or brandy
- 3/4 cup all-purpose flour
- 1 1/2 teaspoons baking powder
- 1/2 teaspoon salt
- 1/4 cup (1/2 stick) unsalted butter, room temperature
- 1/2 cup packed light-brown sugar
- 1/4 cup granulated sugar
- 3 large eggs
- 2 tablespoons honey
- 1 1/2 teaspoons pure vanilla extract
- 1 cup hazelnuts (about 4 ounces), toasted and skinned (see page 323), then coarsely chopped

FOR DECORATING

Seven-Minute Frosting (page 303)

Meringue Mushrooms (page 250)

Cocoa powder, for dusting

1. Preheat oven to 300°F. Line a standard muffin tin with paper liners. Toss apricots, figs, and dates in a bowl with the liqueur. In another bowl, whisk together flour, baking powder, and salt.

2. With an electric mixer on medium-high speed, cream butter and both sugars until pale and fluffy. Add eggs, one at a time, beating until each is incorporated and scraping down sides of bowl as needed. Beat in honey and vanilla. Add flour mixture, and beat until just combined. Fold in fruit mixture and hazelnuts by hand.

3. Divide batter evenly among lined cups, filling each three-quarters full. Bake, rotating tin halfway through, until a cake tester inserted in centers comes out clean, about 30 minutes (if cupcakes start to brown too quickly, tent loosely with foil). Transfer tin to a wire rack to cool completely before removing cupcakes.

4. To finish, use an offset spatula to spread cupcakes with frosting. Dust meringue mushrooms with cocoa and place on top of cupcakes just before serving.

CONTINUED >>

MERINGUE MUSHROOMS
MAKES ENOUGH FOR 12 CUPCAKES

Swiss Meringue (page 317)

2 ounces bittersweet chocolate, finely chopped

3 ounces white chocolate, finely chopped

1. Preheat oven to 200°F. Line rimmed baking sheets with parchment paper. Transfer Swiss meringue to a pastry bag fitted with a small plain tip (#6). For caps, pipe dome shapes in various sizes, from ½ to 1 inch in diameter (the ones shown are larger), onto prepared baking sheets. Flatten tips with a damp finger. Pipe stems onto baking sheets, releasing pressure halfway and pulling up to form a peak. Make one stem for each cap.

2. Bake the meringue shapes 1 hour, rotating baking sheets halfway through; reduce oven temperature to 175°F. Continue baking until meringue is completely dry to the touch but not taking on any color, 45 to 60 minutes more.

3. Melt bittersweet chocolate in a small heatproof bowl set over (not in) a pan of simmering water, stirring occasionally. Using a small offset spatula, spread bottoms of cooled caps with a thin layer of melted bittersweet chocolate, and let set. Melt white chocolate in another heatproof bowl set over (not in) a pan of simmering water. Let cool, stirring, until thickened, then spread over dark chocolate. Use a toothpick to draw lines through the chocolate from center to edge of caps to mimic gills; let set.

4. Using a paring knife, make a small hole in center of each coated cap. Dip one end of each stem in remaining white chocolate, and insert into a hole; let set. Store mushrooms up to 1 week in airtight containers, and keep in a cool, dry place.

PIPING MERINGUE CAPS
AND STEMS

COATING CAPS WITH
CHOCOLATE

DRAWING "GILLS" WITH A TOOTHPICK

Candy Christmas Cupcake Toppers

Whimsical candy cupcake toppers are a gift not only to the lucky recipient, but also to the baker. Children will likely want to lend a hand in putting them together. Use any flavor of cupcakes you like—such as yellow buttermilk (page 26) or one-bowl chocolate (page 152)—and frost with Swiss meringue buttercream (page 304).

NUTTY PENGUINS Made from white Jordan almonds dipped in melted chocolate, a pair of penguins waddle across sweet snowdrifts. A candy-cane pole is a fine place for a sign (secure with double-sided tape). Melt 4 ounces semisweet chocolate (see page 323); cool slightly. Using kitchen tweezers, dip one almond at a time in melted chocolate (leave part under tweezers uncoated). Use a toothpick to dot on melted-chocolate eyes and buttercream to attach a long orange sprinkle beak and tiny pieces of gummy fish for feet. Spread buttercream over cupcake; dip in sanding sugar, then sprinkle more on top. Place two penguins and a candy cane sign on top.

JOLLY HOLLY A trio of sour-cherry candies and two sugar-frosted gummy spearmint leaves (see Sources, page 342) nestled in creamy white buttercream imitate a sprig of holly in the snow. Using an offset spatula, spread a smooth layer of buttercream over cupcakes. Press three candy sour cherries and two gummy leaves onto each cupcake, as shown. If the leaves are too thick, slice them in half.

LE SNOWMAN This snowman wears a fine winter hat: a chocolate-covered mint beret. His plump figure is two marshmallows—cut a slice off the top one and squish to make it smaller. Dabs of buttercream hold the parts together. For the eyes, poke two holes in the marshmallow head with a wet toothpick; insert long chocolate sprinkles with kitchen tweezers. To make the nose, cut a small triangle from an orange gummy fish, and push it directly into the marshmallow. Using an offset spatula, spread a smooth layer of buttercream over cupcakes, then place a snowman on top of each.

CANDY BOWS Cupcakes disguised as little holiday presents, with trim candy bows, appear ready to be "opened" and eaten. Cut red sour belt candy into a 7-inch length; fold ends under to form a 3-inch bow, leaving space between ends. Cut a 2-inch length from sour belt; wrap around middle of bow. Using an offset spatula, spread a smooth layer of buttercream over cupcakes, then arrange two 1¼-inch-long strips of sour belt in middle of cupcake on opposite sides, leaving space in between. Top with candy bow, centering it over the pieces.

Wreath Cupcakes

As an alternative to a platter of Christmas cookies, welcome family and friends with a batch of dainty cupcakes adorned with simple wreath shapes piped from green buttercream. They're just the thing for a caroling or tree-trimming party, or a holiday open house. Tiny red candy dots mimic holly berries to provide the finishing touch. MAKES 24

24 cupcakes, such as White Cupcakes (page 154) or Red Velvet Cupcakes (page 30)

+

Swiss Meringue Buttercream (page 304)

+

Green gel-paste food color

Red pearlized round ball sprinkles (see Sources, page 342)

1. Tint 1 cup buttercream green with gel-paste food color. Transfer to a pastry bag fitted with a small leaf tip (#69).

2. Using an offset spatula, spread each cupcake with a smooth layer of untinted buttercream. Starting at the outside edge of the cupcake, pipe slightly overlapping leaves in a circle, then pipe another layer of leaves overlapping the first; repeat to make one or two more layers. Refrigerate 30 minutes to allow frosting to set. Cupcakes can be refrigerated up to 2 days in airtight containers; bring to room temperature and arrange red sprinkles in several clusters around each wreath before serving.

celebrations

Whenever a special occasion calls for a show-stopping cake, consider cupcakes instead. Not only are the little cakes more playful than a large one, they are easier to serve (in many cases, you can dispense with forks and knives) and infinitely more adaptable. If you wish, you can make multiple varieties of cake flavors and frostings to please a range of tastes and preferences. And since the cupcakes in this section are often intended for grand events (think weddings), there's a bit of license to create over-the-top adornments, including piped meringue flowers, delicate spun-sugar nests, and white chocolate disks marked with a wood-grain pattern. The cupcakes in this section are well suited not just to weddings, but also to showers, anniversary celebrations, engagement parties, and even graduations—save them for any milestone that calls for a dessert as significant as the moment itself.

Monogram Heart Cupcakes

Cupcakes crowned with fondant hearts add charm to any party. The hearts are monogrammed with bride-and-groom initials, but you could also make just one initial for a baby shower, or a birthday or going-away party. You can make the hearts (see page 299 for instructions on working with fondant) up to several months in advance; store at room temperature in an airtight container. You will need a small rolling pin, a two-inch heart-shaped cutter, and new, clean rubber stamps with initials, which can be custom-made (see Sources, page 342). MAKES 48

48 White Cupcakes
   (page 154)

   +

2 recipes Swiss
   Meringue Butter-
   cream (page 304)

   +

   Gel-paste food
   color (teal is
   pictured)

1 pound rolled
   fondant

   Cornstarch, for
   work surface

1. Make fondant hearts: Using a small rolling pin, roll out half the fondant to about ⅛ inch on a work surface lightly dusted with cornstarch. Blot one of the monogram stamps in cornstarch, and quickly but gently press stamp into the fondant. Repeat, blotting stamp each time in cornstarch and leaving about 3 inches between each imprint, until entire surface has been stamped. Cut out hearts by centering and pressing a 2-inch heart-shaped cookie cutter over each imprint. Remove all excess fondant from around the cutout shapes; roll out again, and stamp and cut out more hearts. Repeat with remaining fondant, using the other monogram stamp if making cupcakes for a couple, to make an equal number of hearts with the two stamps.

2. Using an offset spatula, carefully transfer fondant hearts to parchment-lined baking sheets; let stand at room temperature until completely dry and firm, about 1 day. Hearts can be stored in an airtight container, between layers of parchment or waxed paper, until ready to use (they will keep for several months).

3. Tint buttercream desired shade with gel-paste food color. Transfer to a pastry bag fitted with a large French star tip (Ateco #867). Pipe frosting onto each cupcake, swirling the tip and releasing pressure as you pull up to form a peak. Cupcakes can be refrigerated, uncovered, up to 1 day.

4. To finish, bring cupcakes to room temperature and insert fondant hearts upright into frosting.

Nesting Baby Bluebird Cupcakes

A chirping trio of newly hatched birds is a charming ode to a baby's pending arrival (or first birthday). The buttercream bluebirds and coconut nest are perched atop cupcakes frosted with chocolate buttercream. MAKES 12

12 Yellow Buttermilk
    Cupcakes
    (page 26) or
    White Cupcakes
    (page 154)

    +

    Swiss Meringue
    Buttercream
    (page 304)

    +

3   ounces semisweet
    chocolate, melted
    and cooled (see
    page 323)

    Yellow and
    light-blue
    gel-paste food
    colors

1½ cups sweetened
    shredded coconut
    (about 5 ounces),
    lightly toasted
    (see page 323)

1. Reserve 1 teaspoon melted chocolate for decorating. Fold remaining chocolate into 2 cups buttercream with a flexible spatula. Using an offset spatula, spread chocolate buttercream in a smooth layer over each cupcake.

2. Tint ½ cup remaining buttercream bright yellow with gel-paste food color. Transfer to a pastry bag fitted with a small V-leaf tip (#349). Tint remaining buttercream blue. Transfer to a pastry bag fitted with a medium plain tip (#11).

3. Pipe three small blue mounds (about ¾ inch in diameter) for bluebird heads onto each cupcake. Pipe tiny yellow beaks on each head. With a toothpick, paint on melted-chocolate eyes. Refrigerate 30 minutes to allow frosting to set. Cupcakes can be refrigerated up to 1 day in airtight containers; bring to room temperature before proceeding.

4. To finish, form each nest with 2 tablespoons toasted coconut, patting it into frosting around edge of cupcake with your fingertips.

Piped Shells and Pearls Cupcakes

Buttercream shells and pearls, often seen on grand-scale wedding cakes, are a fresh way to present a classic motif on a batch of cupcakes. The piped designs are among the easiest to achieve—the pearls are merely dots, while the tip does most of the work in creating the shells—and the small scale of the cupcakes means that even beginning pipers will find them achievable. Even so, you may want to practice making shells on parchment paper before piping onto the frosted cupcakes; any mistakes piped onto the cupcakes can also be gently scraped away before you try again. **MAKES 48**

48 White Cupcakes
   (page 154)

+

2 recipes Swiss Meringue Buttercream (page 304)

+

   Gel-paste food color (egg yellow is pictured)

1. Tint 5 cups buttercream pale yellow with gel-paste food color. Transfer remaining untinted buttercream to a pastry bag fitted with a coupler. Using an offset spatula, spread yellow buttercream over each cupcake in a smooth layer. Refrigerate 30 minutes to allow frosting to set.

2. Using a small French-star tip (#199), pipe shells with untinted buttercream: Holding bag at a 45-degree angle, with tip close to center of cupcake, squeeze untinted buttercream, lifting tip slightly for the raised side of shell and pulling bag toward you. Stop squeezing to end in a pointed tip. Continue piping four more shells in a circle, with each shell slightly touching the next, and rotating the cupcake as you finish each.

3. Pipe pearls: Switch to a small plain tip (#3), and pipe a series of pearls (or dots) in a U-shape, starting with tip of one shell and working out to edge of cupcake and back to tip of next shell. Repeat until all shells are linked with pearls. Refrigerate 30 minutes to allow frosting to set. Cupcakes can be refrigerated up to 3 days in airtight containers; bring to room temperature before serving.

Meringue Bouquet Cupcakes

Any bride would blush to behold such fanciful cupcakes on her special day. Bakers, too, will relish making the exquisite meringue "flowers," which are first piped onto parchment-lined baking sheets, then baked until firm and dry. Their crisp, delicate texture makes them a delight to eat. MAKES 48

48 White Cupcakes
(page 154)

+

2 recipes Swiss
Meringue
(page 317)

+

2 recipes Seven-
Minute Frosting
(page 303)

1. Preheat oven to 175°F. Line rimmed baking sheets with parchment paper. Transfer Swiss meringue to a pastry bag fitted with a coupler. Pipe flowers and other shapes, such as shells and stars, on lined baking sheets, using different tips to create a variety of shapes and sizes (shown, from left to right): a small multi-opening tip (#233) to pipe drop flowers; two small leaf tips (# 67 and #70) for daisy petals and leaves; a small three-opening tip (#89) for piping plumes; two small plain tips (#4 and #6) for five-petal flowers; a small fluted shell tip (#98) for traditional shells; and a small open-star tip (#17) for more drop flowers. You will need about 16 shapes for each cupcake, depending on their size. Bake until meringue is completely dry to the touch but not taking on any color, at least 30 minutes. Transfer shapes on parchment to a wire rack to cool.

2. To finish, spoon frosting generously on a cupcake, and use an offset spatula to spread into a dome shape. Working quickly (before frosting sets), arrange the baked meringue shapes onto cupcake as desired, gently pressing them into frosting to adhere. Repeat with remaining cupcakes. Cupcakes can be stored up to 1 day at room temperature (do not refrigerate).

PIPING FLOWERS AND OTHER
SHAPES WITH MERINGUE

Chrysanthemum Cupcakes

Although the buttercream chrysanthemums may look difficult, a steady hand and a bit of practice is all it takes to produce a whole bunch of them. Displayed in a group of matching or mixed colors, the cupcakes would be lovely at a bridal or baby shower. **MAKES 24**

24 Yellow Buttermilk Cupcakes (page 26)

+

2 recipes Swiss Meringue Buttercream (page 304)

+

Forest-green, leaf-green, lemon-yellow, egg-yellow, and orange gel-paste food colors

1. Tint 1 cup buttercream forest-green with gel-paste food color for leaves and dots. Divide the remaining buttercream evenly among three bowls. Tint each batch a base-coat shade (for cupcake tops): one chartreuse (mix leaf green, lemon yellow, and a touch of egg yellow), another lemon yellow, and the third orange. Using an offset spatula, spread a smooth layer of buttercream over each cupcake as desired. Transfer remaining tinted buttercreams to pastry bags fitted with couplers.

PIPING CHRYSANTHEMUMS

2. Pipe the leaves first: Fill a pastry bag fitted with a leaf tip (#68) with forest-green frosting. Holding bag at a 45-degree angle with the tip's flat side up, squeeze and pull outward, releasing pressure and lifting to form the end.

3. Form center and petals: Using only the coupler (or a medium plain tip, such as #12) and frosting in the desired flower color, make a raised ½-inch-wide dot to anchor the petals. Change to a specialty fluted tip (#80); holding bag at a 45-degree angle against the edge of the dot, with the tip forming an upright U, gently squeeze the bag while pulling out in a quick stroke to form each petal. Repeat, making petals all around the center dot. Form two or more petal layers over the first, making petals shorter and pulling the bag upward with each layer. With a small plain tip (#3) and forest-green frosting, pipe three tiny dots in the center of the flower. Refrigerate 30 minutes to allow frosting to set. Cupcakes can be refrigerated up to 3 days in airtight containers; bring to room temperature before serving.

Graduation Day Cupcakes

Celebrate commencement day with a diploma of a different sort: tiny replicas made of airy tuile cookies that are curled around a skewer and neatly tied with strips of sour candy. To make the template for the tuile scroll, use the lid of a plastic storage container. MAKES 24

24 Yellow Buttermilk
Cupcakes
(page 26)

+

Chocolate–Sour
Cream Frosting
(page 311)

+

Tuile Scrolls
(recipe follows)

Using an offset spatula, spread frosting on middle of cupcakes. Cupcakes can be refrigerated up to 3 days in airtight containers; just before serving, bring to room temperature and top each with a tuile scroll.

TUILE SCROLLS
MAKES 24

1 large egg white, room temperature

¼ cup sugar

¼ cup all-purpose flour

Pinch of salt

1 tablespoon unsalted butter, melted

1 tablespoon heavy cream

¼ teaspoon pure vanilla extract

2 blue candy sour belts (see Sources, page 342)

1. Preheat oven to 375°F. Prepare template: Cut a 2-by-3-inch rectangle from the center of a piece of flexible plastic (discard cutout center). With electric mixer on medium speed, beat egg white and sugar until combined. Beat in flour and salt. Add butter, cream, and vanilla; beat until just combined.

2. Place template on a Silpat-lined rimmed baking sheet. Spoon 1 teaspoon batter onto center; spread thinly with an offset spatula. Repeat to fit six on a sheet. Bake, rotating sheet halfway through, until pale golden around edges, about 6 minutes. Immediately loosen cookies with offset spatula; turn over, bottom side up. Starting at a short side, quickly roll one cookie halfway around a skewer, then roll up other side around another skewer until two sides meet. Transfer to a wire rack; let cool. Repeat with remaining tuiles. (If cookies become too cool to shape, briefly return to oven.) Repeat with remaining batter to make 24 tuiles.

4. Cut candy belts into quarters lengthwise, then cut crosswise into 4-inch-long strips. Wrap a candy strip around each scroll, and tie to secure. Scrolls can be stored up to 1 week at room temperature in airtight containers.

SPREADING TUILE BATTER
OVER TEMPLATE

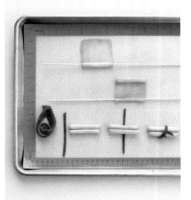

FORMING SCROLLS AND
TYING WITH CANDY STRIPS

Fresh Flower–Topped Pound Cakes

There's no need to perfect your piping skills to create beautiful flower-topped cupcakes. Instead, adorn them with a few fresh, edible flowers. Some of the best-tasting varieties include nasturtiums, pansies, hibiscus, snapdragons, violets, and marigolds (pictured). Use only flowers grown without pesticides, either from your own organic garden or from specialty suppliers. When making the little pound cakes, remember to cream the butter and sugar thoroughly to produce the right texture. **MAKES 36**

3⅓ cups all-purpose flour

2 teaspoons salt

1 pound (4 sticks) unsalted butter, room temperature

2 cups sugar

1 teaspoon pure vanilla extract

9 large eggs, room temperature, lightly beaten

Swiss Meringue Buttercream (vanilla-bean variation, page 305)

Fresh edible flowers, such as marigolds, violets, pansies, or nasturtiums (see Sources, page 342)

1. Preheat oven to 325°F. Line standard muffin tins with paper liners. Whisk together flour and salt.

2. With an electric mixer on medium-high speed, cream butter and sugar until pale and fluffy, scraping down sides of bowl as needed. Reduce speed to medium, and beat in vanilla. Add beaten eggs in four batches, beating until each is incorporated. With mixer on low speed, add flour in four batches; beat until completely incorporated after each.

3. Divide batter evenly among lined cups, filling each three-quarters full. Tap tins on countertop once to distribute batter evenly. Bake, rotating tins halfway through, until a cake tester inserted in centers comes out clean, about 20 minutes. Transfer tins to wire racks to cool 10 minutes; turn out cupcakes onto racks and let cool completely. Cupcakes can be stored up to 2 days at room temperature in airtight containers.

4. To finish, use an offset spatula to spread cupcakes with a generous layer of buttercream, and top each with a few flowers. Serve immediately.

Sunflower Cupcakes

What could be more fitting for a late summer wedding in the country than a bunch of cupcakes masquerading as radiant sunflowers? Chocolate-covered sunflower seeds create the centers, while the petals are piped with bright yellow buttercream. Novice pipers, take note: Just as with real flowers, the petals needn't appear perfect, nor should any two flowers look exactly alike. In fact, you may want to study some real sunflowers to use as inspiration. MAKES 48

48 One-Bowl
   Chocolate
   Cupcakes
   (page 152)

+

2 recipes Swiss
   Meringue Butter-
   cream (page 304)

+

   Egg yellow
   gel-paste food
   color

3 ounces chocolate-
   covered sunflower
   seeds (see
   Sources,
   page 342)

1. Tint buttercream bright yellow with gel-paste food color. Transfer to a pastry bag fitted with a small leaf tip (#66). Starting at the outside edge of a cupcake, pipe slightly overlapping petals in a circle, then pipe another layer of petals overlapping the first; repeat to make one or two more layers. Refrigerate 30 minutes to allow frosting to set (or up to 2 days in airtight containers).

2. To finish, fill centers with chocolate-coated sunflower seeds. Decorated cupcakes can be refrigerated up to 6 hours in airtight containers; bring to room temperature before serving.

PIPING SUNFLOWER PETALS

Honey Bee Cupcakes

Be prepared for guests to buzz with delight at the sight of miniature marzipan bees alighting atop piped buttercream dahlias. Honey (of course!) flavors the cakes. Serve them at a garden reception, shower, or child's birthday party, on their own or with the sunflower cupcakes on page 273. **MAKES 20**

FOR CUPCAKES

- 2 cups all-purpose flour
- 1/2 teaspoon baking soda
- 1 teaspoon baking powder
- 1 teaspoon coarse salt
- 1/2 teaspoon ground cinnamon
- 2 large eggs, room temperature
- 1/2 cup granulated sugar
- 1/4 cup packed light-brown sugar
- 1/2 cup plus 2 tablespoons good-quality honey
- 1/2 cup milk
- 1/2 cup vegetable oil
- 1/2 teaspoon finely grated lemon zest

FOR DECORATING

- 2 ounces marzipan
- Yellow and black gel-paste food colors
- Cornstarch, for work surface
- 1/4 cup sliced unblanched almonds
- 2 recipes Swiss Meringue Buttercream (page 304)

1. Make cupcakes: Preheat oven to 325°F. Line standard muffin tins with paper liners. Whisk together flour, baking soda, baking powder, salt, and cinnamon.

2. With an electric mixer on high, beat eggs and sugars until pale and thick. Whisk together honey, milk, oil, and zest. On low speed, mix honey mixture into egg mixture. Add flour mixture in two batches, mixing until just combined.

3. Divide batter among lined cups, filling each three-quarters full. Bake, rotating tins halfway through, until golden brown and a tester inserted in centers comes out clean, about 25 minutes. Transfer tins to wire racks to cool 15 min-

FORMING MARZIPAN BEES

utes; turn out cupcakes onto racks and let cool completely.

4. Make bees: Divide marzipan in half. Tint one portion yellow and the other black with gel-paste food color (see page 299 for instructions). Roll each portion into a rope, a little less than 1/4 inch thick, on a work surface lightly dusted with cornstarch; cut rope crosswise into 1/4-inch pieces. Alternating between yellow and black, gently press together four pieces to form the body. For the head, roll a small black piece into a ball; press onto yellow end of body. Pinch off two tiny bits of yellow marzipan. Roll into balls; press onto head. Press almonds into bee for wings. Repeat to make 20 bees.

5. Decorate cupcakes: Tint buttercream pale yellow; spread a thin layer of buttercream over cupcakes. Transfer remainder to a pastry bag fitted with a small curved petal tip (#59). Starting at outer edge, pipe petals in a circle, holding tip perpendicular to cupcakes. Pipe more circles of petals inside first to cover. Refrigerate 30 minutes to allow frosting to set. Cupcakes can be refrigerated up to 3 days in airtight containers; bring to room temperature and top with bees before serving.

Almond-Hazelnut Cupcakes with Faux-Bois Toppers

You might want to throw a woodland-themed celebration just to have an excuse to make cupcakes topped with chocolate faux-bois rounds. Faux bois, or imitation woodgrain, is a favorite Martha Stewart Living Omnimedia motif; it can be applied to chocolate using a wood-graining rocker, found at paint-supply stores (see Sources, page 342, for the tool and for acetate sheets). Made with ground almonds and hazelnuts and covered with dark chocolate frosting, the cupcakes are also worth serving on their own, without any other embellishments. MAKES 16

FOR CUPCAKES

- ¹/₂ cup whole unblanched almonds, toasted (see page 323)
- ¹/₂ cup hazelnuts, toasted and skinned (see page 323)
- ³/₄ cup all-purpose flour
- ³/₄ cup cake flour (not self-rising), sifted
- 1¹/₂ teaspoons baking powder
- ¹/₄ teaspoon salt
- ¹/₂ cup (1 stick) unsalted butter, room temperature
- ¹/₄ cup granulated sugar
- ¹/₂ cup firmly packed dark-brown sugar
- 2 teaspoons pure vanilla extract
- ³/₄ cup milk
- 4 large egg whites

FOR DECORATING

Dark Chocolate Frosting (page 302)

Chocolate Faux-Bois Disks (page 279)

1. Make cupcakes: Preheat oven to 350°F. Line standard muffin tins with paper liners. In a food processor, pulse together almonds and hazelnuts until finely ground (do not overprocess, or the nuts will turn into a paste). Into a mixing bowl, sift together both flours, baking powder, and salt. Whisk in the ground nuts.

2. With an electric mixer on medium-high speed, cream butter and both sugars until smooth. Beat in vanilla. Reduce speed to low. Add flour mixture in three batches, alternating with two additions of milk, and beating well after each.

3. In another mixing bowl, with electric mixer on medium speed, whisk the egg whites until soft peaks form. In two additions, gently fold the egg whites into the batter.

4. Divide batter evenly among lined cups, filling each three-quarters full. Bake, rotating tins halfway through, until a cake tester inserted in centers comes out clean, about 25 minutes. Transfer tins to wire racks to cool completely before removing cupcakes. Cupcakes can be stored up to 3 days at room temperature, or frozen up to 2 months, in airtight containers.

5. To finish, use an offset spatula to spread a thin layer of frosting over cupcakes, then transfer remaining frosting to a pastry bag fitted with a large open-star tip (#821). Pipe a ring of frosting around the perimeter of each cupcake, then place a chocolate disk on top. Decorated cupcakes can be refrigerated up to 1 day in airtight containers; bring to room temperature before serving.

CREATING WOOD-GRAIN PATTERN
WITH DARK CHOCOLATE

CHOCOLATE FAUX-BOIS DISKS

MAKES ENOUGH FOR 16 CUPCAKES

- 2 ounces bittersweet chocolate, finely chopped
- 8 ounces white chocolate, finely chopped

1. Cut a piece of acetate (see Sources, page 342) to fit the back of a baking sheet. Tape acetate to inverted baking sheet. Melt bittersweet chocolate (see page 323). Coat the surface of a wood-graining tool with a thick layer of melted bittersweet chocolate. Starting at the top of the acetate, rock the coated tool back and forth while dragging it in one swift motion to make a vertical striation. If you are not satisfied with how it looks, repeat motion over each strip right away. Transfer baking sheet to the freezer and chill until set, about 3 minutes.

2. Melt white chocolate (see page 323). Stir to cool slightly (it should not be piping hot), then pour the white chocolate on top of the coated acetate. Using an offset spatula, quickly but gently spread the melted white chocolate evenly over the entire surface (do not press too hard or the dark chocolate will smear).

3. Freeze baking sheet for 30 seconds to allow the chocolate to set slightly. Remove from freezer, and use a 2¼-inch round cookie cutter (the same size as the top of cupcakes) to cut rounds of chocolate (press down to the acetate), leaving them intact on the baking sheet. Return to freezer and allow chocolate to set completely, at least 10 minutes (or up to 2 days, wrapped well in plastic). Once chocolate has hardened, remove tape from one side of the pan; lifting acetate from that side, punch out the chocolate rounds (leave on baking sheet). Refrigerate until ready to use, up to 2 hours. To avoid leaving any fingerprints on the surface, use an offset spatula to transfer rounds to cupcakes.

SPREADING WHITE CHOCOLATE OVER DARK

CUTTING OUT FAUX-BOIS DISKS

Strawberry Basket Cupcakes

Fashioned by hand from marzipan and cradled in piped-buttercream baskets, tiny, rosy-red strawberries evoke a visit to the berry patch. A basketweave tip produces a thick weave, but you can experiment with different tips, such as ruffle or even plain tips, to create other patterns. See Sources, page 342, for where to find the tools (shown below) for forming the strawberries. MAKES 24

24 Strawberry Cupcakes (page 146)

+

Swiss Meringue Buttercream (page 304)

+

7 ounces marzipan

Red and green gel-paste food colors

Cornstarch, for work surface

1. Using an offset spatula, spread a thin layer of buttercream over each cupcake. Transfer remaining buttercream to a pastry bag fitted with a coupler and a small basketweave tip (#47). Working from top to bottom, pipe a series of lines across top of cupcake, leaving about ¼ inch between piped lines. Working from left to right, and starting at bottom of cupcake, pipe short horizontal lines over vertical ones, filling in all gaps to create a basketweave effect. Repeat with remaining cupcakes and buttercream. Refrigerate 30 minutes to allow frosting to set. Cupcakes can be refrigerated up to 2 days in airtight containers; bring to room temperature before topping with marzipan strawberries.

2. Tint half of marzipan red with gel-paste food color (see page 299 for instructions). Make 24 pea-size balls, and 48 slightly larger balls. Roll balls on work surface dusted with cornstarch, elongating them to mimic a strawberry shape. Using a toothpick, poke indentations all over the strawberries. Tint remaining marzipan green. Pinch off some; roll into 24 thin vines, about 2 inches long. Roll out remaining green marzipan ⅛ inch thick on a work surface lightly dusted with cornstarch; cut out tiny leaves with a calyx cutter. Attach a leaf to the top of each strawberry, poking in the centers with a taper-cone modeling tool and draping the leaf points down the sides of the strawberries. Cut some leaves into halves or quarters, and attach to vines.

3. To finish, drape the marzipan vines over buttercream basketweave patterns on cupcakes; attach strawberries and arrange leaves along the vines.

PIPING BASKETWEAVE PATTERN

FORMING MARZIPAN STRAWBERRIES

Piped-Buttercream Rose Cupcakes

A rose is not just a rose when it is lovingly piped onto a frosted cupcake to celebrate a bride-to-be, a sweetheart, or your parents on their anniversary. Besides the realistically replicated blooms, the monochromatic color scheme makes for an ultra-elegant dessert. Or, for a more casual event, pipe the flowers in one color, and frost the cupcakes with another. A flower nail is essential, as you can turn the nail with one hand while piping the roses with the other. The flowers can be refrigerated up to two days before placing them atop cupcakes. MAKES 24

24 White Cupcakes (page 154) or Devil's Food Cupcakes (page 34)

+

2 recipes Swiss Meringue Buttercream (page 304)

+

Gel-paste food color (red is pictured)

1. Cut parchment paper into squares to fit on top of flower nail (#7). Tint buttercream red with gel-paste food color. Dab buttercream on top of nail to secure parchment. Fit a pastry bag with only a coupler; fill with buttercream. Squeeze pastry bag gently; pull up slowly to make an acorn-shape mound on top of the square.

2. Secure a small petal tip (#103) to the coupler. (If you need both hands to attach the tip, anchor the nail in a block of polysterene or in a potato with a flat-cut bottom.) Holding tip against the point of the buttercream mound, wide end down and the narrow end angled in toward the acorn's center, pipe a wide strip as you turn the nail, enveloping the top completely.

3. Turning the nail as you go, make two slightly arched petals that each reach around half of the circumference of the acorn.

4. Continue turning the nail, making longer petals that overlap, and angling farther outward as you go, until you have piped a full rose. Gently slide the parchment with the rose off the nail and onto a baking sheet, and refrigerate at least 20 minutes (or up to 2 days). Repeat to make 24 roses.

5. Using a serrated knife, trim tops of cupcakes to make level. Using an offset spatula, spread buttercream over cupcakes. Use a clean offset spatula to gently transfer buttercream roses onto frosted cupcakes (discard parchment). Cupcakes can be refrigerated up to 3 days in airtight containers; bring to room temperature before serving.

BUTTERCREAM ROSES, IN STAGES

Candied-Hazelnut Cupcakes

Add a sleek touch to a significant celebration, such as an engagement party, with cupcakes topped with striking caramel-dipped hazelnut spikes. Dark chocolate frosting is shown, but caramel buttercream (page 307) is another option (and would complement the toppers). MAKES 24

24 Almond-Hazelnut
Cupcakes
(page 277)

+

Dark Chocolate
Frosting
(page 302)

+

Caramel-Dipped
Hazelnuts
(recipe follows)

Using an offset spatula, spread frosting over each cupcake. Cupcakes can be refrigerated up to 3 days in airtight containers; bring to room temperature and top with caramel-dipped hazelnuts just before serving.

CARAMEL-DIPPED HAZELNUTS
MAKES ENOUGH FOR 24 CUPCAKES

24 hazelnuts, toasted and
     skinned (see page 323)
3   cups sugar
³/₄ cup water

1. Gently insert pointed end of a long wooden skewer into the side of each hazelnut. Place a cutting board along the edge of a counter-top; place newspaper on the floor, directly under cutting board.

2. Prepare an ice-water bath. Heat sugar and the water in a heavy saucepan over medium heat, stirring occasionally, until sugar is dissolved and syrup is clear. Stop stirring; cook until syrup comes to a boil, washing down sides of pan with a wet pastry brush to prevent crystals from forming. Continue to boil, gently swirling occasionally, until medium amber. Plunge pan into ice bath to stop the cooking; let stand until thickened, about 10 minutes. (To test: Dip a skewer in caramel and lift a few inches; if a thick drip slowly forms and holds a string, the caramel is ready.)

3. Dip a skewered hazelnut into caramel, letting excess drip back into pan. When dripping syrup becomes a thin string, secure opposite end of skewer under cutting board. Repeat with remaining hazelnuts. (If caramel hardens before all hazelnuts have been dipped, rewarm it over low heat.) Let stand until caramel string has hardened, about 5 minutes; break each string to desired length. Carefully remove skewers. Candied hazelnuts should be used the same day; store, uncovered, at room temperature until ready to serve cupcakes.

DIPPING HAZELNUTS INTO CARAMEL

CREATING CARAMEL SPIKES

Spun-Sugar Crowned Cupcakes

Golden tendrils of spun sugar formed into a "nest" make a dramatic cupcake topper. Despite its delicate appearance, spun sugar is actually pliable and requires no special handling (except during the cooking stage, when the caramel must be cooked to the proper temperature). The spun sugar should be used the same day; let it drape over the spoon, then shape threads into balls just before placing on a frosted cupcake. MAKES 12

12 Devil's Food
    Cupcakes
    (page 34)

+

    Dark Chocolate
    Frosting
    (page 302)

+

    Spun Sugar
    Crowns (recipe
    follows)

Using an offset spatula, spread frosting over middle of each cupcake. Refrigerate up to 3 days in airtight containers; bring to room temperature and top with spun sugar crowns just before serving.

SPUN SUGAR CROWNS
MAKES ENOUGH FOR 12 CUPCAKES

    2 cups sugar
    ¼ cup light corn syrup
    ¼ cup water

1. Secure a long-handled wooden spoon under a heavy cutting board on the edge of counter, with the handle facing out and extending over the edge. Place newspaper on the floor, directly under the cutting board.

2. Prepare an ice-water bath. Bring sugar, corn syrup, and the water to a boil in a heavy saucepan over medium-high heat, stirring until sugar has dissolved. Stop stirring. Clip a candy thermometer to side of pan. Cook until mixture turns pale amber and registers 300°F (hard-crack stage) on the candy thermometer. Plunge pan into ice bath to stop the cooking; let cool, stirring occasionally, until caramel registers 250°F.

3. Dip the tines of a fork into caramel. Holding fork about 2 feet above spoon handle, swing caramel back and forth like a pendulum in long arcs, allowing strands to fall in threads over the handles. Let stand until ready to use, then gently gather some of the strands into a ball, shaping with the palms of your hands. Repeat to make 12 crowns.

SPUN SUGAR THREADS

FORMING CROWNS

the basics

Anyone—whether a dedicated hobbyist or the occasional home baker—can make cupcakes. Most people have all the necessary equipment already in their kitchen cabinets: measuring cups and spoons, a sturdy mixing bowl or two—and, of course, muffin tins. If you're considering buying new items, invest in the best ones you can afford; good-quality pans and tools will withstand years or even generations of baking. In addition to laying out the supplies you'll need, these pages will familiarize you with the basic ingredients and take you step by step through techniques for mixing and decorating. You'll also find ample recipes for frostings, fillings, and other embellishments. Use them where suggested throughout this book—or adapt them as you wish to create something new and unexpected.

DUTCH-PROCESS
COCOA POWDER

CAKE FLOUR

ALL-PURPOSE FLOUR

BAKING POWDER

BAKING SODA

NATURAL COCOA
POWDER

DARK-BROWN
SUGAR

LIGHT-BROWN
SUGAR

GRANULATED SUGAR

(TABLE) SALT

COARSE SALT

CONFECTIONERS'
SUGAR

essential dry ingredients for mixing

COCOA POWDER Cocoa powder is made by removing anywhere from 65 to 90 percent of the cocoa butter from chocolate, then finely grinding what remains. The result is an intensely flavored powder that gives baked goods a deeper, rounder flavor than when made with solid chocolate alone. You'll find two types of cocoa powder: natural cocoa (sometimes called "nonalkalized cocoa"), and Dutch-process cocoa, which is treated with an alkaline solution that reduces cocoa's natural acidity and gives the powder a milder flavor and redder color. Unless a recipe specifically calls for a particular type of cocoa, you can use either. Before using any cocoa powder, you may want to sift it with a fine sieve to remove any lumps.

BAKING SODA AND BAKING POWDER Baking soda and baking powder are chemical leavening agents that add volume and lightness to the texture of cakes and other baked goods. Baking soda is usually combined with an acid, such as sour cream, buttermilk, honey, or even brown sugar (due to the presence of molasses), to hasten the leavening action and to produce better flavor. Baking powder essentially takes care of this by combining baking soda with the precise amount of acid (usually cream of tartar) needed to achieve the same result. For this reason, baking soda and baking powder are not interchangeable (although they are often combined in recipes to produce the proper texture). Store both in a cool, dry place, and note the use-by date on the label. To test for potency, stir $1/4$ teaspoon baking powder into $1/2$ cup hot water; the water should instantly form bubbles. For baking soda, add $1/4$ teaspoon white vinegar to the hot water before testing.

FLOUR Most home cooks reach for all-purpose flour when it's time to bake, but other types—especially cake flour—are also common. With its higher protein content, all-purpose flour produces a coarser crumb (or texture) in cupcakes and other baked goods, while cake flour, which contains much less protein, will result in a finer texture. A combination can be used to achieve the right results. For the recipes in this book that call for cake flour, do not buy the self-rising kind; it contains baking powder and salt. Always sift cake flour, which is prone to clumping, as indicated in each recipe; all-purpose flour does not need to be sifted (unless specifically instructed). Use only dry measuring cups for flour, and never shake the cup or tap it on the counter to make level; both actions will lead to inaccurate measurements. Instead, fill the cup to overflowing, then level with a straightedge.

SUGAR

White granulated sugar is the most widely used sugar, especially for baking. Made from refined sugarcane or sugar beet, it serves as a base for most other types of sugars.

Brown sugar is a combination of granulated sugar and molasses. Because dark-brown sugar has a higher molasses content than light-brown sugar, it is deeper in color and flavor. Use light-brown sugar when you want a milder molasses taste. Brown sugar labeled "granulated" is processed so the grains flow freely; do not substitute it in recipes. Pack brown sugar tightly in the measuring cup to eliminate air pockets. After opening, seal the package securely, so the sugar does not harden. To soften, place a wedge of apple in bag, and reseal; leave a day or two, until sugar is sufficiently soft again, then remove apple.

Confectioners' sugar (also called powdered sugar) is made by grinding granulated sugar to a fine powder, then sifting and adding a small amount of cornstarch to prevent caking. It is primarily used to make frosting, or for dusting over baked desserts. Confectioners' sugar often forms clumps, so you may want to sift it with a fine sieve before using.

SALT A small amount of salt is usually added to cake batters (and some frostings) to enhance their flavors. Our recipes call for "salt" (table salt) or "coarse salt" (kosher salt). If substituting one for the other in a recipe, use a bit less table salt than the amount of coarse salt called for (and vice versa).

more essential ingredients for mixing

DAIRY Dairy products give cupcakes richness, and different kinds provide different flavors and textures. Cream, for example, produces a much more velvety texture than whole milk; buttermilk creates a more tender crumb and, like sour cream and yogurt (which also keep baked goods moist), adds subtle flavor. Although some dairy products can be substituted for others, it is best to use what the recipe calls for to ensure proper results, especially for buttermilk (as the amount of baking soda would have to be adjusted). In a pinch, you can make your own buttermilk by adding 1 tablespoon white vinegar or lemon juice to 1 cup regular milk (adjust the amounts of each depending on how much buttermilk is called for); let milk mixture sit for 10 minutes, or until sufficiently thickened, before using in a recipe.

CHOCOLATE Chocolate, used alone or in combination with cocoa powder, produces baked goods that are moist and wonderfully dense (think brownies). It also creates frostings that are rich and satiny (such as ganache). When buying chocolate for baking, look for the best quality bar, block, or chips you can find; the higher the percentage of cacao (or chocolate liquor), the richer and deeper the taste. Milk chocolate must only contain 10 percent chocolate cacao, while dark chocolate (unsweetened, bittersweet, and semi-sweet), as its name suggests, has a higher cacao content—anywhere from 35 to 70 percent, depending on the quality. (White chocolate is not technically considered to be chocolate, since it contains no cacao.) Some premium brands to look for are Valhrona, Callebaut, El Ray, and Scharffen Berger. Chocolate chips are simply morsels of chocolate that are designed to hold their shape during baking, so they contain less cocoa butter than block or bar chocolate.

EXTRACTS Extracts are concentrated flavorings made by steeping and aging an ingredient in liquid (usually alcohol). Always choose extracts labeled "pure," which have a sharper, cleaner flavor. Vanilla extract is the one most commonly used in baking, as it adds subtle but distinctive flavor; extracts made with vanilla beans from Madagascar, Tahiti, and Mexico are worth the extra cost. Some of the recipes in this book call for vanilla beans instead of extract, as the seeds import a deeper, more complex flavor and fragrance (but you can generally substitute 1 tablespoon extract for each whole bean called for). To release the seeds, lay the bean flat on a cutting board; holding one end, slice it open lengthwise with a paring knife, then run knife along each cut side. You can save the pod for making vanilla sugar to use in baking or sweetening drinks: Place split pod in a jar of sugar, seal lid, and leave for at least a week (shake daily to distribute flavor); use sugar within several months.

BUTTER AND OIL Butter and oil keep baked goods moist and also contribute or enhance flavor. Unsalted butter has the purest flavor and is usually fresher than salted (because salt is added as a preservative). Whipped and light butters—mixed with air and water, respectively—won't produce the same results. When butter is used in making cake batter, it should be at a cool room temperature before you begin; this ensures that it will develop as many fine bubbles as possible during the creaming stage, a crucial step in producing a light cake with a velvety crumb. Some recipes in this book call for vegetable oil instead of butter, as it produces a soft (or fine) crumb. Make sure to use only neutral-tasting oils, such as safflower or sunflower.

EGGS Eggs play a critical role in baking: The whites act as leaveners, especially when beaten to stiff peaks separately before being folded into batter, while yolks are emulsifiers, which enable fats and liquids to hold together and produce a smooth texture and rich flavor. Use large eggs (the color indicates the type of hen they came from, not the quality). Eggs are easiest to separate when they are cold, but they should generally be brought to room temperature before using to allow them to blend more easily with other ingredients. For the most volume, whites are best beaten when at room temperature (or warm, as when making meringue and some buttercreams).

YOGURT

BUTTERMILK

MILK

BUTTER

SOUR CREAM

HEAVY CREAM

VANILLA
EXTRACT

CHOCOLATE

VEGETABLE OIL

EGGS

tools for baking

PASTRY BRUSH For recipes that call for muffin tins to be buttered and floured (instead of using paper liners), use a small pastry brush to coat the cups with softened (or melted) butter, as the bristles can readily reach into crevices. Use a clean brush with firmly attached bristles; wash after every use in warm, soapy water, and let dry completely before storing.

CAKE TESTER Most often, the best way to determine doneness is by inserting a wooden skewer or thin metal cake tester into the center of a cake or cupcake. If it comes out clean, or with only a few moist crumbs clinging (as some recipes instruct), the cupcakes are finished baking. Some cupcakes, such as those that are intentionally moist and dense, should not be tested this way, so follow the recipe to see which method to use.

MUFFIN TINS Muffin tins come in mini, standard, and jumbo sizes. Each cup of a mini tin holds 2 ounces of batter, a standard cup holds 4 ounces, and a jumbo cup holds 8 ounces. If you choose dark or nonstick cake pans, reduce your oven temperature by 25 degrees to avoid burning (and begin checking for doneness a little earlier than the recommended baking time). You can, of course, substitute tin sizes, but you will need to adjust the cooking times (see below).

PAPER LINERS Liners, which keep cupcakes from sticking to baking tins, are made of glassine paper, greaseproof paper, or foil laminated with waxed paper. Also called baking cups, these liners eliminate the need to butter and flour the tins, and ensure easy cleanup. Paper liners come in solid colors and a variety of prints (see Sources, page 342). If you can't find mini or jumbo liners, butter and flour the cups instead.

OVEN THERMOMETER Oven temperatures are rarely accurate. Use an oven thermometer—they are widely available and often inexpensive—to monitor the temperature of your oven, and adjust accordingly.

WIRE RACK A wire rack is the perfect tool for cooling baked goods, as it allows air to circulate freely so they cool quickly and evenly. Look for a rack with heavy-duty stainless steel wires. If you bake frequently, or plan to make large batches, you may want to invest in two or three racks, or a larger one that folds up neatly for storing.

ICE-CREAM SCOOP An ice-cream scoop with a quick-release mechanism is a convenient tool for filling muffin tins with batter; it will make uniform scoops to encourage even baking. Look for different sizes that can be used for standard and jumbo muffin tins (a soup spoon or tablespoon is best for mini cups). A small cup with a spout (such as a dry-measure cup) is a suitable alternative.

ADAPTING RECIPES TO MAKE MINI, STANDARD, OR JUMBO CUPCAKES

It's easy to adapt almost any cupcake recipe to make treats of different sizes. Generally, a recipe that results in 12 standard cupcakes will yield enough batter for anywhere from 32 to 46 mini cupcakes; minis should take 10 to 15 minutes to bake in a 350°F oven. The same amount of batter will produce 5 to 8 jumbo cupcakes, which should bake for about 25 minutes. Unless otherwise instructed in a recipe, the muffin cups should be filled three-quarters full, regardless of size. And remember to check the cupcakes a little early, and watch for visual cues.

CAKE
TESTER

PASTRY BRUSH

MUFFIN TINS

PAPER LINERS

ICE-CREAM SCOOP

TAYLOR

OVEN THERMOMETER

WIRE RACK

GEL-PASTE
FOOD COLORS

CANDIES AND SPRINKLES

PAPER
CORNET

KITCHEN
TWEEZERS

PASTRY BAGS

FLOWER NAIL

TIPS

PLASTIC COUPLER

OFFSET
SPATULA

tools and ingredients for decorating

GEL-PASTE FOOD COLORS More concentrated than the liquid variety, these gels are a good choice for tinting frostings (and royal icing) without diluting them. They are also easier to use with fondant and marzipan, which require kneading to incorporate the food color (and only a few drops or dabs of gel paste is generally needed for even the deepest of shades). Gel-paste food colors are available in a wide range of colors and are sold in either drop bottles or lidded containers (in which case you will need to use a toothpick or wooden skewer to add color to frostings or fondant). Look for them at baking-supply stores and online retailers. They are inexpensive and will keep, tightly sealed, indefinitely (this is important, since a little goes a long way).

CANDIES AND SPRINKLES Practically any type of candy will do; page 296 shows those commonly used to decorate the cupcakes in this book. Long sprinkles and nonpareils (round candy sprinkles) are all-purpose, while licorice, taffy tape, and marshmallows, among other candies, can be used to make any manner of embellishment.

PASTRY BAGS Pastry bags come in disposable and reusable varieties. Disposable bags are inexpensive and can be purchased in quantity; having multiples on hand makes it possible to use one for each shade of frosting (and they are clear, so you can easily tell which one is which). Reusable bags—made from pliable nylon or plastic-lined cloth—can be more economical and are more environmentally friendly if you decorate cakes and cupcakes often. For easy handling, choose a pastry bag that is between 10 and 14 inches long; any larger and the bag may be unwieldy. Once the bag is filled with frosting, use a rubber band to seal its open end.

PAPER CORNET Piping cones made of parchment paper are usually used for making fine details, such as when writing or piping little dots with royal icing or melted chocolate, or when you are piping only a very small amount. They are also disposable, for easy cleanup. See page 298 for how to make a cornet.

FLOWER NAIL This tool is convenient when piping buttercream roses for adorning cakes and cupcakes. Rather than having to pipe each rose on a cupcake, you pipe the flower on the nail (lined with a square of parchment), which can be slowly turned with one hand while you pipe with the other. Any mistakes can easily be swept back into the pastry bag, and you can also pipe the roses in advance.

OFFSET SPATULA The thin metal blade and angled design of a small offset spatula is just right for spreading and smoothing frosting onto cupcakes. It is also efficient for lifting and placing piped designs, such as dried royal icing letters and piped roses, and other small decorations (including those made from marzipan or fondant) onto frosted cupcakes, and for loosening and lifting cupcakes from tins.

KITCHEN TWEEZERS Inexpensive and just the right size, kitchen tweezers are very helpful when attaching little candies or other fine details onto frosted cupcakes. Look for the kind with curved pincers for greater precision.

TIPS Piping tips are sold individually or in sets; choose based on how often you plan to use them and the types of designs you want to create. If you are just getting started, you may want to buy a set of 10 basic tips (most sets include a coupler and come in a handy storage box), and then pick up any additional ones as needed. See pages 300–301 for a glossary of basic tips used in this book.

PLASTIC COUPLER A coupler allows you to easily remove and replace a pastry tip, helpful when you will be piping different patterns with the same frosting. Couplers come in two parts: the tube that rests on the inside tip of the bag, and a ring that screws onto the tube to fasten the tip to the bag. Sometimes, as when piping frosting in a swirled peak to cover a cupcake, the coupler is used alone, without any tip; make sure the coupler does not have a slit at the tip.

how to prepare a piping bag

1. If using a new pastry bag, cut the end of the bag so that the narrow end of the plastic coupler aligns with the hole. Place the coupler inside the bag; the coupler's grooves should be visible and the bag should fit snugly on the base of the grooves (if not, snip off a bit more). Attach the tip and screw on the outer ring. Unscrew the ring to change tips as needed.

2. To fill the pastry bag, cuff the open end over one hand and use a flexible spatula to transfer icing to the bag. For best results, fill the bag only halfway.

3. Squeeze out air from the open end of the bag, and twist the bag closed to prevent the icing from leaking out; use a rubber band to securely seal after twisting. When not in use, store the filled bag, tip down, in a glass lined with a damp paper towel. This is especially important when using royal icing, which hardens quickly. If a tip becomes clogged, use a toothpick or straight pin to clear it.

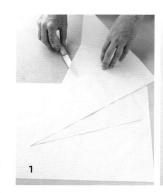

HOW TO MAKE A PAPER CORNET

Cut parchment into a 12-by-16-by-20-inch triangle, as shown (or an 8-by-12-by-14½-inch triangle for piping melted chocolate). With the mid-length side closest to you, curl the upper right-hand point down toward the middle of the shortest side to form a cone shape; form the cone's point at the middle of the longest side. Wrap the slack around the cone shape, while pulling the inside flap of parchment taut to keep the point tight and completely closed. Tuck the top flap inside the cone, and use tape to secure it, or make a small tear in the folded side you have just created. Snip the tip of the cone after filling it.

working with fondant and marzipan

In most cases, fondant (firm sugar icing) and marzipan (a paste of ground almonds, sugar, and sometimes egg whites) can be used interchange-ably. The only exception is when you desire a pure white color (as with the springerle Easter bunny cupcakes on page 217, in which case you will need to use fondant). Both can be easily tinted and used to cover a cupcake for a smooth topping or to shape into animals, fruit, or any other objects imag-inable. Work with fondant and marzipan as you would modeling clay; each is sticky enough that you can press the parts together and they'll adhere.

While they are largely treated in the same manner, fondant calls for a few extra steps. Fondant must be at room temperature before you can use it. And because it picks up the tiniest speck of lint, keep your workspace as clean as possible. Also, fondant must be kneaded until it feels soft and pliable (at which point you may add coloring). Follow these steps to tint and roll out fondant and marzipan.

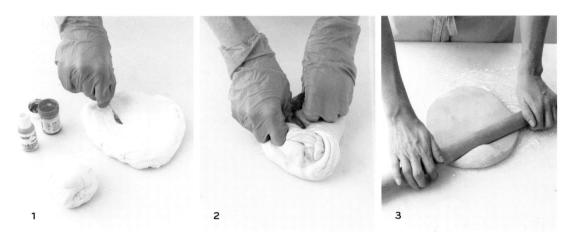

1   2   3

1. Divide fondant or marzipan into parts, one for each color you need; leave some untinted to lighten colors if necessary. Use gel-paste food color and a toothpick or wooden skewer to dab with color. (You may want to wear latex gloves when tinting.)

2. Begin kneading to distribute color, adding more gel paste a little at a time as you go. Avoid adding too much color too soon; the intensity will increase as you knead. Continue kneading until the color is uni-form and the desired shade is reached. If necessary, knead in a bit of untinted fondant or marzipan to tone down the color.

3. If rolling out to cut into shapes, dust the work sur-face lightly with cornstarch to keep fondant or mar-zipan from sticking. Roll out to $\frac{1}{8}$ inch thick (or as instructed in a recipe) with a rolling pin. If you notice any air bubbles in the fondant or marzipan as you roll, prick them with a clean straight pin.

pastry tips

With a bowl of buttercream and a basic collection of pastry tips, you can create countless designs. Piping tips are sold individually or in small sets with pastry bags and couplers, and are categorized by family according to the decorative effects they produce (as listed below). Tips are also designated by number; the recipes in this book include suggestions for Ateco and Wilton tips by number (unless a brand name is specifically mentioned, the numbers are the same for both); other companies may use different numbers. Nearly every category of tip comes in a range of sizes to create even greater variety; oversize (large) tips are perfect for making dramatic decorations or to quickly cover a cupcake in a swirly peak. If your set doesn't have the number shown here, a tip from the same category and of an approximate size will produce similar results.

PLAIN TIPS

(SUCH AS #1, #4, #11, AND ATECO #806)

Plain, or round, tips are the most versatile and are used for making thin or thick lines, letters, dots, beads, delicate vines, and simple flowers.

STAR TIPS

(SUCH AS #14, #17, #20, #199, AND ATECO #828, #863, AND #867)

There are three basic styles of star tips: open, closed, and French (or fine-ribbed) stars. The tips of open stars are used to create the traditional star shape, while French stars are most often used to create shells. The tips of closed stars are crimped inward slightly, and are the ones to use for creating rosettes.

LEAF TIPS

(SUCH AS #66, #67, #68, #349, AND #352)

A leaf tip can be used to make foliage-like designs or ribbons with a vein down the middle. Standard leaf tips will make a flat shape, while a V-leaf tip will create a more textured, raised design. Both tips are also good for making soft ruffles and borders.

PETAL TIPS

(SUCH AS #102, #103, AND #104)

A petal tip is essential for forming flowers and also works well for making ruffles and ribbons.

MULTI-OPENING TIPS

(SUCH AS #233)

Also known as grass tips, these multi-holed tips make fast work of piping lots of little strands at once.

BASKETWEAVE TIPS

(SUCH AS #44 AND #47)

As its name suggests, a basketweave tip makes lattices and fancy edges, as well as ribbon-like lines. Straight tips make smooth designs, such as ruffles, while the others can be piped with the ridged side facing up for textured lines, or with the straight (back) side up for smooth ones; you can even switch back and forth for variety. These tips are also good for forming pleats and ribbon borders.

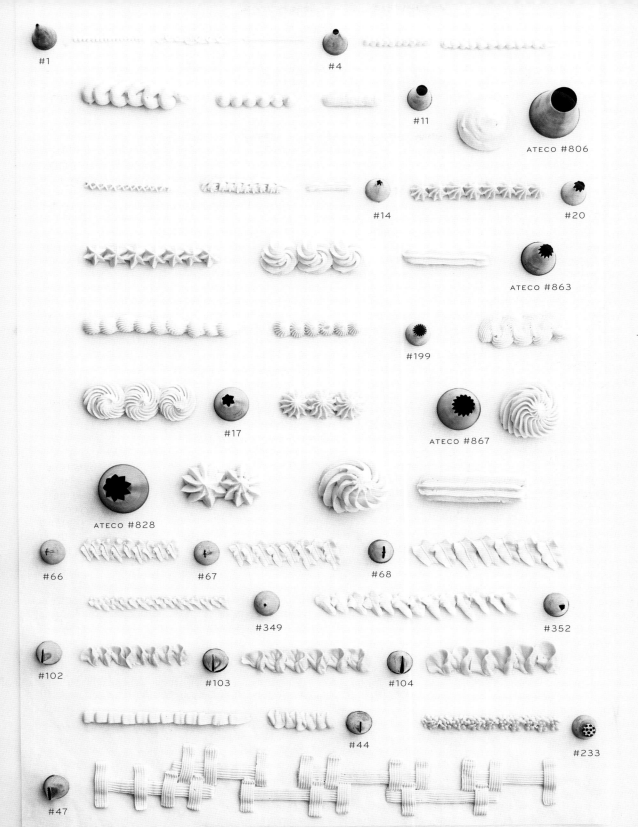

#1

#4

#11

ATECO #806

#14

#20

ATECO #863

#199

#17

ATECO #867

ATECO #828

#66

#67

#68

#349

#352

#102

#103

#104

#44

#233

#47

frostings, fillings, and embellishments

FLUFFY VANILLA FROSTING

Memories of childhood birthday cakes will be evoked by this sweet frosting, made quickly with just three ingredients and a handheld mixer (a standing mixer will take even less time). This frosting can also be tinted with food color; add a drop at a time and stir with a flexible spatula until well combined before adding more. MAKES ABOUT 4 CUPS

1½ cups (3 sticks) unsalted butter, room temperature

1 pound (4 cups) confectioners' sugar, sifted

½ teaspoon pure vanilla extract

1. With an electric mixer, beat butter on medium-high speed until pale and creamy, about 2 minutes.

2. Reduce speed to medium. Add the confectioners' sugar, ½ cup at a time, beating well after each addition and scraping down sides of bowl as needed; after every two additions, raise speed to high and beat 10 seconds to aerate frosting, then return to medium. This process should take about 5 minutes. Frosting will be very pale and fluffy.

3. Add vanilla, and beat until frosting is smooth. If not using immediately, frosting can be refrigerated up to 10 days in an airtight container. Before using, bring to room temperature, and beat on low speed until smooth again, about 5 minutes.

DARK CHOCOLATE FROSTING

This deep, dark, satiny frosting (thanks to the addition of melted semi-sweet chocolate) is a favorite of *Martha Stewart Living* food editors, since it has just the right consistency for spreading or piping into beautiful swirls. It also has a wonderful sheen. MAKES ABOUT 5 CUPS

½ cup plus 1 tablespoon unsweetened Dutch-process cocoa powder

½ cup plus 1 tablespoon boiling water

2¼ cups (4½ sticks) unsalted butter, room temperature

¾ cup confectioners' sugar, sifted

¼ teaspoon salt

1½ pounds best-quality semi-sweet chocolate, melted and cooled (see page 323)

Combine cocoa and the boiling water, stirring until cocoa has dissolved. With an electric mixer on medium-high speed, beat butter, confectioners' sugar, and salt until pale and fluffy. Reduce speed to low. Add melted and cooled chocolate, beating until combined and scraping down sides of bowl as needed. Beat in the cocoa mixture. If not using immediately, frosting can be refrigerated up to 5 days, or frozen up to 1 month, in an airtight container. Before using, bring to room temperature, and beat on low speed until smooth again.

SEVEN-MINUTE FROSTING

Made with beaten egg whites, this frosting is similar to meringue, but is more stable and sturdy enough for piping. And, like meringue, it also takes well to browning with a small kitchen torch. Use immediately, as the frosting will harden quickly (have your piping bag ready). MAKES ABOUT 8 CUPS

1½ cups plus 2 tablespoons sugar

⅔ cup water

2 tablespoons light corn syrup

6 large egg whites, room temperature

1. Combine 1½ cups sugar with the water and corn syrup in a small saucepan; clip a candy thermometer to side of pan. Bring to a boil over medium heat, stirring occasionally, until sugar dissolves. Continue boiling, without stirring, until syrup reaches 230°F.

2. Meanwhile, in the bowl of a standing electric mixer fitted with the whisk attachment, whisk egg whites on medium-high speed until soft peaks form. With mixer running, add remaining 2 tablespoons sugar, beating to combine.

3. As soon as sugar syrup reaches 230°F, remove from heat. With mixer on medium-low speed, pour syrup down side of bowl in a slow, steady stream. Raise speed to medium-high; whisk until mixture is completely cool (test by touching the bottom of the bowl) and stiff (but not dry) peaks form, about 7 minutes. Use immediately.

. . . .

COCONUT VARIATION: Add ½ teaspoon pure coconut extract at the end of step 3, whisking to combine.

COFFEE VARIATION: Add 2 tablespoons pure coffee extract (see Sources, page 342) at the end of step 3, whisking to combine.

CREAM-CHEESE FROSTING

Versatile, tangy, and quick to prepare, cream-cheese frosting has a perfectly soft consistency for swirling or swooping. It's the classic choice for topping many cupcakes, including carrot and red velvet, and is also especially good with others, such as zucchini-spice and applesauce-spice. MAKES 4 CUPS

1 cup (2 sticks) unsalted butter, room temperature

12 ounces cream cheese, room temperature

1 pound (4 cups) confectioners' sugar, sifted

¾ teaspoon pure vanilla extract

With an electric mixer on medium-high speed, beat butter and cream cheese until fluffy, 2 to 3 minutes. Reduce speed to low. Add sugar, ½ cup at a time, and then vanilla, and mix until smooth and combined, scraping down sides of bowl as needed. If not using immediately, frosting can be refrigerated up to 3 days in an airtight container; before using, bring to room temperature, and beat on low speed until smooth again.

SWISS MERINGUE BUTTERCREAM

If there is one frosting recipe a home baker should always have on hand, this is it. This all-purpose buttercream has an ultra-silky, stable texture that spreads beautifully over cakes and cupcakes, and can be piped into perfect peaks and patterns. Swiss meringue buttercream is also less sweet than other types of frosting, with a wonderful buttery taste. It can be varied with different extracts, juices, zests, and other flavoring agents, and tinted any shade. Don't worry if the mixture appears to separate, or "curdle," after you've added the butter; simply continue beating on medium-high speed, and it will become smooth again. **MAKES ABOUT 5 CUPS**

5 large egg whites

1 cup plus 2 tablespoons sugar

Pinch of salt

1 pound (4 sticks) unsalted butter, cut into tablespoons, room temperature

1½ teaspoons pure vanilla extract

1. Combine egg whites, sugar, and salt in the heatproof bowl of a standing mixer set over a pan of simmering water. Whisk constantly by hand until mixture is warm to the touch and sugar has dissolved (the mixture should feel completely smooth when rubbed between your fingertips).

2. Attach the bowl to the mixer fitted with the whisk attachment. Starting on low and gradually increasing to medium-high speed, whisk until stiff (but not dry) peaks form. Continue mixing until the mixture is fluffy and glossy, and completely cool (test by touching the bottom of the bowl), about 10 minutes.

3. With mixer on medium-low speed, add the butter a few tablespoons at a time, mixing well after each addition. Once all butter has been added, whisk in vanilla. Switch to the paddle attachment, and continue beating on low speed until all air bubbles are eliminated, about 2 minutes. Scrape down sides of bowl with a flexible spatula, and continue beating until the frosting is completely smooth. Keep buttercream at room temperature if using the same day, or transfer to an airtight container and refrigerate up to 3 days or freeze up to 1 month. Before using, bring to room temperature and beat with paddle attachment on low speed until smooth again, about 5 minutes.

4. (Optional) To tint buttercream (or royal icing), reserve some for toning down the color, if necessary. Add gel-paste food color, a drop at a time (or use the toothpick or skewer to add food color a dab at a time) to the remaining buttercream. You can use a single shade of food color or experiment by mixing two or more. Blend after each addition with the mixer (use the paddle attachment) or a flexible spatula, until desired shade is achieved. Avoid adding too much food color too soon, as the hue will intensify with continued stirring; if necessary, you can tone down the shade by mixing in some reserved untinted buttercream.

MAKING SWISS MERINGUE BUTTERCREAM

CHOCOLATE VARIATION: Using a flexible spatula, fold 4½ ounces semisweet chocolate, melted and cooled (see page 323), into buttercream mixture in step 3, along with the vanilla extract.

COFFEE VARIATION: Mix 2 tablespoons good-quality instant espresso powder (do not use instant coffee) with the vanilla extract, and add in step 3.

VANILLA-BEAN VARIATION: Split 1 vanilla bean lengthwise and scrape seeds into a food processor (reserve pod for another use); pulse with the sugar in the recipe until combined, then pass through a fine sieve to separate the larger pieces (discard these). Heat vanilla-bean sugar with the egg whites in step 1.

RASPBERRY VARIATION: Beat in 1 container (6 ounces) fresh raspberries (or other berries) after all butter has been added, until buttercream is streaky (do not overbeat).

STRAWBERRY MERINGUE BUTTERCREAM

This fruit-flavored buttercream is made using the same technique as Swiss meringue buttercream, so you can refer to the step-by-step photos on page 305 as you proceed. **MAKES ABOUT 5 CUPS**

1½ cups fresh strawberries (8 ounces), rinsed, hulled, and coarsely chopped

4 large egg whites

1¼ cups sugar

1½ cups (3 sticks) unsalted butter, cut into tablespoons, room temperature

1. Puree strawberries in a food processor. Combine egg whites and sugar in the heatproof bowl of a standing electric mixer set over a pan of simmering water. Whisk constantly by hand until mixture is warm to the touch and sugar has dissolved (the mixture should feel completely smooth when rubbed between your fingertips).

2. Attach the bowl to the mixer fitted with the whisk attachment. Starting on low and gradually increasing to medium-high speed, mix until stiff (but not dry) peaks form. Continue mixing until the mixture is fluffy and glossy, and completely cool (test by touching the bottom of the bowl), about 10 minutes.

3. With mixer on medium-low speed, add the butter a few tablespoons at a time, mixing well after each addition. Once all butter has been added, scrape down sides of bowl with a flexible spatula and switch to the paddle attachment; continue beating on low speed until all air bubbles are eliminated, about 2 minutes. Add strawberries and beat until combined. Stir with a flexible spatula until the frosting is smooth. Keep buttercream at room temperature if using the same day, or transfer to an airtight container and refrigerate up to 3 days or freeze up to 1 month. Before using, bring to room temperature and beat with paddle attachment on low speed until smooth again, about 5 minutes.

CARAMEL BUTTERCREAM

This is another variation of Swiss meringue buttercream, only you cream the butter before incorporating it into the beaten egg-white mixture; caramel is added at the end, resulting in a buttercream that is at once rich and ethereal. MAKES ABOUT 4 CUPS

1 cup plus 2 tablespoons sugar

¼ cup water

¼ cup heavy cream

1½ cups (3 sticks) unsalted butter, room temperature

4 large egg whites

1 teaspoon pure vanilla extract

1. Combine ½ cup plus 2 tablespoons sugar and the water in a heavy saucepan. Heat over medium, stirring occasionally, until sugar is dissolved and syrup is clear. Stop stirring, and cook until syrup comes to a boil, washing down sides of pan with a wet pastry brush to prevent crystals from forming. Continue to boil, gently swirling pan occasionally to color evenly, until mixture is very dark amber. Remove from heat; add cream in a steady stream (the mixture will spatter), stirring with a wooden spoon until smooth and combined. Let cool.

2. With an electric mixer on medium-high speed, cream butter until pale and fluffy. In the heatproof bowl of a standing electric mixer, combine remaining ½ cup sugar and the egg whites. Set bowl over a pan of simmering water; whisk constantly by hand until mixture is warm to the touch and sugar has dissolved (the mixture should feel completely smooth when rubbed between your fingertips).

3. Attach bowl to the mixer fitted with the whisk attachment. Starting on low and gradually increasing to medium-high speed, mix until stiff (but not dry) peaks form. Continue whisking until egg mixture is fluffy and glossy, and completely cool (test by touching the bottom of the bowl), about 10 minutes. Reduce speed to medium-low. Add beaten butter, about ¼ cup at a time, mixing well after each addition. Mix in vanilla.

4. Switch to the paddle attachment. With mixer on medium-low speed, very slowly pour in caramel; beat 5 minutes. Scrape down sides of bowl, and continue to beat until caramel is fully incorporated. Keep buttercream at room temperature if using the same day, or transfer to an airtight container and refrigerate up to 3 days or freeze up to 1 month. Before using, bring to room temperature and beat with paddle attachment on low speed until smooth again, about 5 minutes.

MINT BUTTERCREAM

The lovely white shade of this frosting belies the bright mint flavor, achieved by first steeping fresh mint in milk when making the custard base, and then adding extract at the end. **MAKES ABOUT 3½ CUPS**

2 large eggs, separated

½ cup sugar

⅔ cup milk

⅓ teaspoon pure vanilla extract

⅔ cup coarsely chopped fresh mint leaves

1 pound (4 sticks) unsalted butter, room temperature

¼ teaspoon pure peppermint extract

1. In the bowl of a standing electric mixer fitted with the whisk attachment, mix egg yolks and ¼ cup sugar on high speed until pale and thick, 2 to 3 minutes.

2. Prepare an ice-water bath. Bring milk, vanilla, and mint leaves just to a boil in a medium saucepan. Remove from heat. Whisk about one third of milk mixture into yolk mixture (this is called tempering, which keeps the yolks from curdling). Pour yolk mixture into pan with remaining milk mixture, and whisk to combine. Clip candy thermometer to side of pan. Cook over medium heat, stirring constantly, until mixture registers 185°F. Remove from heat; strain through a fine sieve into a heatproof bowl (discard solids). Set bowl in ice bath, stirring mixture until cool.

3. In another bowl of an electric mixture fitted with the paddle attachment, cream butter on medium-high speed until pale and fluffy. Beat in chilled egg-yolk mixture.

4. Heat egg whites and remaining ¼ cup sugar in the clean heatproof bowl of an electric mixer set over a pan of simmering water, whisking constantly by hand until mixture is warm to the touch and sugar has dissolved (the mixture should feel completely smooth when rubbed between your fingertips). Attach bowl to the mixer fitted with the clean whisk attachment; starting on low speed and gradually increasing to medium-high speed, whisk until stiff (but not dry) peaks form and mixture is completely cool (test by touching bottom of bowl), about 10 minutes.

5. Add egg-white mixture to butter mixture; switch to the paddle attachment, and beat on medium-high speed until smooth. Beat in peppermint extract. Keep buttercream at room temperature if using the same day, or transfer to an airtight container and refrigerate up to 3 days or freeze up to 3 months. Before using, bring to room temperature, and beat with the paddle attachment on low speed until smooth again, about 5 minutes.

MAPLE BUTTERCREAM

Before adding the maple syrup to the beaten eggs, it should be heated to 240 degrees. If you don't have a candy thermometer, you can test by adding a drop of syrup to cold water; it should immediately form a soft ball. Be sure to buy only pure maple syrup, not a brand labeled "pancake syrup" or "maple-flavored syrup," which is actually corn syrup flavored with maple extract. Pure maple syrup is graded according to color and flavor; grade B has a robust flavor that works well in baking and other recipes.

MAKES 4 CUPS

6 large egg yolks

2 cups pure maple syrup, preferably grade B

1 pound (4 sticks) unsalted butter, chilled and cut into tablespoons

1. In the bowl of a standing electric mixer fitted with the whisk attachment, mix egg yolks on high speed until pale and thick, about 5 minutes.

2. Meanwhile, bring maple syrup to a boil in a saucepan over medium heat; clip a candy thermometer to side of pan. Cook until syrup registers 240°F, about 15 minutes. Remove from heat.

3. With mixer on medium speed, carefully pour the syrup in a slow, steady stream down the side of the bowl until it is completely combined, about 1½ minutes. Continue mixing until the bottom of the bowl is only slightly warm to the touch, 5 to 6 minutes.

4. Add the butter, a few tablespoons at a time, mixing until completely incorporated after each addition. Once all butter has been added, scrape down sides of bowl with a flexible spatula, and continue beating until buttercream is fluffy, about 4 minutes more. Keep buttercream at room temperature if using the same day, or transfer to an airtight container and refrigerate up to 3 days or freeze up to 1 month. Before using, bring to room temperature and whisk on low speed until fluffy again, about 5 minutes.

MASCARPONE FROSTING

Made with mascarpone cheese, this frosting is similar to cream-cheese frosting, but with a slightly richer flavor. **MAKES ABOUT 2 CUPS**

1 cup heavy cream

8 ounces mascarpone cheese, room temperature

1/2 cup confectioners' sugar, sifted

With an electric mixer on medium speed, whisk heavy cream until stiff peaks form (be careful not to overbeat, or cream will be grainy). In another bowl, whisk together mascarpone and confectioners' sugar until smooth. Gently fold whipped cream into mascarpone mixture until completely incorporated. Use immediately.

. . . .

BROWN-SUGAR CREAM-CHEESE FROSTING **MAKES 2 1/2 CUPS**

1/2 cup (1 stick) unsalted butter, room temperature

8 ounces cream cheese, room temperature

1 cup packed light-brown sugar

With an electric mixer on medium-high speed, beat butter, cream cheese, and brown sugar until smooth. Use immediately, or refrigerate up to 3 days in an airtight container. Before using, bring to room temperature, and beat on low speed until smooth.

. . . .

CREAMY PEANUT BUTTER FROSTING **MAKES ABOUT 3 CUPS**

6 ounces cream cheese, room temperature

1/3 cup confectioners' sugar

1/2 teaspoon salt

1 cup creamy peanut butter

1/2 teaspoon pure vanilla extract

1/2 cup heavy cream

1. With an electric mixer on medium-high speed, beat cream cheese and confectioners' sugar until pale and fluffy. Add salt and peanut butter, and beat to combine. Beat in vanilla.

2. In another bowl, with an electric mixer on medium speed, whisk cream until medium-stiff peaks form. Fold cream into peanut-butter mixture. Use immediately, or refrigerate, covered tightly, up to 2 days. Before using, bring to room temperature and stir with a flexible spatula until smooth.

CHOCOLATE–SOUR CREAM FROSTING

Similar to dark chocolate frosting (page 302), this topping gets its intense color from the addition of semisweet chocolate. Sour cream and cream cheese impart tangy flavor and ultra-creamy consistency. This frosting would pair well with any chocolate cupcake, particularly devil's food (page 34; also made with sour cream), as well as those made with banana, such as the roasted banana cupcakes on page 141. MAKES ABOUT 8 CUPS

1	pound (4 cups) confectioners' sugar, sifted
1/2	cup unsweetened Dutch-process cocoa powder
1/4	teaspoon salt
12	ounces cream cheese, room temperature
3/4	cup (1 1/2 sticks) unsalted butter, room temperature
18	ounces bittersweet chocolate, melted and cooled (see page 323)
1 1/2	cups sour cream

Sift together confectioners' sugar, cocoa, and salt. With an electric mixer on medium-high speed, beat cream cheese and butter until pale and fluffy. Reduce speed to low. Gradually add sugar mixture; mix until combined. Mix in melted and cooled chocolate and then sour cream; scrape down sides of bowl and continue beating until smooth. Use immediately, or frosting can be stored in the refrigerator up to 5 days, or frozen up to 1 month, in an airtight container. Before using, bring to room temperature and beat on low speed until smooth.

. . . .

COCONUT-PECAN FROSTING MAKES ABOUT 4 CUPS

3	large egg yolks
1	can (12 ounces) evaporated milk
1 1/4	cups packed light-brown sugar
3/4	cup (1 1/2 sticks) unsalted butter, cut into small pieces, room temperature
1	teaspoon pure vanilla extract
1/4	teaspoon salt
1	package (7 ounces) sweetened flaked coconut
1 1/2	cups pecans (6 ounces), toasted (see page 323) and coarsely chopped

1. Heat egg yolks, evaporated milk, brown sugar, and butter in a saucepan over medium, stirring constantly, until thick, about 10 minutes (it should reach the consistency of sour cream). Strain through a fine sieve into a bowl.

2. Stir vanilla, salt, coconut, and pecans into frosting. Let cool completely, stirring occasionally. Frosting can be refrigerated up to 1 day in an airtight container. Before using, bring to room temperature and stir with a flexible spatula until smooth.

CHOCOLATE GANACHE GLAZE

This rich, thick chocolate glaze may remind you of hot fudge sauce in its flavor and consistency. Avoid overmixing when stirring the chocolate into the hot-cream mixture, as this can cause the ganache to become dull and grainy. To make a thinner glaze for coating the handwritten valentine cupcakes on page 212, see variation below. **MAKES ABOUT 1 ¼ CUPS**

6 ounces semisweet chocolate, finely chopped

⅔ cup heavy cream

1 tablespoon light corn syrup

1. Place chocolate in a medium heatproof bowl. Bring cream and corn syrup just to a simmer in a small saucepan over medium-high heat; pour mixture over chocolate. Let stand, without stirring, until chocolate begins to melt.

2. Using a flexible spatula, gently stir chocolate and cream until totally combined; begin near the center of the bowl and gradually work your way toward the edge, pulling in as much chocolate as possible, until the mixture is smooth and glossy. (If any chocolate pieces remain, strain mixture through a fine sieve and discard solids.) If not using immediately, glaze can be refrigerated up to 5 days in an airtight container. Reheat gently before using.

POURING WARM CREAM MIXTURE OVER CHOCOLATE

STIRRING UNTIL CHOCOLATE IS COMBINED

SHINY CHOCOLATE GLAZE VARIATION: Reduce amount of chocolate to 2 ounces. Follow step 1 of recipe above, letting mixture stand 5 minutes before slowly whisking until smooth and combined. Use immediately, without straining.

CHOCOLATE GANACHE FROSTING

Ganache—a smooth mixture of chocolate and cream—is one of the richest, most luscious of all chocolate frostings. The frosting is made in the same manner as the chocolate ganache glaze (opposite), and then allowed to thicken until the frosting is spreadable. Achieving the perfect consistency can be tricky; if the frosting becomes too firm to spread, re-heat in a bowl over a pan of simmering water until it begins to melt around the edges, then remove from heat and stir until smooth. **MAKES 4 CUPS**

1 pound good-quality bittersweet chocolate, finely chopped

2⅓ cups heavy cream

¼ cup corn syrup

1. Place chocolate in a large heatproof bowl. Bring cream and corn syrup just to a simmer over medium-high heat; pour mixture over chocolate. Let stand, without stirring, until chocolate begins to melt.

2. Beginning near the center and working outward, stir melted chocolate into cream until mixture is combined and smooth (do not overstir).

3. Refrigerate, stirring every 5 minutes, until frosting just barely begins to hold its shape and is slightly lighter in color. Use immediately (ganache will continue to thicken after you stop stirring).

HONEY FROSTING MAKES ABOUT 2 CUPS

½ cup (1 stick) unsalted butter, room temperature

8 ounces cream cheese, room temperature

¼ cup good-quality honey

Blend butter, cream cheese, and honey with a flexible spatula until smooth. If not using immediately, frosting can be refrigerated up to 5 days in an airtight container; before using, stir with a flexible spatula until smooth.

BROWN-BUTTER ICING

This delicious icing has a tendency to separate. If it does, warm it in a heat-proof bowl over a pan of simmering water; whisk until smooth, adding a bit more milk, if necessary, to achieve the right consistency. MAKES 1 CUP

½ cup (1 stick) unsalted butter

2 cups sifted confectioners' sugar

2 teaspoons pure vanilla extract

2 tablespoons milk, plus more if needed

1. Melt butter in a small saucepan over medium heat, swirling pan occasionally, until nut-brown in color, about 10 minutes. Remove from heat, and pour butter into a bowl, leaving any burned sediment behind.

2. Add confectioners' sugar, vanilla, and 2 tablespoons milk to brown butter; stir until smooth. If necessary, add more milk (up to 2 tablespoons) a little at a time, just until icing is spreadable. Use immediately.

POURING OFF BROWN BUTTER

CITRUS GLAZE

Follow this recipe to make a glaze with any citrus flavor, such as orange, lemon, or lime. MAKES ABOUT 1 CUP

1½ cups confectioners' sugar, sifted, plus more if needed

¼ teaspoon finely grated citrus zest

3 tablespoons fresh citrus juice, plus more if needed

Whisk together all ingredients until smooth. If necessary, add more sugar to thicken or more juice to thin the glaze. Use immediately.

ROYAL ICING

Using meringue powder (or powdered egg whites), instead of raw egg whites, eliminates food-safety concerns. Look for the powder at baking-supply stores and many supermarkets. Royal icing hardens quickly, so if not using immediately, transfer to an airtight container and store in the refrigerator, up to one week; before using, stir with a flexible spatula until smooth. MAKES ABOUT 2½ CUPS

1 pound (4 cups) confectioners' sugar, sifted

¼ cup plus 1 tablespoon meringue powder

Scant ½ cup water, plus more as needed

With an electric mixer on low speed, beat all ingredients until smooth, about 7 minutes. If icing is too thick, add more water, a little at a time, beating until icing holds a ribbon on the surface for a few seconds when beater is lifted; if too thin, continue mixing 2 to 3 minutes more.

PASTRY CREAM

Contrary to its name, pastry cream—a classic custard filling for cakes, tarts, pastries, and other baked goods—contains no cream, only milk. Be sure to bring the mixture to a full boil to activate the cornstarch and ensure proper thickening. **MAKES ABOUT 3 CUPS**

4 large egg yolks
½ cup sugar
¼ cup cornstarch
  Pinch of salt
2 cups milk
1¼ teaspoons pure vanilla extract

1. Whisk egg yolks until smooth in a large bowl. Combine sugar, cornstarch, and salt in a medium saucepan, and heat over medium. Stirring constantly, gradually add milk in a slow, steady stream, and cook until mixture thickens and begins to bubble, about 5 minutes.

2. Whisking constantly, slowly pour one third of the milk mixture into egg yolks (this step is called tempering, which keeps the yolks from curdling). Pour mixture into remaining milk mixture in saucepan. Cook over medium heat, whisking constantly, until mixture comes to a full boil and is thick enough to hold its shape when lifted with a spoon, 2 to 4 minutes. Remove from heat; stir in vanilla.

3. Strain mixture through a fine sieve into a heatproof bowl. Cover with parchment paper or plastic wrap, pressing it directly on surface to prevent a skin from forming. Refrigerate until chilled and firm, at least 2 hours (or up to 2 days).

WHIPPED CREAM

This familiar dessert topping makes a versatile last-minute embellishment for cupcakes. It can be dolloped on top as an alternative to heavier frostings, or used as a filling for split cupcakes. Whether you use a handheld whisk or an electric mixer to whip the cream, be sure not to overmix, or the consistency can become grainy. For unsweetened whipped cream, simply omit the sugar. **MAKES ABOUT 4 CUPS**

2 cups heavy cream
¼ cup confectioners' sugar, sifted

Whisk heavy cream until soft peaks form. Add confectioners' sugar, and whisk until combined. If not using immediately, whipped cream can be refrigerated, covered tightly, up to 3 hours in an airtight container.

LEMON CURD

A high proportion of lemon juice gives curd its intense flavor. As an acid, the juice also prevents the yolks from curdling when heated (unlike when making pastry cream, which requires the extra step of tempering). You can substitute an equal amount of juice from other citrus, such as lime, grapefruit, or blood orange. **MAKES ABOUT 2 CUPS**

2 whole eggs plus 8 egg yolks

1 cup sugar

$2/3$ cup fresh lemon juice (about 6 lemons)

2 tablespoons unsalted butter, cut into small pieces, room temperature

Combine whole eggs and yolks, sugar, and lemon juice in a heatproof bowl set over a pan of simmering water. Cook, whisking constantly, until mixture is thick enough to coat the back of a spoon. Remove from heat. Add butter, a few pieces at a time, whisking until smooth after each addition. Strain through a fine sieve into another bowl, and cover with parchment paper or plastic wrap, pressing it directly on surface to prevent a skin from forming. Refrigerate until chilled and firm, at least 2 hours (or up to 2 days).

SWISS MERINGUE

This billowy meringue is used to pipe the "mushrooms" for the fruitcakes on page 249 as well as the flowers for the meringue bouquet cupcakes on page 264. (It is also serves as the foundation for Swiss meringue butter-cream on page 304.) **MAKES ABOUT 4 CUPS**

4 large egg whites

1 cup sugar

Pinch of cream of tartar

1 teaspoon pure vanilla extract

1. Combine the egg whites, sugar, and cream of tartar in the heatproof bowl of a standing electric mixer; set over a pan of simmering water. Clip a candy thermometer to side of bowl. Cook, whisking constantly by hand, until the mixture registers 140°F and the sugar is dissolved (it should feel completely smooth when rubbed between your fingertips), about 3 minutes.

2. Transfer bowl to a mixer fitted with the whisk attachment. Starting on low and gradually increasing to high speed, mix until the meringue is completely cool (test by touching the bottom of the bowl), and forms stiff, glossy (but not dry) peaks, about 10 minutes. Mix in the vanilla. Use immediately.

CHOCOLATE COOKIE CUTOUTS

This all-purpose dough bakes rich and dark cutouts, and it can be rolled again and again with little compromise in texture. Follow the recipe below to make your own designs, or cut and bake as directed in specific cupcake recipes. **MAKES 3 TO 4 DOZEN 3-INCH COOKIES**

1½ cups all-purpose flour, plus more for work surface

½ cup plus 2 tablespoons unsweetened Dutch-process cocoa powder

⅛ teaspoon salt

¼ teaspoon ground cinnamon

¾ cup (1½ sticks) unsalted butter, room temperature

1½ cups sifted confectioners' sugar

1 large egg, lightly beaten

½ teaspoon pure vanilla extract

1. Sift together flour, cocoa, salt, and cinnamon. With an electric mixer on medium-high speed, cream butter and confectioners' sugar until pale and fluffy. Add egg and vanilla, and beat to combine. Reduce speed to low. Gradually add flour mixture, beating until just combined.

2. Divide dough in half; flatten each half into a disk, and wrap in plastic. Refrigerate until firm, at least 1 hour (or overnight). Dough can be frozen, wrapped tightly in plastic and placed in a resealable plastic bag, up to 3 months; thaw overnight in the refrigerator before using.

3. On a lightly floured work surface (or a piece of parchment paper), roll out one disk of dough to just under ¼ inch thick. Transfer to a baking sheet; freeze until firm, about 15 minutes.

4. Preheat oven to 350°F, with racks in upper and lower thirds. Using a 3-inch cookie cutter, quickly cut out shapes from dough (if dough begins to soften, chill in freezer 5 minutes), and transfer shapes to parchment-lined baking sheets, spacing them 2 inches apart, as you work. Reroll scraps and cut out more shapes. Brush off excess flour. Freeze until firm, about 15 minutes. Repeat with remaining disk of dough.

5. Bake cookies until crisp, about 8 minutes, firmly tapping down sheets once and rotating them halfway through. Let cool completely on sheets on wire racks before decorating as desired. Cookies can be stored up to 1 week at room temperature in an airtight container.

SUGAR COOKIE CUTOUTS

Buttery and crunchy, sugar cookies are delicious on their own and make delightful cupcake toppers when decorated with royal icing. This dough is a favorite of *Martha Stewart Living* food editors for its flavor and texture, which is just right for rolling out and cutting into shapes. Follow the recipe below to make your own designs, or cut and bake as directed in specific cupcake recipes. **MAKES 4 DOZEN 2-INCH COOKIES**

4 cups sifted all-purpose flour, plus more for work surface

1 teaspoon baking powder

½ teaspoon salt

1 cup (2 sticks) unsalted butter, room temperature

2 cups sugar

2 large eggs, room temperature

2 teaspoons pure vanilla extract

1. Sift together flour, baking powder, and salt. With an electric mixer on medium-high speed, cream butter and sugar until pale and fluffy. Add eggs and vanilla, and beat to combine. Reduce speed to low. Gradually add flour mixture, beating until just combined.

2. Divide dough in half; flatten each half into a disk, and wrap in plastic. Refrigerate until firm, at least 1 hour (or overnight). Dough can be frozen, wrapped tightly in plastic and placed in a resealable plastic bag, up to 3 months; thaw overnight in the refrigerator before using.

3. Let one disk of dough stand at room temperature until soft enough to roll, about 10 minutes. On a lightly floured work surface (or a piece of parchment paper), roll out dough to just under ¼ inch thick, adding more flour as needed to keep dough from sticking. Transfer to a baking sheet; freeze until firm, about 15 minutes.

4. Preheat oven to 350°F, with racks in upper and lower thirds. Using a 2-inch cookie cutter, quickly cut out shapes from dough (if dough begins to soften, chill in freezer 5 minutes), and transfer shapes to parchment-lined baking sheets, spacing them 2 inches apart, as you work. Reroll scraps and cut out more shapes. Brush off excess flour. Freeze until firm, about 15 minutes. Repeat with remaining disk of dough.

5. Bake until edges turn golden, 15 to 18 minutes, firmly tapping down sheets once and rotating them halfway through. Let cool completely on sheets on wire racks before decorating as desired. Cookies can be stored up to 1 week at room temperature in an airtight container.

GINGERBREAD COOKIE CUTOUTS

Use this dough to make gingerbread boys and girls—or other shapes, such as giant dinosaurs—for topping cupcakes (adjust baking time as necessary). The crisp cookies are flavored with a blend of spices—ginger, cinnamon, cloves, and nutmeg—and sweetened with a combination of molasses and brown sugar. Follow the recipe below to make your own designs, or cut and bake as directed in specific cupcake recipes. **MAKES 4 TO 5 DOZEN 2-INCH COOKIES**

5½ cups all-purpose flour, plus more for work surface

1 teaspoon baking soda

1½ teaspoons salt

1 tablespoon plus 1 teaspoon ground ginger

1 tablespoon plus 1 teaspoon ground cinnamon

1½ teaspoons ground cloves

1 teaspoon freshly grated nutmeg

1 cup (2 sticks) unsalted butter, room temperature

1 cup packed dark-brown sugar

2 large eggs

1½ cups unsulfured molasses

1. Whisk together flour, baking soda, salt, and spices. With an electric mixer on medium-high speed, cream butter and brown sugar until pale and fluffy. Add eggs and molasses, and beat to combine. Reduce speed to low. Gradually add flour mixture, beating until just combined.

2. Divide dough into thirds; flatten each piece into a disk, and wrap in plastic. Refrigerate until firm, at least 1 hour (or overnight). Dough can be frozen, wrapped tightly in plastic and placed in a resealable plastic bag, up to 3 months; thaw overnight in the refrigerator before using.

3. On a generously floured piece of parchment paper, roll out one disk of dough to just under ¼ inch thick. Brush off excess flour and freeze until firm, about 15 minutes.

4. Preheat oven to 350°F, with racks in upper and lower thirds. Using a 2-inch cookie cutter, quickly cut out shapes from dough and transfer to parchment-lined baking sheets, spacing them 2 inches apart, as you work. Freeze until firm, about 15 minutes. Repeat with remaining disks of dough.

5. Bake cookies until crisp but not darkened, 8 to 10 minutes, firmly tapping down sheets once and rotating them halfway through. Transfer cookies to wire racks to cool completely before decorating as desired. Cookies can be stored up to 1 week at room temperature in airtight containers.

CHOCOLATE MINT LEAVES

MAKES ENOUGH FOR 24 CUPCAKES (ABOUT 6 LEAVES PER CUPCAKE)

1 to 2 bunches fresh mint, leaves picked from stems

8 ounces bittersweet chocolate, melted and tempered (see below)

1. Gently clean leaves with a damp paper towel, and let dry completely. Using a small, dry pastry brush, coat underside of each mint leaf with a thick layer of tempered chocolate. (If chocolate drips onto top of leaf, gently wipe it away with your fingertip.)

2. Drape leaves, chocolate sides up, over a large skewer or the handle of a wooden spoon set on a parchment-lined baking sheet. Refrigerate until set, about 10 minutes.

3. Gently grasp the chocolate layer of each leaf with kitchen tweezers (to prevent melting, don't touch the chocolate with your hands). Holding the stem, peel the leaf away with your fingers. Chocolate leaves can be refrigerated up to 2 days in a single layer in airtight containers.

COATING AND SHAPING LEAVES

PEELING MINT LEAVES FROM CHOCOLATE

TEMPERING CHOCOLATE

All chocolate is in temper when you buy it: It breaks cleanly, melts smoothly, and has a lovely sheen. But as soon as you melt chocolate, it goes out of temper, so when making leaves or other designs with chocolate, you need to follow these steps to ensure the proper results. Temper only the best-quality brands, such as chocolate made by Valrhona, Callebaut, or El Rey. Start by finely chopping 8 ounces chocolate. Reserve $1/2$ cup chopped chocolate; transfer remaining chocolate to a medium heatproof bowl set over (not in) a pan of barely simmering water. Heat, stirring occasionally, until melted and a chocolate or candy thermometer registers 131°F. (Many brands of dark chocolate should not be heated to more than 118°F; check the label.) Remove from heat; stir in reserved $1/2$ cup chopped chocolate until melted. Continue stirring until it cools to 82°F to 84°F. Return to pan of warm water; reheat to 88°F. Use immediately.

BROWNIE CUPCAKES

This recipe is used to make the brownie hearts on page 213; some of the batter is baked in muffin tins, the rest in an 8-inch pan for cutting into heart-shaped toppers. MAKES 24 CUPCAKES PLUS 24 HEARTS

Nonstick cooking spray

3 cups all-purpose flour

1½ teaspoons baking powder

1½ teaspoons coarse salt

1 cup (2 sticks) plus 1 tablespoon unsalted butter, cut into pieces, room temperature

12 ounces unsweetened chocolate, coarsely chopped

3 cups sugar

6 large eggs, room temperature

1 tablespoon pure vanilla extract

1. Preheat oven to 350°F. Line 24 cups of standard muffin tins with paper liners. Spray an 8-inch square pan with nonstick cooking spray. Line bottom of pan with parchment paper; spray parchment. In a mixing bowl, whisk together flour, baking powder, and salt.

2. Heat butter and chocolate in a heatproof mixing bowl set over (not in) a pan of simmering water, stirring occasionally, until melted. Remove from heat, and add sugar. With an electric mixer on medium-high speed, whisk until mixture is smooth. Add eggs, one at a time, beating until each is incorporated, scraping down sides of bowl as needed. Add vanilla, and beat 3 minutes more. Reduce speed to low. Gradually add two thirds of the flour mixture; beat until just combined. Remove bowl from mixer. Add remaining flour mixture, and fold in by hand, just to combine.

3. Divide batter evenly among lined cups, filling each two-thirds full. Spread remaining batter in prepared baking pan, smoothing top with an offset spatula. Bake, rotating tins and pan halfway through, until just set (but still feels soft), and top is shiny, about 17 minutes for cupcakes and 25 minutes for square pan. Transfer tins and pan to wire racks and let cool completely before removing cupcakes and square.

SALTED CARAMEL FILLING

MAKES ABOUT 2 CUPS

2½ cups sugar

⅔ cup water

1 tablespoon light corn syrup

¾ cup heavy cream

2½ teaspoons sea salt, preferably fleur de sel

Heat sugar with the water and corn syrup in a heavy saucepan over high, stirring occasionally, until syrup is clear; clip a candy thermometer to side of pan. Stop stirring, and cook until syrup comes to a boil, washing down sides of pan with a wet pastry brush as needed. Boil, gently swirling pan occasionally, until mixture is caramelized and just reaches 360°F. Remove from heat; slowly pour in cream (mixture will spatter) and stir with a wooden spoon until smooth. Stir in sea salt. Use immediately; if at any time caramel begins to harden, reheat gently until pourable.

CANDIED CARROT CHIPS

MAKES 24 CHIPS

½ cup pure maple syrup, preferably grade B

1 slender carrot, peeled and sliced into 24 very thin rounds

Bring maple syrup to a simmer in a saucepan over medium heat. Working in four batches, add carrot rounds to pan, and submerge to coat with syrup. Cook until edges curl and centers are slightly translucent, about 2 minutes. Using a slotted spoon, transfer to a sheet of parchment paper, and flatten with a spatula. Let cool completely. Carrot chips can be stored up to 3 days at room temperature in an airtight container.

CRYSTALLIZED FLOWERS

MAKES ENOUGH FOR 24 CUPCAKES

1 large egg white

1 teaspoon water

Pesticide-free edible flowers, such as pansies and violas, stems removed (6 per cupcake)

Superfine sugar, for sprinkling

Whisk egg white with the water in a small bowl. Working with 1 flower at a time and holding it with kitchen tweezers, brush egg wash over entire surface of flower using a small paintbrush. Sprinkle with superfine sugar to coat completely. Transfer to a baking sheet or wire rack; let set. Crystallized flowers can be stored up to 3 months at room temperature, in single layers between waxed paper, in airtight containers.

. . . .

DRIED PINEAPPLE FLOWERS
MAKES 24 FLOWERS

2 large or 4 small pineapples, peeled

Preheat oven to 225°F. Line two baking sheets with nonstick baking mats or parchment paper. Using a small melon baller, remove and discard pineapple "eyes." Use a sharp knife to cut pineapple crosswise into very thin slices. Place slices on baking sheets. Bake until tops look dried, about 30 minutes. Flip slices; bake until completely dried, 25 to 30 minutes more (or longer, depending on their thickness). Pinch center of each pineapple slice to shape into a cone; let cool in a clean muffin tin to form flower shown on page 223. Once cool, flowers can be stored (stacked) up to 3 days at room temperature in an airtight container.

. . . .

CANDIED PECAN PIECES
MAKES ABOUT 2 CUPS

$1/2$ cup sugar

$1/4$ cup water

1 cup coarsely chopped pecans (4 ounces)

Line a rimmed baking sheet with a nonstick baking mat. Heat sugar and the water to a simmer in a heavy saucepan over medium heat, stirring occasionally, until sugar is dissolved. Stop stirring; cook until syrup comes to a boil, washing down sides of pan with a wet pastry brush to prevent crystals from forming. Boil, gently swirling pan occasionally, until mixture is light amber. Remove from heat. Stir in pecans with a wooden spoon to coat completely. Immediately remove pecans from caramel; spread in a single layer on prepared baking sheet. Let cool completely before using or storing; break into small pieces, if necessary.

TOASTED NUTS
Preheat oven to 350°F. Spread nuts evenly on a rimmed baking sheet; toast, stirring occasionally, until fragrant, 8 to 10 minutes. (Watch carefully to prevent burning.) Transfer nuts to a plate; let cool completely.

. . . .

TOASTED AND SKINNED HAZELNUTS
Preheat oven to 250°F. Spread hazelnuts on a rimmed baking sheet. Toast in oven, stirring halfway through, until fragrant and skins begin to crack, about 20 minutes. Remove from oven. While nuts are still hot, place in a kitchen towel; rub to remove skins. Return any unskinned nuts to oven for a few minutes, then rub again. Let cool completely.

. . . .

TOASTED COCONUT
Preheat oven to 350°F. Spread coconut evenly on a rimmed baking sheet; toast, stirring occasionally, until starting to brown, about 10 minutes (or longer if darker color is desired). Transfer sheet to a wire rack; let cool completely.

. . . .

MELTED CHOCOLATE
Place finely chopped (white or dark) chocolate (or use whole chocolate chips if called for in a recipe) in a heatproof bowl set over (not in) a pan of simmering water (do not let any water come into contact with the chocolate, or it may seize, or harden). Heat until chocolate is almost melted, then stir with a flexible spatula until completely melted. Remove bowl from pan, and let chocolate cool, stirring occasionally, about 30 minutes before using.

. . . .

CHOCOLATE CURLS
Use a vegetable peeler to slice strips from a slightly warm block of good-quality chocolate (heat in microwave for 5-second intervals, checking after each, until just warm to the touch; do not overheat). To produce tight curls, start from the far edge of the chocolate and move the peeler toward you. The delicate curls are best used immediately; you can even shave the curls right onto a cupcake.

displaying AND giving

Any lovingly prepared home-baked treat calls for a proper presentation. This doesn't mean fancy tableware or linens; on the contrary, the display can be casual or dramatic, stately or whimsical. And likewise, when giving individual and groups of cupcakes, consider the manner in which you will offer them, including delivery options. Because of their frosting, most cupcakes don't stack well, the way cookies do; in transit they are also prone to sliding about, upsetting any carefully wrought toppings and decorations. On the following pages, you'll find crafty display ideas, including clever do-it-yourself flags and other toppers, and suggestions for transporting the cakes securely—and in style.

PUNCHED PAPER FLAGS Paper flags offer an easy way to decorate even the most simply frosted cupcakes—or those with no frosting at all. Craft punches (see Sources, page 342) make quick work of cutting shapes such as hearts, stars, and circles. Punch desired shapes out of heavy paper or card-stock, then adhere two identical pieces back to back, using double-sided tape, with a toothpick or skewer sandwiched in between.

PARTY HAT CLIP-ART TOPPERS Dress up a bunch of birthday cupcakes in jaunty striped party hats. Color-photocopy the clip art on page 338, and cut out. Gently curl into a cone shape, lining up edges and securing with double-sided tape. There should be a small hole at the tip of each cone. Insert a frilled toothpick, top first, into each cone from underneath. Tape thread or twine to each hat to mimic a strap.

BIRTHDAY CLIP-ART FLAGS Flags featuring stylish clip-art illustrations in bold colors make a delightful display for a birthday celebration. Color-photocopy the images on page 339, then cut them out using a 2-inch-circle craft punch (turn the craft punch upside down so you can easily center the design), or by hand. Attach to toothpicks with tape.

WRAPPING PAPER DECORATIONS Cheerful wrapping paper can be used to make coordinating party decorations. Here, cupcake flags are made by cutting out shapes from playful paper using craft punches (see Sources, page 342). A square of paper in the same pattern serves as a charming liner for a cake stand (a larger section can even become a make-shift runner or tablecloth). Since wrapping paper comes in so many designs and colors, you can adapt this idea for any celebration.

TIERED DESSERT DISPLAY
Cupcakes needn't always be the main attraction: use them to round out a bounty of similarly colored confections for a dessert buffet. Here, silver paper–lined cupcakes in three sizes (see Sources, page 342, for liners), capped with snowy white icing and coconut flakes, are nestled among iced penguin-shaped cookies and silver bowls of almond candies for a wintry holiday display.

SILVER SNOWFLAKE COASTERS Give each cupcake a place of honor atop a glossy silver star cut from delicate foil paper (see Sources, page 342). Photocopy the template on page 340 and cut out. Cut a 5½-inch circle from foil paper. Fold circle in half, then in half again. Fold into thirds (you should have a wedge shape). Place template on wedge and cut along dotted lines. Repeat until you have the desired number of coasters; you can make other shapes for variety or repeat a single pattern, as shown.

GILDED CUPCAKE BASKETS

Trimmed with piped latticework and paper ribbon handles, a cluster of cupcakes is cleverly transformed into a display of gift baskets, each one waiting to be picked by a lucky party guest. For the ones shown, golden-hued buttercream is piped in a variety of basketweave motifs, and the cupcakes are set atop cake stands for a significant celebration. Other shades of frosting and plain paper liners would be appropriate for a less formal occasion. You can easily adapt the cupcake handle idea for the strawberry basket cupcakes on page 280. Before adding handles, refrigerate cupcakes until frosting is set.

To make a basket: Fold a 14$\frac{1}{4}$-inch piece of $\frac{3}{8}$-inch-wide paper ribbon in half, and crease lightly to mark the center. Measure 2$\frac{1}{2}$ inches down from the center on each side; fold ribbon outward at those points, and crease firmly. Bring side creases up to meet at center crease, forming bow shape. Affix to center crease with glue dots (see Sources, page 342). Do not crease loops of bow. To finish bow, wrap a piece of 1-inch-long ribbon over center; secure ends on underside with glue dots. Fold ends of ribbon inward by 1$\frac{1}{4}$ inches and crease. Affix double-sided tape to inside of tabs; gently press to bottom of liner.

GOLDEN CUPCAKE TOWER
Tiers of cupcakes in burnished foil liners create a lustrous display suitable for a wedding or golden anniversary. Small, slightly crinkled pieces of edible gold leaf and a sprinkling of luster dust add additional notes of sparkle and shine to the swirled frosting. You can find both at baking-supply stores and online (see Sources, page 342); gold leaf is available in sheets, flakes, and sprinkles.

PLACE CARD FLAGS (above) Whether it's part of a group on a buffet table or a place card on an individual table setting, a cupcake marked with a guest's name is sure to be appreciated. Inscribe each name on a plain gift tag (see Sources, page 342). Most tags come with one hole punched at the top; punch another at the bottom, and slip a toothpick through the two holes. Stamp with a motif appropriate to the occasion—in this case, Christmas.

CUPCAKE ORNAMENTS DISPLAY (opposite) Trim a two-dimensional tree made from a leftover evergreen branch with jolly mini cupcakes piped to resemble holiday ornaments. Set the branch on an oversized serving platter, then arrange the "ornaments" among the "boughs." Finish the arrangement with tiny fudge "presents" tied with thin red ribbons.

PHOTO TOPPERS Commemorate an anniversary, birthday, shower, or wedding with personalized cupcake toppers made from a favorite photograph. Photocopy (or download and print) images onto card stock (you will need two for each topper), then affix them back to back with double-sided tape around large toothpicks or coffee stirrers.

MONOGRAM CUPCAKE TOWER A many-tiered mountain of cupcakes is a less traditional—but no less striking—alternative to a multilayered wedding cake. Cupcakes adorned with monogrammed stamped-fondant hearts (see page 258 for recipe and instructions) are displayed on stacked cake boards supported by Styrofoam rounds and trimmed in blue satin ribbon, held in place with dots of hot glue. The doily trim, also attached with hot glue, is reminiscent of lace details on a wedding gown.

KEEPSAKE CARRIER A muffin tin is a natural holder for a gift of cupcakes—and the pan will be used long after the last crumb has been eaten. Wrap the tin in colored paper, tenting the paper to avoid marring the frosting.

To make a wrapper: To cover a six-cup muffin tin, you will need to cut an 8-by-24-inch rectangle out of parchment or glassine paper (see Sources, page 342). Fold paper in half lengthwise. Fold top edges down about 3/4 inch. Lay a 25-inch piece of twine along the folded-down edge, then fold edge again (the twine should now be in the top fold). Turn corners down. Hold the paper sleeve open (or get a friend to help you), and slide the muffin tin into place. Tie twine in a bow and add a gift tag, if desired.

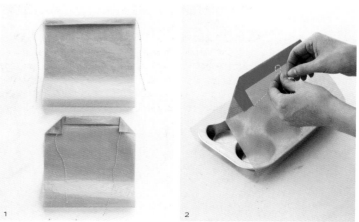

1

2

TO-GO BOXES Small, wire-handled cartons—most often associated with Chinese food—are just the right size for individual cupcakes. Give them as gifts or party favors, or—true to their original purpose—send guests home with leftovers. Easy-to-make inserts keep cupcakes in place so decorations won't get damaged. To make custom cupcake inserts, photocopy the template on page 341 onto card stock in the color of your choice, and cut out. Use a craft knife or 2⅛-inch circle punch to remove the center. Copy the template onto more cardstock until you have enough inserts; cut out. Fold sides on dotted lines, and place each insert into a 1-pint carton (see Sources, page 342).

TASTY TRIO Three standard size cupcakes will fit in a small wooden baking pan, known as a Panibois mold, available at craft and baking-supply stores (see Sources, page 342). To embellish the mold, wrap the long sides in seasonal or patterned paper, and finish by tenting with plain paper in a complementary color.

templates AND clip art

Photocopy all artwork at 100 percent.

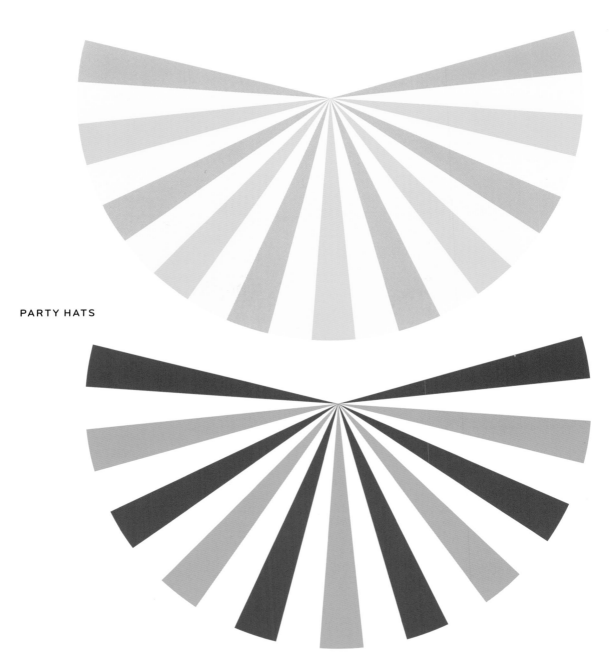

PARTY HATS

CLOCK HANDS

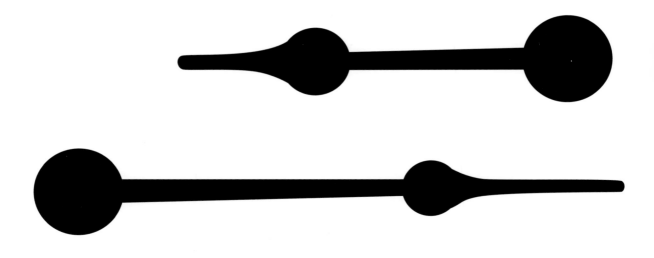

SILVER SNOWFLAKE

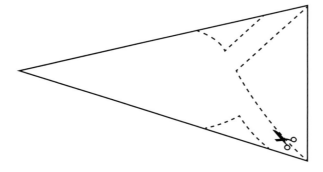

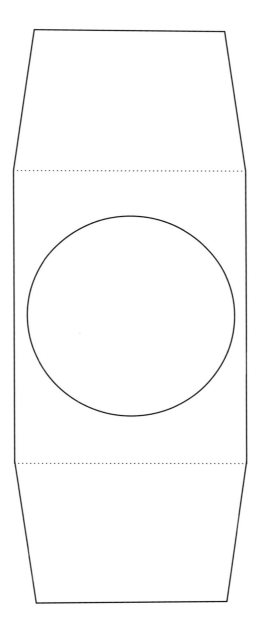

sources

The following is a list of the trusted vendors the editors turn to most often for ingredients, tools, equipment, and supplies. The list beginning opposite contains more specific source information for the recipes and the photographs on the pages indicated. All addresses, phone numbers, and websites were verified at the time of publication; this information is subject to change.

CANDY AND SPRINKLES

Economy Candy
800-352-4544
www.economycandy.com
Chocolate-covered sunflower seeds, chocolates, gumdrops, gummy candy, licorice

Macy's
800-289-6229
www.macys.com
Martha Stewart Collection sanding sugars and sprinkles

Sugarcraft
513-896-7089
www.sugarcraft.com
Candy sprinkles, nonpareils, sanding sugars

The Sweet Life
212-598-0092
www.sweetlifeny.com
Chocolates, gummy candy (including sour belts), licorice

DRIED FRUIT, NUTS, SPICES, AND EXTRACTS

Adriana's Caravan
800-316-0820 or 617-649-4749
www.adrianascaravan.com
Extracts, whole and ground spices

A. L. Bazzini
212-334-1280
www.bazzininuts.com
Dried fruit, nuts

Kalustyan's
212-685-3451
www.kalustyans.com
Dried fruit, extracts, nuts

Penzeys Spices
800-741-7787
www.penzeys.com
Spices, extracts

Russ & Daughters
800-787-7229 or 212-475-4880
www.russanddaughters.com
Dried fruit, nuts

TOOLS AND EQUIPMENT

Bridge Kitchenware
800-274-3435 or 212-688-4220
www.bridgekitchenware.com
Baking pans (standard, jumbo, and mini muffin tins), pastry bags and tips, pastry brushes, rubber spatulas, whisks

Broadway Panhandler
866-266-5925 or 212-966-3434
www.broadwaypanhandler.com
Baking pans (standard, jumbo, and mini muffin tins), spatulas, pastry bags and tips, whisks

Candyland Crafts
877-487-4289
www.candylandcrafts.com
Baking pans (standard, jumbo, and mini muffin tins), pastry bags and tips

CopperGifts.com
620-421-0654
www.coppergifts.com
Cookie cutters

Macy's
800-289-6229
www.macys.com
Martha Stewart Collection baking pans (standard and mini muffin tins), cookie cutters, cupcake carriers, measuring cups and spoons, whisks

Sugarcraft
513-896-7089
www.sugarcraft.com
Paper liners

Williams-Sonoma
877-812-6235
www.williams-sonoma.com
Baking pans (standard and mini muffin tins), kitchen torches, pastry bags and tips, rubber spatulas, whisks

DISPLAYING AND PACKAGING SUPPLIES

GlerupRevere Packaging
866-747-6871
www.glerup.com
Boxes, paper

Macy's
800-289-6229
www.macys.com
Boxes, cake stands, cupcake carriers, cupcake trees

Martha Stewart Crafts
877-882-0319
www.marthastewartcrafts.com
Boxes, craft punches, ribbons, paper

Michaels
800-642-4235
www.michaels.com
Martha Stewart boxes, craft punches, ribbons, paper

The Container Store
800-786-7315
www.containerstore.com
Boxes, ribbon

CUPCAKES FOR ANY DAY

Page 15: Martha Stewart Collection 8″ square whiteware cake stand, from Macy's, 800-289-6229 or www.macys.com for stores

Page 43: BLUEBERRIES-AND-CREAM CUPCAKES Martha Stewart Collection 10″ whiteware cake stand, from Macy's, see above

Page 57: PEANUT BUTTER AND JELLY CUPCAKES Martha Stewart "Candy Shop" 12″x12″ crafting paper, from Michaels, 800-642-4235 or www.michaels.com for stores

Page 67: COCONUT-PECAN CUPCAKES WITH CHOCOLATE GANACHE Creamed coconut, from Foods of India, Sinha Trading, 212-683-4419

Page 68: ICED PISTACHIO CUPCAKES Pistachio slivers, from Pariya Food, www.pariya.com

Page 83: CHOCOLATE-SPICE CUPCAKES Martha Stewart Collection 8″ whiteware cake stand, from Macy's, see above

Page 86: LAVENDER-ICED BROWNIE CUPCAKES Dried lavender (#511062), from Dean & DeLuca, 800-221-7714 or www.deandeluca.com

Page 134: BLACK FOREST CUPCAKES Adro sour cherries in light syrup (#14093), from Parthenon Foods, 877-301-5522 or www.parthenonfoods.com

Page 139: SNICKERDOODLE CUPCAKES Patisserie cups (set of 30 standard and 30 mini), from Sur La Table, 866-328-5412 or www.surlatable.com

Page 142: LEMON MERINGUE CUPCAKES Kitchen torch, from Williams-Sonoma, 877-812-6235 or www.williams-sonoma.com

Page 147: STRAWBERRY CUPCAKES Pink greaseproof cupcake liners (#7100-BC-PG-1), from Fancy Flours, 406-587-0118 or www.fancyflours.com

Page 151: S'MORES CUPCAKES Kitchen torch, from Williams-Sonoma, see above

CUPCAKES FOR SPECIAL DAYS

Page 164: GELATO-TOPPED MINI CUPCAKES 1¼-ounce paper nut cups (#415-500), from Sugarcraft, 513-896-7089 or www.sugarcraft.com

Page 170: LADYBUG CUPCAKES Martha Stewart Crafts cupcake liners, from Michaels, see above

Page 176: JELLIED-CANDY FLOWER CUPCAKES Fruit slices, assorted gumdrops, and spice drops, from Economy Candy, 800-352-4544 or www.economycandy.com

Page 177: SUGAR-COOKIE FLOWER CUPCAKES Similar daisy cookie cutter (#94), from CopperGifts.com, 620-421-0654; lollipop sticks (#300-500C), from Sugarcraft, see above

Page 178: COOKIE MONOGRAM CUPCAKES Similar circle cookie cutters (#416) and set of 26 alphabet cookie cutters (#871), from CopperGifts.com, see above

Page 182: MOUSE CUPCAKES Chocolate-covered sunflower seeds, from Economy Candy, see above

Page 186: DINOSAUR CUPCAKES Similar dinosaur cookie cutter (#77), from CopperGifts.com, see above; lollipop sticks (#300-500C), from Sugarcraft, see above

Page 190: PLAYFUL PUPPY Martha Stewart "Candy Shop" 12″x12″ crafting paper (in background), from Michaels, see above

Page 191: WISE OWLS Martha Stewart "Café" 12″x12″ crafting paper (in background), from Michaels, see above

Page 213: CANDY SPRINKLE HEARTS Red heart sprinkles (#78-13101), from Sugarcraft, see above

Page 217: SPRINGERLE EASTER BUNNY CUPCAKES Bunny springerle mold (#M5630), from House on the Hill, 877-279-4455 or www.houseonthehill.net

Page 225: FATHER'S DAY TEE-TIME CUPCAKES Parisian mints (for "golf balls"), from Economy Candy, see above

Page 226: FOURTH OF JULY CUPCAKES Similar cupcake liners (#7100-VI-PR-1), from Fancy Flours, see above

Page 236: PUMPKIN PATCH CUPCAKES Similar mini leaf cutter (set of 6; #FR4790) from Golda's Kitchen, 866-465-3299 or www.goldaskitchen.com

Page 242: CANDIED SWEET POTATO CUPCAKES Orange cupcake liners (#BCA0850064), from Confectionery House, 518-279-4250 or www.confectioneryhouse.com; kitchen torch, from Williams-Sonoma, see above

Page 244: SPARKLY STAR OF DAVID CUPCAKES Blue cupcake liners (#BCA0850056), from Confectionery House, see above

Page 248: FRUITCAKES WITH MERINGUE MUSHROOMS Pisa gold cupcake liners (#7100-VI-PG-1), from Fancy Flours, see above

Page 252: JOLLY HOLLY Sour-cherry candies and gummy spearmint leaves, from Groovy Candies, 888-729-1960 or www.groovycandies.com

Page 253: CANDY BOWS Red stripe cupcake liners (#7100-QP-RD-1), from Fancy Flours, see above

Page 258: MONOGRAM HEART CUPCAKES Similar mini heart cookie cutter (#264), from Copper Gifts .com, see above; custom rubber stamp with initial, from Stampworx 2000, 800-998-7826 or www.stampworx2000.biz

Page 269: GRADUATION DAY CUPCAKES Blue raspberry sour belt (#gutslsb1), from The Sweet Life, 212-598-0092 or www.sweetlifeny.com; Martha Stewart Collection 10″ whiteware cake stand, from Macy's, see above

Page 270: FRESH FLOWER–TOPPED POUND CAKES Edible flowers, from Sid Wainer & Son, 888-743-9246 or www.sidwainer.com

Page 273: SUNFLOWER CUPCAKES Chocolate-covered sunflower seeds, from Economy Candy, see above; dark green cupcake liners (#BCA0850060), from Confectionery House, see above

Page 277: ALMOND-HAZELNUT CUPCAKES WITH FAUX-BOIS TOPPERS 4″ wood-grain rocker tool (#B905-10), from J.B. Prince, 800-473-0577 or www.jbprince.com; 12″ by 18″ clear acetate sheets (#559900), from Pfeil & Holing, 800-247-7955 or www.cakedeco.com

Page 280: STRAWBERRY BASKET CUPCAKES Set of 3 calyx cutters (#242L) and taper cone modeling tool (#PME8), from Sugarcraft, see above; red cupcake liners (#BCA0850052), from Confectionery House, see above; similar gum paste cutter (#260MN), from Creative Cutters; 888-805-3444 or www.creativecutters.com

Page 282: PIPED-BUTTERCREAM ROSE CUPCAKES Medium brown cupcake liners (#7100-BC-BM-1), from Fancy Flours, see above

THE BASICS
Page 298: HOW TO MAKE A PAPER CORNET Ateco parchment triangles, from BakersTools.com, 866-285-2665 or www.bakerstools.com

DISPLAYING & GIVING
Page 324: Martha Stewart Collection cupcake tree, from Macy's, see above

Page 326: PUNCHED PAPER FLAGS Martha Stewart Crafts snowflake, heart, and cornflower craft punches, from Michaels, see above

Page 327: WRAPPING PAPER DECORATIONS Martha Stewart Crafts 1″ circle, scalloped circle, heart, and classic butterfly craft punches, from Michaels, see above

Page 328: TIERED DESSERT DISPLAY Mini (#85-70121), standard (#6432), and jumbo (#680620) silver foil liners, from Sugarcraft, see above

Page 329: SILVER SNOWFLAKE COASTERS 6″ silver foil origami paper, from Paper Jade, paperjade.com

Page 330: GILDED CUPCAKE BASKETS Mini glue dots, from Michaels, see above; standard gold foil cupcake liners (#415-206), from Sugarcraft, see above

Page 331: GOLDEN CUPCAKE TOWER Standard gold foil cupcake liners (#415-206), from Sugarcraft, see above; edible gold leaf flakes and luster dust, from Technobake, 732-656-0888 or technobake.com

Page 332: PLACE CARD FLAGS Red 1¾″ by 1 5/32″ marking tags (#11060), from Avery, 800-462-8379 or www.avery.com; set of 12 holiday rubber stamps (#CV3001), from RedStamp.com, 877-405-2270; Gel Xtreme white pen, from Yasutomo, www.yasutomo.com

Page 336: KEEPSAKE CARRIER German tissue in rose pink, from Kate's Paperie, 800-809-9880 or www.katespaperie.com

Page 337: TO-GO BOXES 1-pint white wire-handled boxes, from Paper Mart, 800-745-8800 or www.papermart.com. TASTY TRIO Large panibois basket (set of 6), from GourmetBetty.com, 513-309-5506; similar Martha Stewart Crafts tissue paper, from Michaels, see above

photo credits

All photographs by
CON POULOS except:

SANG AN 87, 229, 230, 231, 234, 235, 252 (left), 312

JAMES BAIGRIE 207

CHRISTOPHER BAKER 328

MELINDA BECK 339
 (birthday flags illustrations)

ALAN BENSON 222

REED DAVIS 192, 193

LAURIE FRANKEL 185

DANA GALLAGHER 94, 116

GENTL & HYERS 162, 163, 169, 172, 174, 175, 176 (left), 190 (right), 191 (left), 196, 197, 212 (right), 213 (right), 227, 232, 238, 252 (right), 253 (left), 266, 267, 333

RAYMOND HOM 47, 48, 104, 121, 129, 151, 152, 166, 168, 171, 181–184, 190 (left), 191 (right), 198, 206, 217, 218, 245, 264, 269, 273, 274, 278–280, 283, 284, 287, 290, 293, 295, 296, 298, 299, 301, 305, 314, 321, 326, 329, 332, 334, 336, 337

LISA HUBBARD 215

YUNHEE KIM 327 (left)

ANDERS KRUSBERG 327 (right)

RICK LEW 330

STEPHEN LEWIS 179

DAVID LOFTUS 132

WILLIAM MEPPEM 259, 335

MARCUS NILSSON 331

VICTORIA PEARSON 164, 236, 237

TOSCA RADIGONDA 177 (left)

TINA RUPP 202

CLIVE STREETER 27, 45

WENDELL T. WEBBER 176 (right), 250, 251

ANNA WILLIAMS 177 (right), 187, 194, 195, 199–201, 260

index

Note: *Italicized* page numbers indicate photographs.